895

40

The
Future of
Nineteen Eighty-Four

THE
FUTURE OF
NINETEEN EIGHTY-FOUR

Edited and with an Introduction by
Ejner J. Jensen

Ann Arbor
The University of Michigan Press

Copyright © by The University of Michigan 1984
All rights reserved
Published in the United States of America by
The University of Michigan Press and simultaneously
in Rexdale, Canada, by John Wiley & Sons Canada, Limited
Manufactured in the United States of America

1987   1986   1985   1984   4   3   2   1

Library of Congress Cataloging in Publication Data
Main entry under title:

The Future of Nineteen eighty-four.

   Includes bibliographical references.
   Contents: Nineteen eighty-four, satire or prophecy? /
Bernard Crick—George Orwell and the English
language / Richard W. Bailey—"I'm not literary,
dear" / Leslie Tentler—[etc.]
   1. Orwell, George, 1903–1950. Nineteen eighty-four—
Congresses.   I. Jensen, Ejner J.   II. Title: The Future
of 1984.
PR6029.R8N533   1984   823'.912   83-23355
ISBN 0-472-10048-3
ISBN 0-472-08047-4 (pbk.)

Preface

This volume brings to a formal close an enterprise begun in 1980 when Gorman Beauchamp, William Steinhoff, and I first spoke about planning a conference on George Orwell's *Nineteen Eighty-Four*. The conference at which these essays were first presented was held at the University of Michigan on March 10–12, 1983. That meeting was made possible through the support and assistance of a great many individuals and agencies, and it was the success of the conference that led in turn to the publication of this volume. The Michigan Council for the Humanities and its executive director, Ron Means, provided major financial support. Within the University, the Horace H. Rackham School of Graduate Studies and its board of governors, the College of Literature, Science and the Arts, and the offices of the Vice-Presidents for Academic Affairs and for Research all contributed generously. Dean Alfred Sussman, Associate Dean Eugene Feingold, Dean Peter O. Steiner, Vice-President Billy E. Frye, and Vice-President Charles G. Overberger all served as beneficent advocates of this project.

Jay L. Robinson and John R. Knott provided support from the Department of English, and the staff of the department gave extraordinary assistance at every stage of this work. Gloria (Cain) Parsons assisted at its inception; Linda Blaess helped it along the way; and Karen Van Raalte brought it to a financially successful conclusion. Kate Clark was a constant source of assurance and cheer. Jackie Harvey shared nearly all the work of preparing for the conference and of planning for this volume; she deserves special thanks.

Several participants in the conference who served as moderators or respondents also contributed to this volume indirectly and should be mentioned here. They include Keith Cushman, the Reverend Douglas Evett, Czeslaw Milosz, Lana Pollack, and Marilyn J. Shatz. Bob Holbrook very graciously stepped in at the last minute to transform what is often a merely ceremonial occasion into a thoughtful and well-focused beginning for the conference. Shirley Smith, who likes to translate ideas into action, provided good advice at an early stage of this work; and Daniel P. Sorensen was an indispensable guide and editorial consultant at its close. Theresa Krier was an efficient, resourceful typist. Throughout, we have benefited from the strong aid and encouragement of Andrea Roberts Beauchamp and Lineve McKie Jensen. To all these and to many others who helped we extend our sincere gratitude.

Ejner J. Jensen

Contents

Introduction

Ejner J. Jensen

Certain works of literature exist in the popular imagination with such vivid power that they seem always, for many of us, to have been part of our awareness and to have shaped our perceptions of the world. George Orwell's *Nineteen Eighty-Four* is preeminently a work of this kind. Published in 1949, the novel has become a symbol of the nightmare world of totalitarian oppression and of our worst fears about what the future may hold. *Big Brother, Newspeak,* and *doublethink* are part of our vocabulary. The influence of *Nineteen Eighty-Four* is in fact so great that it has appropriated to itself most of the horrors foreseen in other pessimistic fictions about the future. Thus the excesses of Huxley's *Brave New World,* for example, are often attributed to Orwell's novel; and "Orwellian" is used to signify threatening developments in science and technology that have no place in the society of *Nineteen Eighty-Four.* That a novel so concerned with abstractions—with such matters as personality and the nature of the self, history, objective reality, the nature of power and the motives animating power seekers—should have had such influence testifies both to the power of art and to Orwell's genius.

If *Nineteen Eighty-Four* is in some measure a timeless book, it is also peculiarly timebound, since Orwell gave to his imagined future a precise date. Now 1984 is upon us. What happens to a book set in the future when that future becomes our present? That question provided the initial impetus for a conference held at the University of Michigan on March 10–12, 1983. "The Future of *Nineteen Eighty-Four*" brought together a variety of experts to explore the significance of Orwell's novel on the eve of 1984. Contributors worked from the beginning on the assumption that their essays would be published; thus the present volume offers a full, original version of what the conference audience heard in a somewhat abbreviated form rather than a fleshing-out of arguments originally designed for oral presentation. Bernard Crick's paper, as he explains, was not written especially for the conference; but the meeting's organizers were delighted to have a preview of his introduction to the Clarendon Press edition of the novel. William Steinhoff wrote his short essay, printed here as an afterword, especially for this volume. Though it was not part of the conference proceedings, it is in my view an essential contribution;

"The Future of *Nineteen Eighty-Four*" would never have been proposed if it were not for Professor Steinhoff's presence at the University of Michigan and the example of his fine study, *George Orwell and the Origins of* Nineteen Eighty-Four.

In the initial invitation, participants were asked to consider George Orwell's book as much for its significance as a cultural phenomenon as for its merits as a novel, and all the participants seemed to take up the challenge of the invitation. By soliciting contributions from scholars in such diverse fields as law, psychology, history, political science, politics, literature, and language, the conference organizers hoped to assemble essays that would provide a variety of special angles for approaching *Nineteen Eighty-Four*. At the same time, in stressing the interdisciplinary nature of the conference we hoped that individual contributors would stretch beyond their own fields and make an appeal to a heterogeneous audience. In our view the collection that has resulted is both rich and varied, responsible to the demands of particular academic disciplines and yet accessible to a wide public interested in learning about George Orwell and his extraordinarily popular and influential novel, *Nineteen Eighty-Four*.

The essays appear in this volume in an order designed to allow for the greatest possible range of reciprocal illumination, though the categories used to designate their groupings are meant to be only generally descriptive and not to imply limitations. The first three essays focus in quite different ways on issues involved in our reading of *Nineteen Eighty-Four*. The next three concern matters of psychology: two concentrate on Orwell's own psychological makeup and the sources of his fiction, the third on the struggles of his character, Winston Smith. Following these are two essays on the prophetic elements in Orwell. The two concluding essays offer strikingly contrasting views of Orwell's value system as it relates to the issues of privacy and the importance of the autonomous self.

"Reading" is a general and in many ways unsatisfactory term for the very different critical enterprises carried out by the first three writers. To cover them all, the word must be understood to mean an analysis of the novel's genre, a study of its language and its linguistic themes, and a speculative discussion of its possible future reception. In the case of Bernard Crick's essay, "*Nineteen Eighty-Four*: Satire or Prophecy?", it denotes first an uncovering of Orwell's literary intention and then a demonstration of how that intention—to write a Swiftian satire—is fulfilled in the design and details of his novel. Professor Crick is especially concerned to dispel the notion that the book is a prophetic fiction, and he does so with characteristic vigor and directness. Richard W. Bailey's reading of *Nineteen Eighty-Four* is attentive not only to the novel's language but also to what Orwell said elsewhere about language and what others have said on that topic. He makes clear in "George Orwell and the English Language" that the views of Orwell the essayist are not a sure guide to the purposes of Orwell the novelist, and he looks closely at the role language plays in *Nineteen Eighty-Four*. Writing on ". . . George Orwell on Women and the Family," Leslie Tentler reads widely in the Orwell canon to determine the author's attitude toward her subject. Her concern is twofold: first, through a careful analysis, to discover the evidence for Orwell's views; second, having assembled that evidence, to speculate about how the author's attitude will affect audiences whose ideas and values are sharply different from his. Perhaps more than any of the other writers in this collection, Tentler raises in an explicit way the question of the future—here, the future reception—of Orwell's novel.

The three essays in the next group share a field of discourse pointed to by the vocabulary of their titles: ". . . Power and Sadism," ". . . Psychopolitics," and "The Self and Memory. . . ." They all owe a debt to psychology and psychiatry, though each makes use of knowledge of those disciplines for distinct purposes. Gorman Beauchamp's essay, "From Bingo to Big Brother: Orwell on Power and Sadism," explores the connection between "Such, Such Were the Joys," Orwell's account of life in his first boarding school, and *Nineteen Eighty-Four*. This relationship was discussed in considerable detail by Anthony West over twenty-five years ago and it has remained a central issue in interpreting the novel. West's account, argues Beauchamp, "trivializes and thus undermines Orwell's depiction of totalitarian tyranny," whereas he proposes that the difference between the two systems—the abhorrent public school tyrannized over by "Bingo" and the repressive political world of Oceania dominated by Big Brother—is only a matter of degree, distinguished by the available scope for the exercise of power. Alex Zwerdling, in "Orwell's Psychopolitics," addresses many of the issues treated in Beauchamp's essay, seeking to understand the irrational political world of Oceania, a world in which the exercise of power in its most brutal manifestations requires no justification beyond itself and in which the future is summed up in the image of a "boot stamping on a human face—forever." This "motiveless malignity" and the horrors to which it gives rise are neither the products of Orwell's diseased imagination nor vivid projections of imagined future horrors; they arise, argues Zwerdling, from the writer's response to the actual horrors of World War II and more particularly from his awareness of the monstrous evil of the death camps, an evil documented for the first time just at the point when Orwell was writing *Nineteen Eighty-Four*. Professors Beauchamp and Zwerdling, both literary scholars, use psychology as a means to understanding *Nineteen Eighty-Four*. Joseph Adelson, a psychologist, employs terms drawn from William James and an analysis grounded in personality theory to construct an essay that seems as "literary" as any in this collection. Adelson's analysis of Winston Smith provides new insight into the complexities of his character and a rich understanding of his frustrated journey to salvation. In his analysis, which manages to be both economical and moving, Adelson offers a challenge to those critics who fault Orwell for his inadequate command of the novelist's art.

In the popular imagination, *Nineteen Eighty-Four* enjoys a special status as a kind of secular prophetic book. Almost any encroachment on personal freedom, no matter how trivial, is likely to be attributed to creeping "Big Brotherism." Thus a recent decision in San Francisco to mandate separate working areas for nonsmoking city employees was attacked as yet another sure sign of the arrival of a 1984 destined to fulfill Orwell's worst fears. While both Alfred Meyer and Eugene McCarthy discuss the prophetic dimensions of *Nineteen Eighty-Four*, they do so on a level far removed from the reflexive complaining that tends to regard most of the evils in the contemporary world as "Orwellian." Professor Meyer draws an extended contrast between the pessimism of Orwell in his novel and that of Herbert Marcuse, chiefly as set forth in *One-Dimensional Man*. Meyer sees both writers responding to the problem of a broken ideal: the idea of progress. But in the values they profess and in the methods with which they propose to confront this shattered world view, they are opposed at every point. Senator McCarthy, in "George Orwell: A Prophet Honored Just after His Time," deals explicitly with the predictive element in *Nineteen Eighty-Four*. He concentrates on political Newspeak and the manipulation of the historical record through euphemism and obfuscation. Set as it is among a collection of academic essays, Senator McCarthy's discussion—sprinkled with allusions to public figures (Robert McNamara, Henry Kissinger, Jimmy Carter, Walter Cronkite)—is likely to seem a bit anomalous; but for that very reason it has a special value in this collection. It provides a firsthand account of one public official's confrontation with the bureaucratization of language. Moreover, it does so in an essay that is itself primarily satiric. What Senator McCarthy seems to suggest is that the grim levity of satire is the one sane response open to us in a time when missiles are called "peacekeepers" and an order "not to generate any prisoners" is a command to kill.

The final essays from the conference, by Francis A. Allen and W. Warren Wagar, present a striking contrast. Each writer concentrates on Orwell as a political thinker, each focuses on the issue of personal freedom and the value of the autonomous self, and each ranges widely over related literature to provide an intellectual context for his discussion of *Nineteen Eighty-Four*. But while Professor Allen documents contemporary attacks on the ideal of privacy and the integrity of the autonomous self, and while he sees Orwell's novel as providing a salutary reminder of the losses such attacks may lead to, Professor Wagar regards Orwell as an apologist for a dominant world view that makes no sense in the nuclear age. "Nineteen Eighty-Four and the Eclipse of Private Worlds" reflects Professor Allen's commitment to the study of law, but it reflects as well the interests and concerns of political philosophy, psychology, sociology, and—not least—ethics. In a volume devoted to Nineteen Eighty-Four, especially one in which the contributors' analyses lead generally to praise of Orwell, it may seem odd to close with an essay so pronouncedly anti-Orwell as Professor Wagar's. Yet the great value of "George Orwell as Political Secretary of the Zeitgeist" lies just in this: it calls into question the very grounds for celebrating Orwell as prophet and political thinker and demands that he be judged in 1984 in the light of the political and social realities of 1984. Many readers will quarrel with Professor Wagar's view—indeed, his presentation gave rise to the most heated debate of the entire conference. His paper was the final presentation of the conference's closing day. At the end of that last session the moderator was forced to "claim the privilege of the chair" repeatedly before the debate generated by Professor Wagar's essay subsided. The palpable rise in temperature that warmed the last minutes of the conference was only the strongest sign among many that it had fulfilled its purposes: to gain a fuller understanding of Nineteen Eighty-Four as a living cultural force and to discover a deeper critical awareness of the issues it raises for our society. I hope that this volume will have a similar effect: that readers of the essays included here will be challenged to sharpen both their own views of Nineteen Eighty-Four and their understanding of the thought and achievement of George Orwell.

Nineteen Eighty-Four:
Satire or Prophecy?

Bernard Crick

As we approach the year 1984, we must ask ourselves what is the enduring significance of Orwell's novel *Nineteen Eighty-Four?* I have already made two assumptions: first, that we will reach 1984 and, secondly, what is reasonably obvious but often forgotten, that the book is a novel, not a monograph. I have given the correct title fully spelled out, which he deliberately favored because, presumably, he meant it as a title of fiction rather than as a date in a calendar or a prophecy. But notwithstanding it being a novel, I assume that its content may have some enduring significance as well as its still often underestimated artistic achievement.

Writing before the year 1984, I see the need to warn against too literal an interpretation of the text and any melodramatic desires to read it primarily as a prophecy rather than primarily as a satire. I will try to make good this warning by putting the text into both its contemporary setting and into the wider context of the whole of Orwell's works. Yet even if it is a consciously Swiftian satire of great strength, the emotional shock is not ordinary and, whether satire or prophecy, it does not reflect well on the world. From my life of Orwell, I am reasonably sure of three things.

1. The novel *Nineteen Eighty-Four* was not his last will and testament—it was simply the last book he wrote before the poor man happened to die.[1]
2. It was not a work of unnatural intensity dashed off hastily by a dying man choked with death wish and regressing through the novel to childhood memories of his preparatory school (as some assert to be the importance often attached to his essay "Such, Such Were the Joys").[2]
3. It does not represent a repudiation of his socialism, since he continued to write for the *Tribune* and American left-wing journals right up to his final illness, during the time of the composition of *Nineteen Eighty-Four*.[3]

This essay will form part of an introduction to a critical edition of *Nineteen Eighty-Four* which the author is preparing for Clarendon Press.

Nonetheless, it remains the most complex of his books and the one attracting the most diverse interpretations. It has been read as a deterministic prophecy, as a conditional projection, as a humanistic satire (he said, but of what?), as nihilistic misanthropy, as a total rejection of socialism, and as a libertarian-socialist—almost an anarchist—protest against totalitarian tendencies both in his own and in any other society.

Czeslaw Milosz, the Polish poet and writer, wrote in 1953 in his *Captive Mind* about Orwell's *Nineteen Eighty-Four* (having himself recently defected from the Communist party):

> because [*Nineteen Eighty-Four*] is both difficult to obtain and dangerous to possess, it is known only to certain members of the Inner Party. Orwell fascinates them through his insight into details they know well, and through his use of Swiftian satire. Such a form of writing is forbidden by the New Faith because allegory, *by nature manifold in meaning*, would trespass beyond the prescriptions of socialist realism and the demands of the censor. For those who know Orwell only by hearsay are amazed that a writer who never lived in Russia should have so keen a perception into its life. The fact that there are writers in the West who understand the functioning of the unusually constructed machine of which they are themselves a part astounds them and argues against the "stupidity" of the West.[4] [Emphasis added.]

Few of the above viewpoints, rather like those famous many causes of the French or American Revolutions over which students are annually invited to exercise their judgment, can be rejected completely: it is a question of proportion and relative weight. There is no single message of *Nineteen Eighty-Four*: it contains multiple messages. It is a novel, the most complex Orwell ever attempted, and more complex in its variety of themes than most commentators and critics still appreciate. If he had wanted to write a straight or even a more or less nonfiction book, he would have done so as he had done before. But a general difficulty with satires is that they depend greatly on contemporary references (now often missed), and warnings depend on plausibility in the circumstances of the day (now sometimes half misunderstood and underestimated).[5] And there is a special difficulty of the genre that satire and warning are a difficult mixture to bring off; it is difficult to judge how specific and precise the author is being. H. G. Wells, for example, wrote novels of both kinds, but on the whole, he kept them well apart. Orwell attempted something artistically very difficult in (as I called it in my biography) a "flawed masterpiece," an attempt to combine satire and warning in this extraordinarily powerful and complex book, but certainly not the best thing he wrote artistically.

Nineteen Eighty-Four is already in the canon of modern English literature, and teachers of English in schools wrestle with it annually. It is also rapidly entering into the canon of political thought and the social sciences. Some of the above difficulties are made worse because academic political thinkers can be uncertain or inept in handling satire and in relating meaning to structure. (By all means study political concepts as found in novels as well as in monographs and tracts; but remember then that the meaning of those ideas is defined by the context of the fiction as a whole.) Or, if students of politics have critical ability, as shown by the way they can handle seventeenth- and eighteenth-century texts, they can also make the common mistake—as many literary critics have done—of thinking that Orwell is always a simple writer with a clear message wrapped up in costume. *Nineteen Eighty-Four* is, I will endlessly repeat, a novel; but of a certain kind. Presumably he wrote it in the form of a novel rather than a monograph either because he thought some of the issues raised are inherently unresolvable, or at least because he had not as yet resolved them himself. But literary critics are often equally uncertain or inept in handling political ideas, and usually underestimate the originality of two of his major themes: the totalitarian hypothesis (even if it is found far more clearly—as I will argue—in his essays) and the complex epistemological argument he makes for relating both liberty and historical truth to plain language.

As well as a picture of a certain kind of totalitarianism, *Nineteen Eighty-Four* is obviously a picture of a hierarchical society, which in itself has created a foolish misunderstanding. If Orwell was still a socialist, where in the text does he assert his libertarian and egalitarian values? Some ask this question rhetorically and assume that somehow, because he does not mention these things, he has abandoned them: certainly that he has abandoned his egalitarianism. This view is strengthened if one "locates," as has become a routine English literature exercise, *Nineteen Eighty-Four* in the tradition of Huxley's *Brave New World*, Zamyatin's *We*, Jack London's *Iron Heel*, and H. G. Wells's *The Sleeper Awakes*. The issue is a complex one. Certainly there are borrowings from and echoes of all these books—and many more—in *Nineteen Eighty-Four*.[6] But finally it is arbitrary and foolish to limit one's interpretation of a text in this way. *Nineteen Eighty-Four* owes as much to Swift's *Gulliver* as to any of them, and, in any case, also needs locating both in the political events of the 1930s and 1940s and in Orwell's reading of nonfiction (particularly, as will soon be argued, of James Burnham's *The Managerial Revolution*). However, let us compare

Nineteen Eighty-Four to *Brave New World* even in the broadest features of their plots: Huxley was satirizing equality, he disliked and feared equality, therefore equality is an explicit theme in his satire which shows equality through happiness carried rather too far. Orwell also disliked "happiness," or rather he often railed against "mere hedonism" both as a proper motive for life and as an explanation of human conduct,[7] although doubtless to Huxley's horror he located true happiness in the ordinary, decent life of a working man in good employment, not in the hyped-up higher moments of the literary intelligentsia. But Orwell is far from satirizing equality, he is at least (we can refine this in a moment) satirizing hierarchy. More precisely he satirizes the pretensions of intellectuals to exercise power nominally for other people's good, but adds the sardonic twist that they are really enjoying power for its own sake. Therefore in the rigid hierarchical structure of *Nineteen Eighty-Four* it is authority and power hunger which are carried too far. There isn't a word about equality (except, significantly, in Goldstein's book), but equality is surely the thing denied by such hierarchy: the implicit message is that men should behave in a more egalitarian manner. A satire has a moral presupposition: it is not cynical or totally pessimistic (which is why so much contemporary so-called satire is simply nihilistic, which Orwell's never was).

The satire is so consistent that the dictator is actually called "Big Brother": "Big Brother is watching you." Satires turn the truth upside down. It is both comfort and threat—a perfect piece of "doublethink." It has a touch of the Stalinist perversion of early Communism about it, but also has a touch of the *Volksgemeinschaft* and *Brudersband* of the Nazis, their false fraternity and contempt for individual liberty. In a satire, the positive values of a writer emerge as the contrary of what he is attacking, or of the fanatical and usually disgusting world which he portrays.

Consider for a moment *Nineteen Eighty-Four* simply as a story. It is a story of a man, Winston Smith, trying to struggle against a new kind of despotism. But the story makes clear right from the beginning that effective resistance is impossible, if things are ever allowed to reach such a pass. On one level, Winston attempts to resist by activism and rebellion, seeking out the enemies of the regime; but on another level, he simply struggles to maintain his individuality (the original title was to have been *The Last Man in Europe*). In this struggle, which for a weak and unheroic man he pursues with surprising courage and tenacity, right up to the final torture, *memory* and *mutual trust* are the positive themes. That he is finally defeated is inevitable in the satire of total power, but Orwell believes that that can happen only if we are utterly alone: while we have someone to trust, our individuality cannot be destroyed. For man is a social animal, our identity arising from interaction, not autonomy. Mutual trust is that virtue praised by Aristotle, asserted to be necessary to true citizens and the very thing that a tyrant must smash (he tells us in book 5 of *Politics*) if he is to perpetuate his rule successfully. Mutual trust is a component of that overworked word in Orwell, that essential concept, "decency" (Orwell's equivalent of "fairness" in John Rawls's moral philosophy or "mutual respect" in Kant's).

Decency[8] is mutual trust, toleration, behaving responsibly toward other people, acting empathetically—all of these. Mutual trust is of supreme importance to a civic culture, for political action is impossible without it. Again the author is no more explicit about "mutual trust" than he is about "equality." In a satire only the contrary or the negation is explicit, but then perfectly explicit. O'Brien tells Winston Smith,

> Already we are breaking down the habits of thought which have survived from before the Revolution. We have cut the links between child and parent, between man and man, and between man and woman. No one dares trust a wife or a child or a friend any longer.[9]

And when Winston and Julia meet again after their torture, defeat, and release, she says,

> "You *want* it to happen to the other person. You don't give a damn what they suffer. All you care about is yourself."
>
> "All you care about is yourself," he echoed.
>
> "And after that you don't feel the same towards the other person any longer."
>
> "No," he said, "you don't feel the same."[10]

And a wretched old man, grieving in an air raid shelter for someone dead, "kept repeating,"

> "We didn't ought to 'ave trusted 'em. I said so, Ma, didn't I? That's what comes of trusting 'em. I said so all along. We didn't ought to have trusted the buggers."
>
> But which buggers they didn't ought to have trusted Winston could not now remember.[11]

"Mutual trust" is thus a minimum demand on us if we want to stay human, but it is also a maximum demand: there is no need to treat one's fellow citizens with more than mutual trust or decency. For instance, there is no need to love everybody equally, which is either impossible or a debasement of "love"; but there is a categorical imperative to treat people equally, as if everyone were an end in themselves and not a means toward some other's ends. Some critics have argued that "love" is asserted as a positive value in *Nineteen Eighty-Four* and is necessary for a good society, as shown by the love affair between Winston and Julia. They then say, not surprisingly, that the portrayal of love is clumsy and shallow. But it begins as simply a "love affair"; if it can be said to be love at all, that only grows on them toward the end. Indeed the love affair is shown in the story to have been a mistake on Winston's part (Julia falls asleep when he reads Goldstein's testimony and she is bored by his tale of the photograph); and on her part, it is a gesture of contempt for the regime (she actually boasts that she has had it off with Party members many times before and that turns Winston on again). She is closer to the proles than Winston is in behavior, because she had come from the proles, but not in sympathies—she wants to get away from them. But Winston is more like the middle-class intellectual who is determined to find hope amid the people. If the affair is not a love affair in a genuine sense, it is, however, exemplary of "mutual trust" right up to the end when they are tortured. Mutual trust, fellowship, fraternity, and decency are recurrent themes in all of Orwell's writings after *Wigan* and *Catalonia*. These themes qualify his earlier individualism.

The second positive and major theme, *memory*, is explicit in the satire, and links *Nineteen Eighty-Four* with *Coming Up for Air* and with Orwell's general view of morality. He held (rightly or wrongly, but so he did) that a good and decent way of life already existed in tradition: an egalitarian or genuine postrevolutionary society would not transfigure values or expect them to be different (his anti-Marxism comes out here) but would simply draw on the past. Quite simply, Orwell did not believe that poverty and class oppression (which he believed were real forces in the history of the West) had dehumanized people completely. Rather these forces had created a genuine fellowship and fraternity in the common people that the middle classes, wracked by competitive individualism, lacked. Hence the importance of the proles in the story, much more positively characterised (if perhaps too briefly for emphasis) than usually noticed.

As Winston Smith observed when he walked among the proles,

What mattered were individual relationships, and the completely helpless gesture, an embrace, a tear, a word spoken to a dying man, could have value in itself. [The proles,] it suddenly occurred to him, had remained in this condition. They were not loyal to a party or to a country or to an idea, they were loyal to one another. For the first time in his life he did not despise the proles or think of them as merely an inert force which would one day spring to life and regenerate the world. The proles had stayed human. They had not become hardened inside. They had held on to the primitive emotions which he himself had to re-learn by conscious effort.[12]

This is a crucial passage in the book, completely consistent with Orwell's moral and social perspectives in *The Road to Wigan Pier* and *Homage to Catalonia*. Thus the authenticity of memory, thus the diary: the attempt to write the diary begins the main thread of the plot in which private memory is defended against the official attempts to rewrite history; and this becomes a parallel action in the plot to the defense of plain language against ideological discourse.

My claim is that both the memory and mutual trust themes and the defense of plain language theme work best as satires of contemporary mass-produced writing (Orwell sees even the nominally nonpolitical writing of prolefeed and prolecult as having a political, deadening, perverting, and pacifying effect) as well as possible parts of a model of a totalitarian society. Indeed, if we see them primarily as part of a future totalitarian society, then we actually distance the thrust at ourselves. Consider this passage from his essay of 1946, "The Prevention of Literature."

It would probably not be beyond human ingenuity to write books by machinery. But a sort of mechanizing process can already be seen at work in the film and radio, in publicity and propaganda, and in the lower reaches of journalism. The Disney films, for instance, are produced by what is essentially a factory process, the work being done partly mechanically and partly by means of artists who have to subordinate their individual style. Radio features are commonly written by tired hacks to whom the subject and the manner of treatment are dictated beforehand. Even so, what they write is merely a kind of raw material to be chopped into shape by producers and censors. So also with the innumerable books and pamphlets commissioned by government departments.[13]

One of the satiric rages that moved Orwell was plainly bitter disappointment that almost a hundred years of the democratic franchise and of compulsory secondary education had not realised the liberal dream of an educated, active, and politically literate citizenry but that industrial society had turned people into proles: "films, football, beer and, above all, gambling filled the horizon of their minds. To keep them in control was not difficult."[14] Several of his essays bristle with contempt for what he still called "the yellow press" and, as a working journalist, he had obviously believed that through writing plain English one could—if not prevented—reach ordinary people with important issues. He implied that most intellectuals now lived off the backs of a debased populace by supplying prolefeed, no longer trying to "educate and agitate"—the old radical slogan. He only erred in his satire of two-way television by seeing its development primarily as a device of surveillance; and, even so, these other things had so debased the proles that "the great majority of the proles did not even have telescreens in their homes." The actual development of mass television would have been added grist to Orwell's satiric mill, prolefeed indeed.

Seen as a projective model of totalitarian society, the text actually works badly. The proles are left passive, they are not mobilized systematically as nearly every author who used the term *totalitarian* had thought was the essence of the concept—including Orwell himself in a whole group of wartime and postwar essays. *Nineteen Eighty-Four* is not his clearest model of a totalitarian society, simply because the demands of the specific satire make the proles debased rather than adequate human material for political mobilization.

The intensity of the writing and his immediate reactions to reviews must convince us that, even if it is not a prophecy of totalitarianism (still less a timetable, nor a precise model), the book is certainly a warning that "something like this could happen even here." Of course, the details of the regime cannot be reviewed as a precise model but only as parts of a satiric story. It is almost as absurd to object to Orwell that the class structure in Oceania is obscure or contradictory as to tell Swift that the babies of the Irish poor would have been too emaciated to serve as food for the starving.

Orwell himself was disturbed when a first wave of American reviews (notably from the Time-Life Corporation's journals) hailed *Nineteen Eighty-Four* as, first and last, an explicit attack on socialism. Not unexpectedly, Communists took exactly the same line. Orwell dictated notes for the following press release:

> It has been suggested by some of the reviewers of *Nineteen Eighty-Four* that it is the author's view that this, or something like this, is what will happen inside the next forty years in the Western World. This is not correct. I think that, allowing for the book being after all a parody, something like *Nineteen Eighty-Four could* happen. This is the direction in which the world is going at the present time, and the trend lies deep in the political, social and economic foundations of the contemporary world situation.
>
> Specifically the danger lies in the structure imposed on Socialist and on Liberal capitalist communities by the necessity to prepare for total war with the U.S.S.R. and the new weapons,

of which of course the atomic bomb is the most powerful and the most publicized. But danger lies also in the acceptance of a totalitarian outlook by intellectuals of all sorts.

The moral to be drawn from the dangerous nightmare situation is a simple one: *Don't let it happen. It depends on you.*

George Orwell assumes that if such societies as he describes in *Nineteen Eighty-Four* come into being there will be several super states. This is fully dealt with in the relevant chapter of *Nineteen Eighty-Four*. It is also discussed from a different angle by James Burnham in *The Managerial Revolution*. These super states will naturally be in opposition to each other or (a novel point) will pretend to be more in opposition than in fact they are. Two of the principal super states will obviously be the Anglo-American world and Eurasia. If these two great blocs line up as mortal enemies it is obvious that the Anglo-Americans will not take the name of their opponents and will not dramatise themselves on the scene of history as Communists. Thus they will have to find a new name for themselves. The name suggested in *Nineteen Eighty-Four* is of course Ingsoc, but in practice a wide range of choices is open. In the U.S.A. the phrase "Americanism" or "hundred per cent Americanism" is suitable and the qualifying adjective is as totalitarian as anyone could wish.

If there is a failure of nerve and the Labour Party breaks down in its attempt to deal with the hard problems with which it will be faced, tougher types than the present Labour leaders will inevitably take over, drawn probably from the ranks of the Left, but not sharing the Liberal aspirations of those now in power. Members of the present British government, from Mr. Attlee and Sir Stafford Cripps down to Aneurin Bevan, will *never* willingly sell the pass to the enemy, and in general the older men, nurtured in a Liberal tradition, are safe, but the younger generation is suspect and the seeds of totalitarian thoughts are probably widespread among them. It is invidious to mention names, but everyone could without difficulty think for himself of prominent English and American personalities whom the cap would fit.[15]

Certainly Orwell thought that something like it could happen, but notice how contemporary—division of the world between the great powers and his fears for the Labour Party—the specific elements of the satire become: and notice his use of the phrase that it was "after all a parody." The problem still remains, a parody of what? Here the book perhaps ceases to speak directly to the modern reader unless a few introductory lines are written. For it is reasonably clear that a major part of the book is a parody of James Burnham's thesis, in particular, and of the power hunger of intellectuals (an old Orwell theme) in general. "Who was James Burnham?" many of the celebrants of *Nineteen Eighty-Four* may well ask.

Burnham had a double thesis: that the two great ideologies and superpowers would one day converge, neither the commisars nor the congressmen winning; and that the state would be taken over not by politicians or party men (of whatever ideology) but by technocrats who would develop a common culture and common interests. Orwell was fascinated by both views. He wrote two major essays on Burnham, although in the end he rejected both views. Nonetheless, if one takes intellectuals as a subclass of managers, as Orwell seems to do, he had considerable ambivalence about them. While he defends intellectual liberties, he seems to dislike intellectuals as a class and suspects them of coming to be more interested in power than in thought. He is vastly impressed by a fear (from his BBC wartime experience) that most intellectuals sell out to the machine all too easily for the sake of a job, rationalizing their positions easily. Bureaucrats in *Nineteen Eighty-Four* are, as it were, types like himself but who had stayed on and made a career in the BBC. And worse,

> The motives of these English intellectuals who support the Russian dictatorship are, I think, different from what they publicly admit, but it is logical to condone tyranny and massacre if one assumes its progress is inevitable.[16]

Orwell packed a lot into that cheerful little aside: not merely his usual polemic against the fellow travelers, but a Karl Popper–like assumption that a belief in inevitable history or in historical prophecy inevitably gets used as an excuse for tyranny. This he linked to the fear of the suppression of truth.

> The fallacy is to believe that under a dictatorial government you can be free *inside*. Quite a number of people console themselves with this thought, now that totalitarianism in one form or another is visibly on the upgrade in every part of the world.[17]

Certainly in *Nineteen Eighty-Four* the Ministry of Truth is doing more than debasing the masses, it is rewriting history: he who controls the present controls the past and the future. On one level, the satire is fairly obvious: anyone at the time who cared to know would have followed the grim and notorious humor of successive editions of the *Soviet Encyclopaedia* which first had Trotsky as a hero of the Civil War, then condemned him as an agent of the Mensheviks and the British, then dealt with the problem in the simplest and sweetest way by removing him entirely from historical record, making him an un-person. Orwell on a deeper level tries to wrestle with the epistemo-logical problem as to whether it is *possible* so to control the past. Although Winston strives to achieve authentic memories, what he finds among the proles is extremely disturbing: their memories are short, ridiculous, wandering, it needs a trained mind to have a trained memory in favorable circumstances. It emerges from some of Orwell's earlier essays that (*a*) he fears totalitarian regimes believe their own propaganda, and (*b*) a contradictory theme, that totalitarian regimes could not possibly work if some of their leaders or functionaries, sci-entists or bureaucrats, did not know what was really happening. Or-well never resolved this profound and difficult epistemological dilemma.

Nor did he fully resolve whether he was satirizing Burnham's view of the primacy of pure power—"It is curious that in all his talk about the struggle for power, Burnham never stops to ask *why* people want power" ("Second Thoughts on James Burnham," 1946[18])—as an im-possibility, or whether he thinks it all too possible that party leaders and civil servants who begin as civilized men end up simply as a regime of officeholders, brutally interested in nothing but power for the sake of power. O'Brien gives the nihilistic reply to Winston Smith when he allows Winston to ask him what it is all for: "If you want a picture of the future, imagine a boot stamping on a human face—forever."[19]

Could there be such a thing as power devoid of ideology? Can history be completely rewritten?

Consider these two views on the possibility of total thought control, in one passage from "The Prevention of Literature" (1946).

The organised lying practised by totalitarian states is not, as is sometimes claimed, a temporary expedient of the same nature as military deception. It is something integral to totalitarianism, something that would still continue even if concentration camps and secret police forces had ceased to be necessary. Among in-telligent Communists there is an underground legend to the effect that although the Russian government is obliged now to deal in lying propaganda, frame-up trials, and so forth, it is se-cretly recording the true facts and will publish them at some future time. We can, I believe, be quite certain that this is not the case, because the mentality implied by such action is that of a liberal historian who believes that the past cannot be altered and that a correct knowledge of history is valuable as a matter of course. From the totalitarian point of view, history is some-thing to be created rather than learned. A totalitarian state is in effect a theocracy, and its ruling caste, in order to keep its position, has to be thought of as infallible. But since, in practice, no one is infallible, it is frequently necessary to re-arrange past events in order to show that this or that mistake was not made, or that this or that imaginary triumph actually happened. Then, again, every major change in policy demands a corresponding change of doctrine and a revaluation of prominent historical figures. This kind of thing happens everywhere, but is clearly likelier to lead to outright falsification in societies where only *one* opinion is permissible at any given moment. *Totalitarianism demands, in fact, the continuous alteration of the past, and in the long run probably demands a disbelief in the very existence of objective truth.*[20] [Emphasis added.]

But then, in the same paragraph, he immediately contradicts himself.

The friends of totalitarianism in this country usually tend to argue that since absolute truth is not attainable, a big lie is no worse than a little lie. It is pointed out to us that all historical records are biased and inaccurate or, on the other hand, that modern physics has proved that what seems to us the real world is an illusion, so that to believe in the evidence of one's senses is simply vulgar philistinism. A totalitarian society which succeeds in perpetuating itself would probably set up a schizophrenic system of thought, in which laws of commonsense held good in everyday life and in certain exact sciences, but could be disregarded by the politician, the historian and the sociologist. Already there are countless people who would think it scandalous to falsify a scientific text-book, but would see nothing wrong in falsifying an historical fact. It is at the point where literature and politics cross that totalitarianism exerts its greatest pressure on the intellectual.[21]

He is contradicting himself here because he is assuming not a total system of false thought but a schizophrenic one. This is undoubtedly the more commonsense view, the mildly less nightmarish. Perhaps, as Czeslaw Milosz once argued, it is possible (indeed common) for even quite high functionaries in a totalitarian regime to be inwardly skeptical. We do still live in the world of Thomas Hobbes, in other words, one of conventional fear, not only of total brainwashing and total reconstituting of character. Totalitarianism may be a temperament and a tendency, but it is not a result: nothing in this world is perfect.[22]

Orwell simply was not sure on both these big issues: can there be a total divorce of power from morality and history and ideology from truth? Few of us are sure. *Nineteen Eighty-Four* raises these two dilemmas acutely. Perhaps he had not got the philosophical ability to resolve them, but he had the literary genius to go right to the heart of the problem as few philosophers have done. Pehaps because they were open-ended dilemmas, he chose to write a novel, not a tract— even though so many people read it as if it were a tract, and a deliberate last message at that.

In "The Prevention of Literature," he brings satire down to earth again: "let me repeat what I said at the beginning of this essay: that in England the immediate enemies of truthfulness, and hence of freedom of thought, are the Press lords, the film magnates and the bureaucrats, but that on a long view the weakening of the desire for liberty among the intellectuals themselves is the most serious symptom of all."[23] He radiates mistrust for the debasing effect of the press and feared that intellectuals were betraying their principles. I see this as the enduring relevance of *Nineteen Eighty-Four* and the main satiric thrust.

Notes

1. See Bernard Crick, *George Orwell: A Life*, rev. ed. (London: Secker and Warburg, 1981), 384–85 and 397. (The Penguin Books edition is identical.) I obviously disagree with William Steinhoff, when he sees *Nineteen Eighty-Four* "as a culminating work which expresses, almost epitomizes, a lifetime's ideas, attitudes, events, and reading." His *George Orwell and the Origins of 1984* (Ann Arbor: University of Michigan Press, 1975) is a magnificent feat of scholarship that puts all serious students of Orwell in his lasting debt, showing precisely the "ideas, attitudes, events, and reading that helped to make up *Nineteen Eighty-Four*," but I must disagree that *Nineteen Eighty-Four* is a "culminating work": it is neither Orwell's best nor did he plan it as his last.
2. Crick, *Orwell*, 2, 410–12, 416–17.
3. Crick, *Orwell*, xiv–xv and 404.
4. Czeslaw Milosz, *The Captive Mind*, trans. Jane Zielonko (New York: Knopf, 1953), 40.
5. When William (now Sir William) Empson wrote to thank Orwell for *Animal Farm*, he pointed out that his son read it as "Tory propaganda," whereas he knew that Orwell intended it as socialism.

I certainly don't mean that is a fault in the allegory, it is a form that has to be set down and allowed to grow like a separate creature, and I think you let it do that with honesty and restraint. But I thought it worth warning you (while thanking you very heartily) that you must expect to be "misunderstood" on a large scale about this book—it is a form that inherently means more than the author means, when it is handled sufficiently well. (Letter of 24 August 1945, quoted in Crick, *Orwell*, 340.)

6. See Steinhoff, *Origins*.
7. Notably in his essay "Wells, Hitler and the World State," in *The Collected Essays, Journalism and Letters of George Orwell*, ed. Sonia Orwell and Ian Angus, 4 vols. (London: Secker and Warburg, 1968), 2:141–44 (hereafter cited as *CEJL*), and that on "Arthur Koestler," *CEJL* 3:234–44. And in a private letter to a reader of *Tribune*, he is explicit.

I think you overestimate the danger of a "Brave New World"—i.e. a completely materialistic vulgar civilisation based on hedonism. I would say that the danger of that kind of thing is past and that we are in danger of quite a different kind of world, the centralised slave state, ruled over by a small clique who are, in effect, a new ruling class, though they might be adoptive rather than hereditary. Such a state would not be hedonistic, on the contrary its dynamic would come from some kind of rabid nationalism and leader-worship kept going by literally continuous war. . . . I see no safe-guard against this except (a) war-weariness and distaste for author-itarianism which may follow the present war, (b) the survival of democratic values among the intelligentsia. (Cited in Crick, *Orwell*, 322–23.)

8. An excellent account of how Orwell used the concept of "decency" is R. Taylor, "George Orwell and the Politics of Decency," in *George Orwell*, Bradford Occasional Papers No. 3 (Leeds: Department of Adult Education and Extra-Mural Studies, October 1981).
9. George Orwell, *Nineteen Eighty-Four* (New York: New American Library, 1981), 220.
10. Orwell, *Nineteen Eighty-Four*, 240.
11. Orwell, *Nineteen Eighty-Four*, 31.
12. Orwell, *Nineteen Eighty-Four*, 136.
13. "The Prevention of Literature," *CEJL* 4:69.
14. Orwell, *Nineteen Eighty-Four*, 61–62.
15. Crick, *Orwell*, 395.
16. *CEJL* 4:17.
17. *CEJL* 3:132.
18. *CEJL* 4:177.
19. Orwell, *Nineteen Eighty-Four*, 220.
20. *CEJL* 4:63–64.
21. *CEJL* 4:64.

22. Orwell's dilemma is mirrored even in Hannah Arendt's uncertainty in her *Origins of Totalitarianism*, 3d ed. (New York: Harcourt, Brace, 1967), as to whether totalitarianism was literally possible, or whether the unique cruelties of what we called "totalitarianism" arose from an attempt to achieve the impossible. See my "On Rereading *The Origins of Totalitarianism*," *Social Research* 44, no. 1 (Spring, 1977):106–26.

23. *CEJL* 4:64.

George Orwell and the English Language

Richard W. Bailey

George Orwell's *Nineteen Eighty-Four* is one of the most influential
literary works of our century, and even people who have not read the
novel are conscious of its picture of a grim, drab totalitarian society
in which individuals are stifled by the power of the state.[1] Evidence
of the vitality of Orwell's influence is now found in the English language itself. Usages compiled and recorded in the new *Supplement* to
the *Oxford English Dictionary* (OED) show that words associated with
Orwell and his novel have achieved widespread currency, not inevitably in reference to him and his work but to ideas that people have
come to regard as "Orwellian." When authors decry "two ugly Orwellian names," "Orwellian grimness," or "Orwellian language," they
have in mind a particular kind of sordidness and brutality that applies
not just to his novel and its world but also to contemporary and future
events wholly unconnected with them. Similarly, *Big Brother* is not
just a character in the novel but, as the OED explains, any "apparently
benevolent but ruthlessly omnipotent, state authority." *Doublethink*,
"the mental capacity to accept as equally valid two entirely contrary
opinions or beliefs," is now in the language and on its own. So is
memory hole. *Newspeak* denotes not only the language Orwell invented in his novel but also virtually any corrupt form of English,
particularly, says the OED, the English used by some politicians,
propagandists, and broadcasters. *Nineteen eighty-four* (the phrase) refers to the only year of our century to have acquired connotations
before its arrival; those connotations are, of course, ominous and
dreadful, and the OED has properly recorded them.

Orwell's novel, then, has become part of contemporary culture not
always by its direct influence but often by second- and thirdhand means.
In examining "The Future of *Nineteen Eighty-Four*," we need first to
identify as precisely as we can Orwell's assumptions about his own
time and his expectations for the future; second, to determine just
how his novel projects those assumptions into a hypothetical future;
and third, to use what we have learned from Orwell to project from
our time—a generation after his—into the future that we now face.
Orwell himself saw his novel not as a forecast of what was likely to
happen (a prediction) but instead as an estimate of what might happen

(a projection) based on trends that he observed in his own time. To treat his novel as if it were a horoscope or tout sheet is to miss the point. Orwell (like Sir Thomas More, Jonathan Swift, or Jules Verne) asked his contemporaries to see what *might* happen given some assumptions about human nature and some estimates of what technology might provide. We too must temper our yearnings toward prophecy by acknowledging that our projections, like his, follow the uniformitarian principle, the conviction that future events will extend trends already in existence.

For my part, I want to direct attention to Orwell's ideas about language in general and the English language in particular, for it is in the way that he regarded language that his influence remains particularly strong. In doing so, I want to begin by discussing his views of spoken language and its varieties, the state of our language today, and what we may expect in the next generation. Then I wish to explore his ideas about language change and innovation (most particularly as they are reflected in Newspeak). Finally, I want to treat the most important of these three issues: the role of language (and particular kinds of language) in forming our ideology and shaping our ethical behavior.

"We have nothing to lose but our aitches."

At the conclusion of the *Communist Manifesto*, Marx and Engels wrote these famous words: "The proletarians have nothing to lose [in a communistic revolution] but their chains."[2] In *The Road to Wigan Pier*, Orwell echoed that slogan in an appeal to those he called fellow members of "the lower-upper-middle class."

> And when the widely separate classes who, necessarily, would form any real Socialist party have fought side by side, they may feel differently about one another. And then perhaps this misery of class-prejudice will fade away, and we of the sinking middle class—the private schoolmaster, the half-starved free-lance journalist, the colonel's spinster daughter with £75 a year, the jobless Cambridge graduate, the ship's officer without a ship, the clerks, the civil servants, the commercial travellers and the thrice-bankrupt drapers in the country towns—may sink without further struggles into the working class where we belong, and probably when we get there it will not be so dreadful as we feared, for, after all, we have nothing to lose but our aitches.[3]

For Orwell, the presence or absence of initial *h* was symbolic of the linguistic gulf that matched the chasm separating the social classes of Great Britain. The feature itself is readily recognizable: Orwell alludes to dialects in which *all* and *hall*, *art* and *heart*, *arm* and *harm* are pronounced the same. Then, as now, these dialects of England were primarily urban and working class, and thus in the opinion of "nearly every Englishman, whatever his origins . . . the most despised of all."[4]

In *Nineteen Eighty-Four*, the same linguistic feature separates members of the Party from the proles. The two men arguing about the lottery in the prole district do not speak in the way that Winston's colleagues at the Ministry of Truth do; one says, disputing the claim that a number ending in seven has recently been a winner: "No, it 'as not! Back 'ome I got the 'ole lot of 'em for over two years wrote down on a piece of paper."[5] Similarly, the old man in the pub disparages the conversion to the metric system by saying: " 'Ark at 'im! Calls 'isself a barman and don't know what a pint is! Why, a pint's the 'alf of a quart, and there's four quarts to the gallon. 'Ave to teach you the A, B, C next" (p. 75).

Orwell does not dramatize his own views of language variety in the novel; instead, he relies on his readers to see the fatal result of Winston's presumption that prole English is despicable and Oldspeak (or "Standard English") is good. In this and in other matters, too many readers have overlooked the difference between Orwell's ideas and those he assigns to his fictional character. Winston, unlike Orwell, despairs of the proles and accepts the values—including the linguistic values—of the lower-upper-middle class; Orwell struggled against temptations to do so. Hence to assume that Winston provides the reference norm for values in the novel is to misread it badly.

Everyone in Oceania suffers from shortages, misery, and capricious violence. Unlike Party members like Winston, however, the proles respond to these circumstances with benevolence: by helping each other (as in the warning that saves Winston from the falling rocket bomb as he walks through the prole district), by encouraging social life (compare the noisy pub with its conversation and dart game to the Chestnut Tree Cafe where talk is drowned by the raucous telescreen and the game of preference is the solitary solution to chess problems), and by giving birth and nurturing families. Only when Winston and Julia's idyll is on the brink of being shattered does Winston have an inkling of his mistake: "The birds sang, the proles sang, the Party did not sing," he thinks to himself, and then voices to Julia his fatal inference "We are the dead" (p. 182).

In *Nineteen Eighty-Four*, speech varieties are the consequence and not the cause of social divisions. Carelessly insensitive to the signs that language provides, Winston presumes that the thought-policeman disguised as Mr. Charrington is somehow cultivated or an aspirant to linguistic respectability because "his accent [is] less debased than that of the majority of proles" (p. 80). Charrington, of course, speaks like a member of Winston's class because he is a member of Winston's class: he is a Party loyalist laying a trap for the two lovers. When Charrington discards his prole disguise, his "cockney accent" disappears (p. 184) and his true voice, "a thin, cultivated voice" (p. 183), emerges as he pronounces the sentence of death. Charrington's accent is, of course, a fake, of a piece with his pretended stoop, his falsely whitened hair, and his altered facial features. In the world of the novel, the nature of one's English is an inevitable consequence of social class. Charrington adopts the "less debased" English that Winston admires as part of his plot, a strategem that ultimately succeeds. The possibility of a similar ruse occurs to Winston and Julia when they consider vanishing among the proles by learning "to speak with proletarian accents" (p. 126). Yet attempting such a disguise would be "nonsense"; their speech, they believe, would immediately expose them and their class origins.

Orwell consistently believed that working-class and habitually unemployed people were insensitive or indifferent to the variations in English speech that mark social class while the middle class (and above) responded to even the subtlest linguistic hints of social origin. In *Down and Out in Paris and London*, Orwell reported that his dialect was immediately identified in a shelter for the homeless destitute by a fellow old Etonian; speaking in "an educated, half-drunken voice," the stranger initiated a conversation by saying "An old public school boy, what?"[6] Similarly, in *A Clergyman's Daughter*, her fellow tramps find Dorothy Hare's accent unremarkable: "The tramps and cockney hop-pickers had not noticed her accent, but the suburban housewives noticed it quickly enough, and it scared them. . . . The moment they had heard her speak and spotted her for a gentlewoman, the game was up."[7] Given that belief, Orwell suggests that Winston and Julia might hide their origins from the proles but could not hope to conceal their accents from an assiduous thought-policeman. On the same basis, he invites his readers to presume that a reasonably vigilant and lower-upper-middle-class Winston should have identified Mr. Charrington as a linguistic anomaly, not upwardly mobile in his speech but as out of place in the prole district as if he had worn his Party uniform.

Orwell's ideology is not always well served by Orwell's fiction. By giving Winston the very attitudes that he despised, Orwell inadvertently sanctions the interpretation of the novel as his dying cry of despair. Yet Winston is a repellent figure who suffers, in part, because he is caught in the pretense and delusion of the lower-upper-middle class. In his evaluation of the spoken varieties of English—his notion that *h*-less speech is ignorant, brutish, and debased while *h*-full speech is wise, benevolent, and cultivated—Winston tumbles into the trap set for him by the Party. He is blinded to the truth by his uncritical acceptance of the conventional wisdom about the connections between accent and aptitude, dialect and decency.

Orwell's own notions about these connections were quite unlike Winston's. In the manuscript diary he kept through his final illness, he persists in his near-lifelong obsession with linguistic varieties. In the entry for April 17, 1949, he writes of his surprise at hearing, after two years in a Scottish sanitarium, the bray of "upper-class English voices."

> And what voices! A sort of over-fedness, a fatuous self-confi-
> dence, a constant bah-bahing of laughter abt nothing, above all
> a sort of heaviness & richness combined with a fundamental ill-
> will—people who, one instinctively feels, without even being
> able to see them, are the enemies of anything intelligent or
> sensitive or beautiful. No wonder everyone hates us so. (*CEJL*
> 4:578)

How poignant are these, virtually the last, words Orwell was able to write: the distance between his loyalties and those enemy voices suggested by "one instinctively feels"; the recognition that he is inextricably joined by language to those he despises: "No wonder everyone hates us so."

In considering the future of spoken English varieties, Orwell did not think profoundly or reach any very persuasive conclusions. He arrived at a position, but did not know quite what to do with its consequences. "The deadliest enemy of good English," he wrote in 1944, "is what is called 'standard English'" (*CEJL* 3:43). What he wished to do, of course, was to remove the connection between language and social class, and the following muddled account (written in 1944) of what ought to happen to sever that connection is not much improved upon in *Nineteen Eighty-Four.*

> The third thing that is needed is to remove the class labels from
> the English language. It is not desirable that all the local accents
> should disappear, but there should be a manner of speaking that
> is definitely national and is not merely (like the accent of B.B.C.
> announcers) a copy of the mannerisms of the upper classes. This
> national accent—a modification of cockney, perhaps, or of one
> of the northern accents—should be taught as a matter of course
> to all children alike. After that they could, and in some parts of
> the country probably would, revert to the local accent, but they
> should be able to speak standard English if they wished to. No
> one should be "branded on the tongue." (*CEJL* 3:51)

In this proposal, Orwell has done little to change the status quo. All he has accomplished, in fact, is to replace one national and class dialect with another, a synthetic "modification of cockney" or "one of the northern accents." The futility of creating a new national dialect was clear enough to him; "all nationalists," he wrote shortly after making his naive proposal, "consider it a duty to spread their own language to the detriment of rival languages, and among English-speakers this struggle reappears in subtler form as a struggle between dialects" (*CEJL* 3:417).

Although he searched for a way to bridge the gap between social classes and between their varieties of spoken English, Orwell failed to find one. Why should there be "a manner of speaking that is definitely national"? Why should some people "revert to local accents" in some parts of Britain but not in others? If "local accents" remain, is it not inevitable that some people "should be 'branded on the tongue' " as long as some accents are more equal than others? Orwell did not discover the answers to these questions. And neither have his successors.

Nonetheless, Orwell did correctly identify the complexity and the centrality of spoken English in maintaining social class distinctions. In the world of *Nineteen Eighty-Four*, there is no government in the usual sense, only the Party; there is no system of laws, only the disabling inhibition of fear; except among the proles, there is no cohesive bond of family and friends, only the mass hysteria that congeals a crowd into a mob. The single binding force that creates the state is, if Goldstein's *Oligarchical Collectivism* is to be believed, language.

> Oceania has no capital, and its titular head is a person whose whereabouts nobody knows. Except that English is its chief lingua franca and Newspeak is its official language, it is not centralized in any way. (p. 172)

"*Except* that English." In Orwell's England, there were national and class loyalties, family and friends, institutions and laws. In the world that he projects into the future, all of these are damaged or destroyed. Only English (and its nascent offspring, Newspeak) remains the element that gives "centralizing force."

Since Orwell's time, little has changed in the structured diversity of spoken English; dialects and accents have not disappeared or diminished, though the features that manifest the distinctions between them may have shifted in frequency or kind. *H*-dropping remains "the single most powerful pronunciation shibboleth in England"[8]; both *h*-droppers and *h*-keepers understand the rules of the game. A London school teacher recently told J. C. Wells of University College, London, that "he has only to look sternly at any child who drops an /h/, and that child will say the word again, this time correctly."[9] Lower-upper-middle-class people today are no more inclined to lose their aitches than they were when Orwell visited Wigan Pier almost fifty years ago; urban working-class people, like the child in Wells's anecdote, retain their tendency to drop aitches even though they "know" the style-shifting rules that enable them to put aitches where middle-class teachers think they belong.

In estimating the future of spoken English diversity, we need to consider the values that given features manifest rather than the features themselves. *H*-dropping emerged into social consciousness in London speech only in the eighteenth century, and it is not surprising that in the colonies settled earlier (like the United States and Canada) the feature is virtually unknown, while in subsequent colonies (like Australia and New Zealand), *h*-loss follows the English pattern. The question for our future speculation should not be: will *h*-loss spread or diminish? Instead, we should ask if the social forces that foster and maintain dialect differences will change.

What projection should we make based on our perception of our present world? On Goldstein's evidence, the people of Oceania were "forbidden the knowledge of foreign languages" (p. 162). Such a measure was designed, of course, to encourage the belief that the enemy was "not like us" (not even fully human, perhaps) and to prevent private alliances between Oceania and the two other superpowers, Eastasia and Eurasia. In the United States, at least, there is little need of prohibition against the knowledge of foreign languages, since our people have grown increasingly reluctant to learn them.[10] Hence we are thrust back on the community of English speakers, perhaps not altogether a disabling act since today some 300 million people speak English as their mother tongue and a nearly equal number make some use of it as a second language.

Our efforts to promote the hegemony of English as a world language, as the proper vehicle for "development" and "modernization," are bound to fail simply as a result of the inexorable shift in the world's population from the countries of the haves to the countries of the have-nots. According to the best demographic estimates, four of the world's ten most populous urban areas in 1960 were predominantly English speaking. Explosive population growth and increasing urbanization will mean that the proportion of the world's people living in cities will increase from 38 percent in 1970 to 45 percent in 1990. By then only one of these much larger urban areas will be English speaking.[11] Hence we should not now imagine, as Orwell did in 1948, an immense alliance of people "centralized" by the use of English as a lingua franca. Instead, we should recognize as he did in 1944 that "the world is growing more and not less nationalistic in language. . . . There is going to be some ugly scrapping before [the choice of an international language] is settled, as anyone who has ever glanced into the subject knows" (*CEJL* 3:108).

Within the English-speaking community, we can project a future in which the varieties of English reflect the shared values of oligarchs. Except for those minor differences that distinguish North American varieties of prestigious English from British ones, world elites using English tend to resemble each other more than they resemble the uneducated and powerless in their own region. Foreign ministers attending a Commonwealth conference in London sound alike, much more alike than the representative of Singapore sounds like the English-speaking cab driver in Singapore or the British Foreign Secretary sounds like the cab driver in London. In Orwell's novel, the proles spoke a uniform variety of English in Airstrip One (or London). In our world and in the future, the proles in various English-speaking areas will grow to be more and more unlike each other. Emerging national standards of English may support some national coherence, but where English survives as a nationally spoken language, it is likely to be more diverse—and hence, for the working class, less and less internationally intelligible.[12]

As for attitudes toward English, we have made little collective progress in escaping from the beliefs that led the hapless Winston into Charrington's trap. Far from increasing our tolerance for linguistic diversity, we regard English different from our own as more or less "debased"—as if a linguistic Gresham's Law governed the values associated with "pure" English and with English "corrupted by base metals." Winston is hoodwinked into trust by O'Brien's "peculiar grave courtesy" (p. 130) and by Charrington's apparently cultivated prole accent. Until the moment of his arrest, he despises the English of the proles. We too have done little to separate our notions of good and bad English from our judgments of whom we ought to trust and admire.

"We're getting the language into its final shape."

In *Nineteen Eighty-Four*, Orwell describes through Winston's thoughts "the sacred principles of Ingsoc. Newspeak, doublethink, the mutability of the past" (p. 25). All three principles have contributed to the current popular notion of the message of the novel, but none of them is more central to the definition of "Orwellian" than the deliberate manipulation of language to serve the ends of obscurantism, manipulation, and control. Newspeak, the emerging revision of language, is the first of these principles of Ingsoc; according to Syme (the lexicographer), the eleventh edition of the Newspeak dictionary will strip

Oldspeak of "its vagueness and its useless shades of meaning" (p. 46). As we learn from the appendix to the novel, Newspeak is designed "not to extend but to *diminish* the range of thought, and this purpose was indirectly assisted by cutting the choice of words down to a minimum" (p. 247).

In the novel itself, we are never given unambiguous examples of Newspeak prose; all the communications we are invited to inspect show only the transition toward the ultimate goal of the Newspeak ideal, to be achieved only in the year 2050. When Winston receives instructions at work, they are presented in "abbreviated jargon—not actually Newspeak, but consisting largely of Newspeak words" (p. 27). Likewise, O'Brien dictates his commands through the speakwrite "in the hybrid jargon of the Ministries," once again employing Newspeak words but not fully employing the evolving ideal language. While we are told that the "leading articles," or editorials, of the *Times* even in 1984 were "written entirely in Newspeak" (p. 40), we are never given an instance that would illustrate that language in extended use. When Winston sets out to rewrite a story that appeared in the *Times* on December 3, 1983, he presents Big Brother's Order for the Day in an English that bears little resemblance to what we know of Newspeak (p. 40).

Even without extended examples, the instances of Newspeak in the novel provide an idea of its grammar and vocabulary. In grammar, according to the appendix, all parts of speech have become interchangeable and all inflections follow the same rules. Though we are told in the appendix that the opening lines of the *Declaration of Independence* could not be rendered into Newspeak "while keeping to the sense of the original," Anthony Burgess has done so in the reflective essay on the novel he titled *1985*. First, let us recall the words of the original text.

> We hold these truths to be self-evident, that all men are created equal, that they are endowed by their creator with certain unalienable rights, that among these are life, liberty, and the pursuit of happiness. That to secure these rights, Governments are instituted among men, deriving their just powers from the consent of the governed.

Here is the Newspeak revision as Burgess has contrived it from Orwell's "principles."

> We say that truth writed is truth unwrited, that all mans are the same as each other, that their fathers and mothers maked them so that they are alive, free from all diseases and following not food but the feeling of having eated food. They are maked like this by their parents but Big Brother makes them like this.[13]

The regularization of the inflectional system is apparent here: *writed* for *written, mans* for *men, maked* for *made*. Yet Burgess has not achieved the aim to which Newspeak aspires, that of making English grammarless, compact, telegraphic, and entirely devoid of eloquence.

The vocabulary of Newspeak is much easier to illustrate, and both the appendix and the novel itself provide abundant examples. Newspeak vocabulary is of three types: the A vocabulary, a limited number of words concerned with everyday life "intended only to express simple, purposive thoughts, usually involving concrete objects or physical actions" (p. 247); the B vocabulary, "deliberately constructed for political purposes . . . [and] intended to impose a desirable mental attitude upon the person using them" (p. 249); and the C vocabulary, consisting "entirely of scientific and technical terms" (p. 254). Most of the instances of Newspeak found in the novel belong to the B vocabulary, and nearly all of them are compounds: *goodthinkful* 'incapable of thinking a bad thought' (p. 110), *facecrime* 'an expression suggesting the criminal has "something to hide"' (p. 54), *duckspeak* 'to quack like a duck' (used of human beings) (p. 48), *goodthinker* 'naturally orthodox' (p. 174). Others are formed from affixes and roots: for instance, *unperson* 'a human being declared officially non-existent' (p. 130), *doubleplusungood* 'extremely unsatisfactory' (p. 40), *fullwise* 'in full' (p. 40). Still others consist of blends joining parts of Oldspeak words: *Minitrue* 'Ministry of Truth', *Minipax* 'Ministry of Peace,' *Miniluv* 'Ministry of Love', *Miniplenty* 'Ministry of Plenty' (p. 8), *Pornosec* 'Pornography Section' (p. 39), *artsem* 'artificial insemination' (p. 57). All of these strive for economy and compact meanings into an abbreviated form. "Oldthinkers unbellyfeel Ingsoc" is glossed for us in the appendix as a Newspeak rendering of "Those whose ideas were formed before the Revolution cannot have a full emotional understanding of the principles of English socialism" (p. 250), an expression in three words of ideas that required twenty in Oldspeak. These words, and others, reflect no straightforward "etymological plan." In the B vocabulary especially, Newspeak words "could be any parts of speech, and could be placed in any order and mutilated in any way which made them easy to pronounce while indicating their derivation" (p. 250).

In exploring the nature of Newspeak and Orwell's own view of linguistic change, we need to keep in mind three immediate consequences of the impulse that animates the linguistic innovations he describes: euphony, telescoped words and phrases, and euphemisms. "Euphony," the appendix explains, "outweighed every consideration other than exactitude of meaning," but *euphony* in Newspeak does not carry its usual meaning of pleasing or harmonious sound; instead it denotes "a gabbling style of speech, at once staccato and monotonous" (p. 253). Stress patterns are thus arranged so that oratory resembles a metronome rather than a melody and speech becomes "independent of consciousness." A political address in Newspeak would be quite different from the two examples of public speaking provided in the novel itself: the voice from the telescreen in the Two Minute Hate and the Hitlerian orator who harangues the crowd during Hate Week. In both cases, language is used to create a mass psychosis. Listeners lose all sense of individual response; "it was impossible," Winston says, "to avoid joining in" (p. 16). At the rally, "every few moments the fury of the crowd boiled over and the voice of the speaker was drowned by a wild beastlike roaring that rose uncontrollably from thousands of throats" (p. 149). With the eventual implementation of Newspeak, however, the need for such oratory would wither away. There would be no reason to create the sort of hysteria the novel describes because the very language itself, with its monotony and its "harsh sound and certain willful ugliness" (p. 253), would guarantee orthodoxy and subservience.

A second result of the impulse that drives Newspeak is telescoped words and phrases. In the appendix, Orwell observes that these words in the twentieth century were "one of the characteristic features of political language . . . , [particularly] in totalitarian countries and totalitarian organizations" (p. 252). As examples, he offers *Nazi* (from *Nationalsozialist*), *Gestapo* (from *Geheime Staatspolizei* 'secret state police'), *Comintern* (from *Communist International*), and *Agitprop* (from *agitatsiya propaganda* 'agitation propaganda'). Orwell does not find these formations ugly in themselves. Instead, he sees them emerging from a desire to cut away "most of the associations that would otherwise cling" to them (p. 253). Echoes, connotations, and history need to be controlled and the underlying forms to be cleansed of the associations that make them powerful, leaving only the neutral denotations.

Of the traits of Newspeak, the most important is the use of euphemism, the substitution of words that, Orwell explains, mean "almost the exact opposite of what they appeared to mean." These include, of course, the *Ministry of Truth* or *Minitrue* responsible for falsehoods, the *Ministry of Plenty* for managing scarcity, the *Ministry of Peace* for conducting war, and the *Ministry of Love* for meting out torture and terror. Here too, the impulse is to shift connotations and associations in a direction that serves the Party's ends, toward passivity and acceptance of lies, misery, warfare, and hatred. What euphemism accomplishes—as do euphony and telescoped words—is to constrain free expression by purging language of associations that do not serve the aims of the Party.

Many people who have read *Nineteen Eighty-Four* (and virtually all Orwellians who have not read it) regard Orwell's description of Newspeak as a mirror of the ideas he actually espoused about language: that grammatical simplification corresponds to intellectual simplicity; that the use of nouns as verbs or verbs as nouns reduces thought to uniform pabulum; that purging ordinary words of their ambiguities and shades of meaning is inevitably damaging; that providing ideological words with pleasant associations is deeply dishonest. Careful inspection of the novel and Orwell's other comments on language suggests that he would not unequivocally endorse any one of these claims. Such examination makes clear that Orwell devised "The Principles of Newspeak" as part of the fictional enterprise that is *Nineteen Eighty-Four*. What he actually thought about the direction that English was taking is very different.

Orwell's outline anticipating *Nineteen Eighty-Four* was written as early as 1943. In it he places "Newspeak" first among the themes and ideas "to be brought in."[14] Though *Animal Farm* (1946) shows little of this fascination with language, his essay "Politics and the English Language" (written in 1946) provides a reference point for his views. In that essay, he identifies two principal qualities that seem to him to explain much that is wrong with contemporary writing: staleness of imagery and lack of precision (*CEJL* 4:158). Further, he praises brevity, the use of words of few syllables, vocabulary from Anglo-Saxon rather than classical sources, and conciseness. All of these traits are, of course, precisely the attributes of Newspeak. Bad political writing, Orwell writes, likewise suffers from excessive abstraction: "as soon as certain topics are raised, the concrete melts into the abstract and no one seems able to think of turns of speech that are not hackneyed" (*CEJL* 4:159). Yet Newspeak, the ultimate political language, thrives on the concrete. Anthony Burgess was following Newspeak principles when he rendered *liberty* as "free from all diseases" in his revision of the Declaration of Independence.

Like Syme, the zealous pruner of Oldspeak, Orwell could grow enthusiastic about reforming the language. For all his satire of Syme's literal-minded objections to "vagueness and useless shades of meaning," Orwell found it possible to assert precisely parallel ideas.

> Notice, I am not saying that *art* would necessarily improve if words conveyed meaning more reliably. For all I know art thrives on the crudeness and vagueness of language. I am only criticizing *words* in their supposed function as vehicles of thought. And it seems to me that from the point of view of exactitude and expressiveness our language has remained in the Stone Age. (*CEJL* 2:21)

Though he approved in principle of the invention of new words, he was more inclined to achieve "exactitude and expressiveness" by expurgating the English vocabulary. In an *As I Please* essay published in 1944, he inveighs against the use of borrowed words when "an English equivalent already exists or could easily be improvised" (*CEJL* 3:157). Where borrowings have already taken hold, he writes, they should be pronounced as fully anglicized and adapted to English spelling conventions (*caffay* instead of *café*, for instance, though "we got on well enough with 'coffee house' for two hundred years"). Even as he wrote *Nineteen Eighty-Four*, he compiled a long list of "foreign words & phrases unnecessarily used in English" and assigned to most of them the label "scrap."[15] Getting the English language out of "the Stone Age" was a task to which he devoted repeated attention. Most people, he thought, share with Winston the conviction that reforming the language is "blasphemy" (*CEJL* 2:23); that opinion is not Orwell's.

In reflecting on language, Orwell was much influenced by ideas that emerged from the work of Count Alfred Korzybski and of C. K. Ogden and I. A. Richards. The former inspired the General Semantics movement and explored the influence of "bad language" on thinking. For Korzybski and his followers, abstractions were misleading or meaningless unless they could be derived by deductive principles from concrete observations, and these ideas reached Orwell through books by Stuart Chase and Lancelot Hogben.[16] While in many ways sympathetic to the ideas of General Semantics, Orwell recognized that a language of nearly pure denotation could not cope with the most significant aspects of human creativity and freedom. In fact, in "Politics and the English Language," Orwell singles out Chases's *Tyranny of Words* for special criticism.

> Stuart Chase and others have come near to claiming that all abstract words are meaningless, and have used this as a pretext for advocating a kind of political quietism. Since you don't know what Fascism is, how can you struggle against Fascism? One need not swallow such absurdities as this, but one ought to recognize that the present political chaos is connected with the decay of language, and that one can probably bring about some improvement by beginning at the verbal end. (*CEJL* 4:169–70)

The very concreteness of the names *Big Brother* and *Emmanuel Goldstein*—whose existence the novel leads us to doubt—is sufficient evidence that unbridled abstraction is not the only source of linguistic tyranny in Oceania. While one might "bring about some improvement by beginning at the verbal end," *Nineteen Eighty-Four* makes it clear that the sorts of ideas that Korzybski and Chase articulated could not in themselves prevent "political chaos" and enforced orthodoxy.

Ogden and Richards realized, as Orwell subsequently would, that "in war-time words become a normal part of the mechanism of deceit,"[17] and they wished to provide a corrective to that "mechanism" by offering a theory of definition that would yield "a means of controlling [words] as symbols, a means of readily discovering to what in the world on any occasion they are used to refer."[18] One consequence of their theory was the system of Basic English designed by Ogden to function as "an international auxiliary language" and "to provide a rational introduction to normal English" for foreign learners.[19] Basic English was designed, as Newspeak is, to reduce radically the number of words in the language, or rather to reduce their necessity for the usual occasions of communication. Within the 850 words of Basic, Ogden argued, anyone could "cover the field; that is to say, the essential minimum in which everything of general interest can be talked about."[20] And like Newspeak, Basic employed a drastically simplified grammar containing only five rules. For many people around the world, Basic English has provided an entry point to the full range of English, and the rationale that led to its adoption continues today in, for instance, the idea of "Nuclear English" promoted by Randolph Quirk.[21]

In his discussion of Basic English in one of his *As I Please* columns in 1944, Orwell was entirely approving. While not especially concerned with Basic as an international auxiliary language, he concluded that "it can act as a sort of corrective to the oratory of statesmen and publicists. High-sounding phrases, when translated into Basic, are often deflated in a suprising way." Above all, he wrote, "in Basic . . . you cannot make a meaningless statement without its being apparent that it is meaningless" (*CEJL* 3:244). Yet it is precisely this quality that is one of the principal attributes of Newspeak. According to the appendix, "in Newspeak the expression of unorthodox opinions, above a very low level, was well-nigh impossible" (p. 254). Both language reforms constrain what is possible to say: in Basic, he suggests, it is impossible to tell lies because their falsity is manifest; in Newspeak, it is impossible to tell the truth since words like *equal* or *free* have been purged of all associations that formerly connected them to social equality or political freedom.[22]

Since Newspeak manifests so many of the ideas that Orwell treated approvingly elsewhere in his writings, we need to examine the status of language reforms in *Nineteen Eighty-Four* with great care. Of course Newspeak and the evolutionary changes in Oldspeak that move toward it are ugly, constraining, and brutal, but it is not obvious that the Party arose because of bad language. Instead, it took its shape for quite different reasons and is shown in the novel midway in its progress toward inventing a language to suit its ideology. To presume that Orwell's critique of language is central to his purposes in *Nineteen Eighty-*

Four—and thus to use *Orwellian* as a way of talking about language of which one does not approve—is to focus on the effects of ideology rather than on causes. This same may be said of his views in "Politics and the English Language." As Harvey A. Daniels points out in an insightful commentary,

> Orwell's essay, in general, is a more effective attack on *what* some people in his world are saying than on *how* they are saying it. For all his talk about staleness of imagery, mixed metaphors, and so forth, Orwell is mainly angry about some people's ideas, their purposes.[23]

Orwell objects to bad motives more than to bad language. Party members brutalize their language because they aspire to turn others into brutes incapable of consciousness. From the Party's perspective, as Syme says, "the Revolution will be complete when the language is perfect" (pp. 46–47).

Contemplating the future of Newspeak provides a nearly irresistible temptation to the Orwellians of popular culture. What is entirely unremarkable is that they find it convenient to attack the politics or persons of those they dislike by attacking their language in a simplistic equation of bad ideas and bad language. This rhetorical strategy is not especially constrained by ideology; both the political right and the political left berate each other on the grounds that their opponents are guilty of debasing the language. Euphemism and telescoped words and phrases are most often attacked, but all sorts of alien ideas can be assaulted with linguistic artillery.

So abundant are the examples of this form of argument that there is virtually no end to the lists of despised examples. William Lambdin, a journalist from Greeley, Colorado, has compiled an entire dictionary to illustrate the kind of language he finds objectionable. A few sample entries give some of the flavor of his lexicography and of his politics: *campaign contributions* 'bribes,' *comsymp* 'communist sympathizer,' *defense department* 'war department,' *doctoral dissertation* 'an assault on the English language.' *English teachers* 'a public enemy,' *public purse* 'a grab bag,' and *scientific paper* 'a cunningly contrived piece of rhetoric.' One need not read far in such a reference work to discern that Lambdin is angry about a variety of things and that his objections to them are only incidentally linguistic.[24]

Arguments *ad linguam* are apparently more abundant than ever. Here are two specimens to show how the same strategy can be used for quite different ends.

> There was often not much that was "free" about many of the states that made up what we used to call, sometimes with capital

letters, the Free World; as there is, alas, very often little that is gay about many of those who seek these days to kidnap that sparkling word for specialized use. Social fluidity, moral pretension, political and literary demagoguery, corporate and academic bureaucratization and a false conception of democracy are leading us into semantic chaos.[25]

The incineration of all life was never really faced; what was faced were the academic problems of the algebra of death, the abstract problems of adjusting, equating, and manipulating the wellbred symbols of annihilation. The minters of nuclear newspeak white-washed the sepulchers with the same jingling slogans ("peace is our profession"), the same crypto-sexuality (SM 72, Goose, Hermes and Nike, GAM 63), the same fudgey endorsings, philosophic, patriotic, theological (Plato, Minuteman, Apollo) as had their mentors, the account execs of the agencies.[26]

Aside from a cosmetic interest in language, these two writers do not share the same views. Both of them chose to vent their fury in 1974 in essays that, through their titles if little else, recall Orwell; the essays are both called "Politics and the American Language."

From the perspective of 1984 (the year), we ought not to imagine that "the English language is in a bad way." Our age is more prone to infelicitous linguistic innovation and mendacity than any earlier one. What is remarkable is that Orwell's novel has invigorated a form of argument in which one attacks opponents through their language rather than through their ideas. To this same end, the National Council of Teachers of English (NCTE) has constituted a "Committee on Public Doublespeak" to give "the George Orwell Award for Distinguished Contribution to Honesty and Clarity in Public Language," a prize honoring writers who dissect and decry the language of advertisers and bureaucrats. The same committee also stages a competition, highly publicized, to pillory the worst offenders against the language among elected officials and public figures. Through filmstrip kits called "Doublespeak Box" and "Ad Analysis," the NCTE abets English teachers in persuading the young that the media are not to be trusted and that our government is staffed by dishonest or incompetent persons.

Orwell would doubtless have approved of the Committee on Public Doublespeak. He was sympathetic to the efforts of Mass Observation, a committee formed by Sir Richard Acland in the early months of the war "to find out what meaning, if any, the ordinary man attaches to the high-sounding abstract words which are flung to and fro in politics" (*CEJL* 3:162). What might surprise and distress him, however, is the way in which these relentless attacks have spawned skepticism and mistrust of government by the governed, of the media by readers and listeners, and of virtually all institutions by vast numbers of the public. The more people are constantly warned to watch out for lies, the more they expect to be lied to. In our time, however, we have been lied to by our leaders, and the residue of public mendacity makes all public language suspect. Our problem is not to find a language that tells the truth, but institutions that make the truth available in whatever linguistic form. *Nineteen Eighty-Four* is clearly a cautionary tale. One of its accidental effects may have been to make us too cautious, too preoccupied with language, too reluctant to act on our convictions.

"All art is propaganda."

Orwellians sometimes forget that Winston Smith is a professional writer, and, to judge from O'Brien's opinion of his efforts, a good one. "Winston's greatest pleasure in life was in his work" (p. 39), and his job of "rectifying" the past consumes the many hours he spends at the Ministry of Truth. Syme correctly detects that "in his heart" Winston enjoys writing but prefers "Oldspeak, with all its vagueness and its useless shades of meaning" (p. 46). One is therefore not surprised to find that the first act of Winston's nascent rebellion is buying a book with blank pages and beginning to write in it. For Winston, writing is a way of finding out the truth, an attitude he evidently shares with the Inner Party which devotes an enormous investment in labor and machinery to "perfecting" the truth by revising the records of the past. However perverse that investment seems to us, it does acknowledge a value we share with the society of Oceania: the belief that documents—acts of reading and writing—provide a source of knowledge and values.

Written documents carry with them a kind of magic in the world of *Nineteen Eighty-Four*. When Julia furtively passes him that "scrap of paper folded into a square," Winston immediately grasps that "there must be a message of some kind written on it" (p. 89). Since it is impossible for him to unfold and read the note without careful concealment and delay, Winston finds himself swept into a spiral of growing terror. He suspects that "the message probably meant death" (p. 90) and is staggered when he finally reads the words written on the paper: "I love you." A book provides another spur to Winston's rebellion—Goldstein's book, *The Theory and Practice of Oligarchical Collectivism*.

Written documents are so important to their readers that the Party has organized its resources to pervert and alter them. But there is a paradox in that program: while manipulating the language to ensure orthodoxy, the Party must struggle to control the unorthodox opinions that are based on documents. We are invited to assume that people bother to read the files of old newspapers so elaborately altered and that the information they contain will form the basis of beliefs. But it is the very process of believing that is a threat to the Party's tyranny. As O'Brien explains during Winston's interrogation, the eventual aim of the Party is to achieve a "collective solipsism," a state in which people can rely only on the constructs of their own minds. Nothing external to the mind, even written records of the past, will then be needed as a source of validation and truth. Hence documents must successively inspire respect, fear, contempt, and, ultimately, indifference. In his work as a writer, Winston ought to be well along in that succession since he is charged with mingling fact and fiction. But he concludes when he has finished creating the life of Comrade Ogilvy, "Comrade Ogilvy, who had never existed in the present, now existed in the past, and when once the act of forgery was forgotten, he would exist just as authentically, and upon the same evidence, as Charlemagne or Julius Caesar" (p. 43). The records that Winston creates continue to yield their evocative power to inspire, even when they are historically inaccurate.

In addition to its efforts to revise the written record of the past, the Ministry of Truth is charged with composing new texts. Some of them, we learn, are composed "without any human intervention whatever on an instrument known as a versificator" (p. 115), the machine used to produce the lyrics of the popular songs that find such favor among the proles.[27] Julia's work in the Fiction Department is to service "the novel-writing machines in the Fiction Department" (p. 108) where pornographic novels—"ghastly rubbish" as she calls them—are produced. Such literally mechanical writing fulfills an important purpose for the Party: the machines ensure both orthodoxy and the withering away of the creative impulse that inspires even the most ordinary written materials. Documents produced by machines are harmless because they consist only of prefabricated elements; these writings, unlike those produced by human beings, can never affirm or deny because they are not animated by conviction or doubt.[28]

When Orwell examined the state of contemporary writing in "Politics and the English Language," he observed that "prose consists less and less of *words* chosen for the sake of their meaning, and more and more of *phrases* tacked together like the sections of a prefabricated hen-house" (*CEJL* 4:159). In Oceania, such mechanical writing is composed by literal machines in the Ministry of Truth, and in that respect, his novel reflects the culmination of a trend in his own time that alarmed him. "Staleness of imagery" and "lack of precision," in other words, were not causes but effects of unreflective thought or deliberate deception. The atrophy of creativity and of freedom thus lies at the heart of the matter for Orwell, and "it is at this point that the special connection between politics and the debasement of language becomes clear" (*CEJL* 4:165).

Writing and reading can be a source of human redemption in the world of *Nineteen Eighty-Four*. When Winston begins to write in his diary, he is freed of the constraints of past texts and bureaucratic directives that shape his writing at the Ministry. His first efforts are fragmentary: sentence fragments and phrases punctuated as sentences; deletion of articles and auxiliary verbs; neglect of the conventions of capitalization and punctuation. Even those maimed literary efforts soon disintegrate, and "he discovered that while he sat helplessly musing he had also been writing, as though by automatic action" (p. 19). The text that he mechanically and unconsciously produces consists of repeating a perversion of Party slogans, and he fills half a page by writing "Down with Big Brother" over and over again. But when he resumes writing, it is with a new conviction. He has found an audience—people living in "a time when thought is free" (pp. 26–27)—and he speaks directly to it: he composes a connected discourse, draws inferences and conclusions from ideas, and achieves the kind of creativity that makes it possible for him to think, and ultimately to act. His writing still mimics the style of public documents, but we should see that transitional style as moving him toward reflection and moral choice. Then, by copying from a children's history textbook, he gains confidence in writing, even though he realizes that the book itself is an unreliable fabrication. Finally, in the last specimen of his private writing that Orwell displays, Winston describes his encounter with the prostitute in a way that is coherent, personal, and ethical. He has used writing to discover himself, to locate and anatomize the moral flaw that led him to a furtive sexual encounter, and to realize his complicity in the corruption of his society: "But I went ahead and did it just the same" (p. 60).

Not all the things that inspire Winston to reflection and right action involve written texts, of course. The glass paperweight that evokes a past world of beauty for its own sake, the half-remembered nursery rhyme "Oranges and Lemons," the steel engraving of St. Clement's Dane in its rosewood frame hung in the room above Mr. Charrington's shop, the idyllic glade with its dappled light and shade—all these inspire his imagination and make him more fully free and more fully human. Nonetheless, the act of writing and the opportunity to read texts uncontaminated (as he believes) by official action provide the only opportunities that Winston ever finds to gain a sense of control over his own destiny.

No one has ever doubted that Orwell was a political writer, even in the novels like *Burmese Days* or *A Clergyman's Daughter* through which he first made his reputation. As an essayist, he was primarily concerned with explaining the "politics" of the cultural scene, and perhaps nowhere better than in his 1939 essay on Charles Dickens did he express his essential conviction.

> Every writer, especially every novelist, *has* a "message," whether he admits it or not, and the minutest details of his work are influenced by it. All art is propaganda. (*CEJL* 1:491–92)

Later, after the war, he was even more explicit about his purposes: "What I have most wanted to do throughout the past ten years is to make political writing into an art." That task, he recognized, "is not easy. It raises problems of construction and of language, and it raises in a new way the problem of truthfulness" (*CEJL* 1:28).

Precisely those "problems of construction and of language" are dramatized in *Nineteen Eighty-Four*. Winston's dilemma as a writer is to solve that "problem of truthfulness" in a society in which truth is more elusive than ever before and in which language and construction seem to conspire to prevent him from gaining any sure grasp of reality. Nonetheless, Orwell shows that even in the most repressive of societies it is possible for the writer to regain freedom by finding a language to express conviction and belief.

In at least one respect, Orwell's projection about writers and their language has come true. Winston's work at the Ministry is solitary, and his writings enter the huge data base of the Records Department by mechanical means. Much more than in Orwell's day, professional writers in bureaucracies are now obliged to conform to standards set by others and to efface their creativity by adapting their documents to a scheme circumscribed by the norms of a computer network. The office of the future, like Winston's workplace, will be even more devoid of direct human contact than is now the case. Written English in the workplace will grow more standardized and more governed by the demands of organized life. We may not find it easy to retain our sense of the power of language; we may even approach that sense of anomie that afflicts Winston and drives him to despair. But language is always available as it was to Winston. Language can allow us to reflect, explore, and grope for the truth; to convey our sense of joy and love and playfulness. We can continue to read *Nineteen Eighty-Four* and to reflect on its "message," if only to remind ourselves that language—reading and writing—is always present to make us free.

Where do we now stand as we project our own beliefs about language into the future? Human language still retains its creativity and power. Only if we succumb to the temptation to allow barbarous language to turn us into barbarians will we find that we have arrived in "1984." That temptation is always present. In the war in Southeast Asia, our military fostered a linguistic environment in which the Vietnamese people were called by such names as *slope, dink, slant, gook,* and *zip*; those names made it so much easier to despise, to fear, and to kill them. When we call women in our own society by the names *gash*, *slut*, *dyke*, *bitch*, or *girl*, we—men and women alike—have put ourselves in a position to demean and abuse them.

As Orwell asserted, we can reform our understanding of the world by reforming our language. The decision to say *women* instead of *ladies* or *blacks* instead of *Negroes* may not change our treatment of other people, but it does acknowledge their right to dignity, to be called by names that they themselves choose. The new names may evolve into euphemistic "code words," as these terms and ones like them have sometimes become in our public discourse. But anatomizing our own language is a step toward thinking that does not make us ashamed of ourselves. Looking closely at our language, caring about it, is a step toward honesty and self-understanding. Orwell wishes us to be attentive to our use of English because he wants us to be alive to our beliefs, most especially those that come to us prefabricated and that we pass along to others without reflection. We cannot blame our language but only ourselves if we allow the linguistic prejudices and preferences we inherit to shape our behavior.

In "Politics and the English Language," Orwell asserted that "if thought corrupts language, language can also corrupt thought" (*CEJL* 4:167). Yet this circle is not closed. Language can be made creative and open for us new thoughts; new thoughts can evoke new language. We are only imprisoned by our language and our thoughts if we choose to be so. *Nineteen Eighty-Four* dramatizes a society in which people have lost their freedom by unreflective acceptance of orthodox thoughts and by employing a language that is deliberately stripped of its creativity. We need not suffer that loss. But if we are to avoid doing so, we must acknowledge our responsibility for our beliefs, for our language, and for our freedom.

Notes

1. Several colleagues and friends have provided helpful comments and advice on an earlier version of this essay. I am especially grateful to Judith C. Avery, Barbara Couture, Bernard Crick, Marsha Dutton, Douglas P. Evett, Robin Melanie Fosheim, Ejner J. Jensen, and Marilyn J. Shatz.

2. Karl Marx and Friedrich Engels, *Basic Writings on Politics and Philosophy*, ed. Lewis S. Feuer (Garden City, N.Y.: Anchor Books, 1959), 41.

3. George Orwell, *The Road to Wigan Pier* (New York: Berkley Medallion Books, 1967), 191.

4. George Orwell, *Nineteen Eighty-Four* (New York: Signet, 1962), 72. Subsequent references to the novel are cited parenthetically in the text.

5. Sonia Orwell and Ian Angus, eds., *The Collected Essays, Journalism and Letters of George Orwell*, 4 vols (Harmondsworth, Eng.: Penguin, 1970), 3:44. Subsequent references are contained in the text with the citation *CEJL*.

6. *Down and Out in Paris and London* (New York: Harper and Brothers, 1933), 218.

7. *A Clergyman's Daughter* (New York: Harbrace Paperbound Library, n.d.), 163.

8. J. C. Wells, *Accents of English* (Cambridge: Cambridge University Press, 1982), 1:254.

9. Wells, *Accents of English*, 1:254.

10. The presumption that a single language is sufficient and normal is a natural consequence of ethnocentrism in the United States. From a global perspective, the situation is quite different: "Bilingualism is present in practically every country of the world, in all classes of society, in all age groups; in fact, it has been estimated that half the world's population is bilingual" (François Grosjean, *Life with Two Languages: An Introduction to Bilingualism* [Cambridge, Mass.: Harvard University Press, 1982], vii).

11. See Richard W. Bailey, "Literacy in English: An International Perspective," in *Literacy for Life: The Demand for Reading and Writing*, ed. Richard W. Bailey and Robin Melanie Fosheim (New York: Modern Language Association, 1983), 30–44.

12. See Richard W. Bailey and Manfred Görlach, eds., *English as a World Language* (Ann Arbor: University of Michigan Press, 1982).

13. Anthony Burgess, *1985* (Boston: Little, Brown and Co., 1978), 41.

14. Quoted by Bernard Crick, *George Orwell: A Life* (Boston: Little, Brown and Co., 1980), 407–9.

15. Some of the words Orwell selects for the scrap heap are fully established as English: *deus ex machina* 'fairy godmother' (Orwell's proposed "substitute"), *agenda* 'business' (to which "substitute" he appends a '?'), *exit* 'way out,' *gratis* 'free,' *optimum* 'best,' *sub rosa* 'under the rose.' Words he wishes to "keep" should be given anglicized plurals: *data* 'treat as singular,' *maximum* and *minimum* 'plural ums.' Here is a brief selection of the words and phrases he regards as "unnecessarily used": *transit, lingua franca, crux, ego, quorum, versus, status, verbatim, avant-garde, de luxe, coup d'état, tour de force, bon mot, en route, cause celèbre, en masse, echelon, bourgeois, cliché, attaché, chic, fracas, camouflage, encore, gaffe, liaison, bloc, fait accompli, sabotage, mystique, kudos, kinesis, dilettante, shiboleth* [sic], *incognito, impresario.*

Quoted by permission of the Orwell estate; the unpublished notebook is housed in the George Orwell Archive, the Library, University College, London. I am grateful to Janet Percival, Assistant Librarian, and to Bernard Crick for their help in my efforts to examine and to quote from these lists.

16. See Stuart Chase, *The Tyranny of Words* (New York: Harvest Books, 1938) and Lancelot Hogben, *Interglossa: A Draft of an Auxiliary for a Democratic World Order, Being an Attempt to Apply Semantic Principles to Language Design* (Harmondsworth, Eng.: Penguin, 1943). Chase viewed the fighting in Spain as partly a result of linguistic associations evoked by *fascism* and *communism*: "Abstract terms are personified to become burning, fighting realities. Yet if the knowledge of semantics were general," he wrote, "and men were on guard for communication failure, the conflagration could hardly start. There would be honest differences of opinion, there might be a sharp political struggle, but not this windy clash of rival metaphysical notions" (p. 20). Hogben was similarly persuaded of "social importance of the language issue *vis-à-vis* world peace and worldwide human cooperation" (p. 7); he went so far as to circumscribe the "impolite imperative" verb form in his artificial language since it would be "rare, except in history books. An international auxiliary of peaceful communication is not for generals or for conversation with the cat" (p. 90). Despite having attacked Hogben's prose in "Politics and the English Language," Orwell thought that he might provide a blurb for the dustjacket of *Nineteen Eighty-Four* (*CEJL* 4:520).

17. C. K. Ogden and I. A. Richards, *The Meaning of Meaning* (1923; reprint, New York: Harcourt, Brace, 1953), 17.

18. Ogden and Richards, *The Meaning of Meaning*, 19.

19. C. K. Ogden, *The System of Basic English* (New York: Harcourt, Brace, 1934), 4.

20. Ogden, *Basic English*, 4.

21. See Randolph Quirk, "International Communication and the Concept of Nuclear English," in his *Style and Communication in the English Language* (London: Edward Arnold, 1982), 37–53.

22. Marilyn J. Shatz, a specialist in language acquisition by children, has pointed out to me that Newspeak could not be transmitted intact to infants; its rigorous elimination of "ambiguities" and "secondary meanings" and its unnatural grammar (Newspeak has only the minimal attributes of an analytic or a synthetic language) make it unlikely that a child could grasp its principles and be socialized into the orthodoxy of Newspeak adults. Though Orwell was probably unaware that he had imagined an "unhuman" language, he would have been encouraged by the likelihood that children would naturally sabotage the "Newspeak" ideal.

23. Harvey A. Daniels, *Famous Last Words: The American Language Crisis Reconsidered* (Carbondale: Southern Illinois University Press, 1983), 191.

24. See William Lambdin, *Doublespeak Dictionary* (Los Angeles: Pinnacle Books, 1979). Even more intemperate "Orwellian" opinions about language are expressed by Donald McCormick: "For a huge proportion of the new words are the creations of the moronic semiliterate members of today's society, whether they are civil servants with no feeling for language, or thugs and drop-outs" (*Approaching 1984* [London: David and Charles, 1980], 161). McCormick appends to his book a "Glossary of

Newspeak" in which he fulminates against institutions and views that offend him (see, e.g., his gloss for *multi-racial society*).

25. Arthur Schlesinger, Jr., "Politics and the American Language," *The American Scholar* 43 (1974):553–62. See also Hugh Rank, "Mr. Orwell, Mr. Schlesinger, and the Language," *College Composition and Communication* 28 (1977):90–96.

26. Justus George Lawler, "Politics and the American Language," in *Language and Public Policy*, ed. Hugh Rank (Urbana, Ill.: National Council of Teachers of English, 1974), 133.

27. For more recent developments, see Richard W. Bailey, "Computer-Assisted Poetry: The Writing Machine is for Everybody," in *Computers in the Humanities*, ed. J. L. Mitchell (Edinburgh: Edinburgh University Press, 1974), 283–95.

28. As Orwell put it in his unpublished 1948 notebook, "Anything is untrue when said by a parrot."

"I'm Not Literary, Dear":
George Orwell on Women and the Family

Leslie Tentler

The major themes in George Orwell's work—social inequality, human freedom—transcend concerns about gender. No feminist could honestly claim that *Nineteen Eighty-Four*, as a cautionary tale, is not meant to be read by women as well as men. Orwell believed himself to be in favor of the emancipation of women, and his understanding of their emancipation included the assumption that women in democracies were part of political life.

But Orwell did not believe that women were as significant political actors as men—at least not on the public stage—and the whole of his work is undergirded by a surprisingly conservative understanding of gender roles and family life. In *Nineteen Eighty-Four* especially he is concerned with the necessary connections between private life and public life—between sex, gender roles, family relations, and politics. And it is on these issues that even a moderate feminist, not only of my generation but of Orwell's too, finds him wanting as a social critic. Orwell may have supported the political and legal emancipation of women, but he did not believe that highly differentiated gender roles were an injustice for women or for men.

Orwell's conservatism on gender roles and family life may well be an important consideration as we deliberate the "future" of *Nineteen Eighty-Four*. Many women, I suspect, are offended by aspects of the book, though it is impossible to say to what extent its major political message is thereby blunted. And increasingly, younger readers may find that Orwell's views on women, sex, and family date the book so thoroughly as to vitiate its political importance. The young will surely assent to Orwell's most obvious sexual theme—that of sex as rebellion, as affirmation of individual identity. Sexual activity is perhaps the most persuasive means of establishing a claim to independent selfhood open to the young in our society. But the young will find a good deal else about Orwell's private morality to puzzle them.

That private morality is rooted in the conviction that large, strong, stable families best serve human needs, and that human beings, when they are free to choose, opt almost instinctively for more or less monogamous, fecund marriages. Within the security of the cohesive family, Orwell believed, personal identity is confirmed, a sense of the past internalized, and the necessary virtues of loyalty, responsibility, and self-discipline are learned. The family, then, is not only a source of stability in the bourgeois state, as leftist social critics have long argued; it is also, in Orwell's words, "the sole refuge from the state" and, in the context of *Nineteen Eighty-Four*, a source of opposition to the state, for which reason the freedom to form and raise a family is severely limited in Oceania.[1]

In Orwell's view, however, the contemporary family is not threatened only by totalitarian regimes. The family is also under attack in the liberal democracies, most consciously by the political left, in the guise of birth control, tolerance for abortion, and attacks on the ideals of monogamy and the permanence of marriage. The rootless individualism characteristic of the modern intellectual, Orwell believed, had generated a personal morality that denied the necessity and desirability of mutual dependence, and hence discredited the only values and experiences which made modern men and women capable of resisting totalitarian ideology. Orwell also argued that the family is undermined by chronic unemployment—a view characteristic of the left— but he parted company with most of the left to worry that chronic unemployment causes a greatly lowered birthrate. This depressed birthrate both weakened England as an economic and political force in the world—a special concern as he looked to the probable balance of world power after 1945—and fostered decadent values that place material comfort above the satisfactions of bearing and rearing many children. On this issue, Orwell often sounds like a die-hard Tory imperialist, though his logic and his goals are very much his own.[2]

Orwell's views on family life never formed a coherent political program. Much as he believed that birth control threatened the procreative instinct, he also recognized the futility of the Catholic Church's ban on contraception. As seriously as he suggested taxing childless couples to stimulate the birthrate, he never integrated this suggestion into a detailed and publicized program to save the family. Orwell was often vague and even inconsistent when it came to translating values into public policy, and efforts to control reproductive behavior—by the church or the state—invariably raise troubling questions about individual freedom, a point which Orwell underscored in *Nineteen Eighty-Four* by creating a Party even more cruelly repressive in its attitudes toward sex and divorce than Orwell believed the church to be. (Orwell never understood his own conservative sexual ethic as remotely comparable to the puritanism of the Party or the church, for he believed that the ethic he endorsed reflected human needs and desires rather than aspirations to social control, and there were no absolute prohibitions in the ethic.) It is not surprising that Orwell failed to produce a clear political program for the family. But his failure must not lead us to think that he did not care deeply about his vision of family life, for he did, and that vision underlies much of his work, especially his understanding of the good society.

Orwell's views on the family rest in large measure on the assumption that men and women are very different kinds of people. Whether these distinctive male and female psychologies are innate or culturally determined is an issue which he never discussed, presumably because he did not consider it important. That woman's temperament fits her best for mothering and at most a minor role in the economy and politics was not for Orwell an injustice; when he considered what political changes would specifically benefit women, indeed, he generally argued for making it easier for women to be full-time wives and mothers. Orwell assumed that domesticity was genuinely satisfying for the great majority of women, that their individuality found full expression in the home, and he defended this view on many occasions by celebrating the "comely" and highly sex-differentiated family roles of the working class. He appeared to regard efforts of upper-middle-class women to find satisfaction outside the family as narcissistic, to see feminism of almost any stripe as one more symptom of the spiritual hollowness of the privileged. His portrait of Elizabeth Lackersteen's mother in *Burmese Days* is a case in point.

> Elizabeth's mother had been an incapable, halfbaked, vapouring, self-pitying woman who shirked all the normal duties of life on the strength of sensibilities which she did not possess. After messing about for years with such things as Women's Suffrage and Higher Thought, and making many abortive attempts at literature, she had finally taken up with painting. Painting is the only art that can be practiced without either talent or hard work. Mrs. Lackersteen's pose was that of an artist exiled among "the Philistines"—these, needless to say, included her husband—and it was a pose that gave her almost unlimited scope for making a nuisance of herself.[3]

The undisguised hostility with which feminists are treated in Orwell's novels and his journalism suggests that feminists—like the birth controllers with whom they are in league—were enemies of the family life he valued and believed essential to the survival of both liberty and social cohesion.

Orwell's assumptions about male and female temperaments and the gender roles that grow naturally from them are evident in all his novels and episodically in his essays and his journalism. In this respect *Nineteen Eighty-Four* is of one piece with his earlier writing. Indeed, it is noteworthy that Orwell's views on gender roles and family do not change appreciably over the course of his career, despite experiences that introduced him to a variety of intelligent, independent women and experiences that might have taught him that happiness in family life is not necessarily easy to define or achieve. I suspect that Orwell, for personal reasons, was unwilling, even unable, to think deeply about issues of gender roles and women's independence, and that the images of women in his work are the product of potent needs and fears and relatively little dispassionate consideration.

Central to Orwell's understanding of women—as *Nineteen Eighty-Four* makes clear—is the assumption that women are essentially creatures of instinct and emotion rather than intellect. Women are evidently almost constitutionally incapable of dealing with the world on any but the limited terms of their own needs and experiences. Orwell's views are essentially those he attributes to George Gissing when he describes the depiction of women in Gissing's novels: "Even the clever and spirited ones, like Rhonda in *The Odd Women* (an interesting early specimen of the New Woman), cannot think in terms of generalities, and cannot get away from ready-made standards." Orwell would doubtless argue that this is true of many men as well, but all Orwell's novels feature men, often not well educated, who are able to consider their lives in abstract terms—usually something approaching political terms. Winston Smith, George Bowling in *Coming Up for Air*, John Flory in *Burmese Days*, even Gordon Comstock in *Keep the Aspidistra Flying* are examples. And Orwell's political hopes clearly rested on an as yet inert elite of lower-middle-class men—rather like Winston Smith and George Bowling—who seemed to him singularly capable of fusing ideas and experience and providing the leadership for a humane socialist politics.[4]

For every George Bowling in Orwell's work, however, there is a woman who cannot understand his ideas. She may be a shrew, like Hilda Bowling, or as charming as Gordon Comstock's Rosemary, but even with the best intentions she cannot share her man's intellectual life. That the unintellectual—or anti-intellectual—woman invariably accompanies Orwell's thinking man suggests that Orwell assumed a clear difference in intellectual capacity between the sexes. This is further suggested by Richard Rees's proposal that Winston Smith and Julia were meant by Orwell to stand as typical members of their sexes so that we as readers can experience their nightmare as immediately as possible. What Orwell offers his female audience in Julia is, of course, a not unflattering portrait. Julia is far more capable of action than Winston—appropriately, Julia, like Winston's mother and his first wife Katherine, is physically robust, while he is weak. Julia is less fear-ridden than Winston. She is pragmatic, resilient, and remarkably able to enjoy the few sensual pleasures her cunning can secure her. For all her immaturity, she is intelligently aware of her emotional needs, quite unlike Winston, who is introduced to us as a man whose emotions are a murky sea of anger, fear, and desire. (At the interview with O'Brien, Julia's prompt refusal to give up her lover for the sake of the Brotherhood—logically inconsistent but emotionally sound—is clearly meant to stand as the quintessential female response against Winston's far more tentative answer to the question.) Julia is a likeable character, even an admirable one, and Orwell is careful to show us that her obvious shortcomings are largely the consequence of the harsh world into which she was born.[5]

But Julia's inability to grapple with the ideas that obsess Winston is not wholly explained by her youth and her revolutionary upbringing. She has sufficient self-awareness to commit her life to resistance; like Winston, she has reason to try to understand the origins and nature of the society she struggles to undermine. But only Winston is interested in Goldstein's book; Julia's resistance is rooted solely in her immediate personal concerns. "She only questioned the teachings of the Party when they in some way touched upon her own life. Often she was ready to accept the official mythology, simply because the difference between truth and falsehood did not seem important to her." She is unashamed, even pleased, to be called "only a rebel from the waist downwards."[6] Like Rosemary in *Keep the Aspidistra Flying,* Julia accepts the world view of the man she loves but never understands it: these "meaningless scruples," as Rosemary puts it, "which she had never understood but which she accepted merely because they were his."[7] Or, as Orwell wrote in quite another context (in the diary that forms the basis of *The Road to Wigan Pier*): "Mrs. M., as usual, does not understand much about politics but has adopted her husband's views as a wife ought to; she pronounces the word 'comrade' with manifest discomfort."[8]

That women are concerned with the immediate consequences of action and the needs of the present is, in Orwell's view, not necessarily bad, especially in a society which is merely ordinarily unjust and not brutal. Women are by their very nature guaranteed a certain immunity to fanaticism, at least as long as they do not repress their instinctive needs to procreate and nurture. Women rarely commit the deadly sin of the intellectuals, which is to elevate abstractions so far above experience as to lose any sense of human limitations. At the worst, women atone for life's disappointments by mindless officiousness and an obsessive clinging to convention.

Women in Orwell's world, moreover, are more often than men the agents of moral regeneration and what modest salvation Orwell will allow. Young women offer their bodies and their affection to troubled, isolated men—as both Julia and Rosemary do—and give warmth and meaning to life. Good mothers love and protect their children despite the arbitrary cruelty of the world—fathers, by contrast, are shadowy, ineffectual figures in Orwell's novels, much as his own absent father was in Orwell's childhood. But if women are able to create small private worlds of meaning and happiness, they can also, by their refusal to love, make men's alienation even more hellish. John Flory, in *Burmese Days*, is condemned to death not only by the intolerable social dynamics of an imperialist society but also by the absence of compassion and imagination in the Lackersteen women.

Women, then, are powerful people, even if they are not, in Orwell's view, destined to achieve very much in the world outside the home. It is presumably the power of women, their ability to grant or deny human happiness, that is at the root of Orwell's evident ambivalence toward women and especially his hostility to those women who are not satisfied to focus their energies exclusively on the family. What he loosely called "feminism" is invariably threatening to men and, by extension, to what little happiness ordinary people can hope for in this life. Bernard Crick in his recent biography of Orwell reprints a remarkable fragment found among Orwell's papers, evidently written shortly before his death. Orwell, perhaps outlining a story, draws on memories of early childhood to equate feminism with rejection of men. Whether the fragment recollects an actual experience is less important than Orwell's view of "feminism" as antithetical to male happiness and his evident conviction that one's opinions on the matter have deep emotional roots.

The conversations he overheard as a small boy, between his Mother, his aunt, his elder sister and their feminist friends. The way in which, without ever hearing any direct statement to that effect, and without having more than a very dim idea of the relationship between the sexes, he derived a firm impression that women *did not like* men, that they looked upon them as a sort of large, ugly, smelly and ridiculous animal, who maltreated women in every way, above all by forcing their attentions upon them. It was pressed deep into his consciousness, to remain there until he was about 20, that sexual intercourse gives pleasure only to the man, not to the woman. He knew that sexual intercourse has something to do with the man getting on top of the woman, and the picture of it in his mind was of a man pursuing a woman, forcing her down and jumping on top of her, as he had often seen a cock do to a hen. All this was derived, not from any remark having direct sexual reference—or what he recognized as a sexual reference—but from such overheard remarks as "It just shows what beasts men are." "My dear, I think she's behaving like a perfect fool, the way she gives in to him."

"Of course, she's far too good for him." And the like. Somehow, by the mere tone of these conversations, the hatefulness—above all the physical unattractiveness—of men in women's eyes seemed to him to be established. It was not until he was about 30 that it struck him that he had in fact been his mother's favourite child. It had seemed natural to him that, as he was a boy, the two girls should be preferred.[9]

It is, of course, not clear what Orwell means by "feminist" in this passage. One might well say that the conversations overheard were a fairly standard litany of middle-class female complaints in a society where men and women were raised in quite different ways. Orwell's mother and especially his aunt, however, were suffragists, and were evidently self-consciously "emancipated" women. The feminism of their generation, moreover, did sometimes include a hostile attitude toward male sexuality. But Orwell is not in fact concerned with the ideological content of his mother's feminism; what matters is the rejection of men and their sexual needs that he sees as the essence of even quite limited claims to female autonomy. By contrast, the truly feminine woman is willing to surrender her whole being to a man. George Bowling remembered his adolescent sweetheart Elsie Waters: "She was really deeply feminine, very gentle, very submissive, the kind that would always do what a man told her, though she wasn't either small or weak."[10]

Orwell, then, drew the boundaries of femininity narrowly, largely because he feared the power of women. Real women, in his view, are submissive, giving, nonintellectual—unable to hurt or threaten men. But when the feminine is narrowly defined, a good many women will inevitably transgress the boundaries; and when a narrow definition of the feminine springs from a fear of female power—as it generally does—women who transgress will be perceived as menacing creatures indeed. A narrow definition of the feminine also defines a threat-filled world. Not surprisingly, Orwell's fiction reflects this. There are in his novels a fair number of women who, in their willful disregard of the limits of true femininity, emerge not as partially successful imitators of men but as potential destroyers of men and of hopes for a humane social order. Orwell is not a misogynist: negative characterizations of women occupy a minor place in his fiction and are linked to attacks on capitalism and class privilege in his essays and journalism. But there is a vein of hostility to women that runs throughout his work, always directed at women who are not "feminine" in the narrow sense that Orwell defines it.

All of Orwell's novels include thoroughly unpleasant female characters—and, to be sure, intolerable males as well. There is, however, a special quality to his detestable women: they are stupid, as are most of their male counterparts, but there is a petty savagery, a hysterical edge to the women that is largely missing from the men. The men may retain a certain geniality despite their stupidity, like Parsons in *Nineteen Eighty-Four*, and the cruel male in Orwell's world is often intelligent—O'Brien is the most famous case in point. But the women not only lack the nurturing, giving qualities that define true femininity, they have paid for the repression of these qualities with a deep sense of frustration and barely controlled anger at the world, and, unredeemed by intellect, they become active enemies of whatever in the world gives pleasure, especially to men. In the middle classes, such women are usually obsessive enforcers of convention—most middle-class conventions, in Orwell's eyes, being designed to frustrate youthful sexuality and keep men tied to a mindless round of boring work and ultimately unfulfillable material aspirations. But when such petty women are the residents of a brutal world, their desire to punish the deviant can make them accessories to murder. Thus the "sandy-haired woman" in *Nineteen Eighty-Four* spends her days deleting the names of the vaporized from the official record and, Winston suspects, scrutinizing her colleagues for lapses from orthodox behavior. She has some years previously deleted her own husband's name, from which we are to understand, I think, not only the savagery of the world in which this woman lives, but something about the nature of women as well. Women who lack the altruism and tenderness that define true femininity, Orwell tells us, have little to save them from becoming as ruthless as the society in which they live.

Orwell tells us much the same thing by giving Oceania's telescreens mostly female voices. The BBC had an almost exclusively male voice in Orwell's day, and he makes clear that women do not have power in the Inner Party. There is, then, no particular reason for him to give women the task of broadcasting spurious production reports and relaying "glorious" news from the battle front, save for dramatic effect and perhaps to make a point about gender and politics. The dramatic effect is real, at least for those of us old enough to remember when women reported only "human interest" stories and never the grim tidings of war. And that dramatic effect happens because many of us still associate nurturing, protective qualities almost exclusively with women and violence exclusively with men, associations Orwell both made himself and assumed in his readers. In Oceania, however, endless war, state control of information, and destruction of the affectionate family have created a world where female emotion—disciplined neither by intellect nor the obligation to nurture—is easily harnessed to the aggressive purposes of the state. Winston's wife Katherine "would unquestionably have denounced him to the Thought Police if she had not happened to be too stupid to detect the unorthodoxy of his opinions."[11] Even Julia, utterly detached from family and condemned to childlessness, is, for all her impulsive affection for Winston, indifferent to suffering which does not directly touch her. A society which successfully detaches women from their nurturing role in the family, it seems, unlooses something quite terrible in the world, and pays dearly for the loss of those feminine qualities which are essential to creating and sustaining humane individuals and tolerably civilized societies.

Because Orwell was strongly attracted to women and dependent on them as well as fearful of them, his deepest convictions about the nature of women are not expressed in negative terms but, appropriately, in an idealization of motherhood. There is no more evocative image in *Nineteen Eighty-Four* than the mother's protective embrace. The futile efforts of the Jewish refugee to comfort and save her child— something Winston sees on film without evident emotion—is echoed in his own mother's despairing embrace of his dying sister, a gesture which has increasingly profound meaning for Winston as the novel progresses.

> He did not suppose, from what he could remember of her, that she had been an unusual woman, still less an intelligent one; and yet she possessed a kind of nobility, a kind of purity, simply because the standards that she obeyed were private ones. Her feelings were her own, and could not be altered from outside. It would not have occurred to her that an action which is ineffectual thereby becomes meaningless. If you loved someone, you loved him, and when you had nothing else to give, you still gave him love. When the last of the chocolate was gone, his mother had clasped the child in her arms. It was no use, it changed nothing, it did not produce more chocolate, it did not avert the child's death or her own; but it seemed natural to her to do it. The refugee woman in the boat had also covered the little boy with her arm, which was no more use against the bullets than a sheet of paper. The terrible thing that the Party had done was to persuade you that mere impulses, mere feelings, were of no account, while at the same time robbing you of all power over the material world.[12]

Winston comes to realize, as he broods on the unconditional nature of his mother's love, that the proles have retained the ability to live according to private standards, to love one another and be loyal. But significantly, the only expressions of unselfish love among the proles that Winston sees come from women. An angry prole woman shouts out in the theater that children should not be shown violent films, a nameless young mother spirits her child to safety as a flying bomb passes over, the sturdy prole woman who sings in the courtyard behind Mr. Charrington's shop washes endless diapers for a presumably vast extended family. Those prole men we see, by contrast, are drunk, quarrelsome, more interested in the lottery than anything else. It is not, perhaps, that Orwell thinks men are normally devoid of paternal tenderness; Gordon Comstock, after all, gives up his revolt against materialism to provide for his unborn child. And Orwell described his own brief experience of fatherhood as a great joy. But the capacity to nurture is evidently, in Orwell's view, more deeply rooted in women than in men, and in the savagery of life among the proles, it is the women alone who keep the spark alive.

It is because Orwell defines femininity as nurturing, instinctual, and fundamentally unintellectual that he can, with no sense of injustice, assign women to a circumscribed and sacrificial role in the family and the society. At the same time, however, Orwell is capable of empathy with the homebound wife and mother, particularly if her trials are exacerbated by poverty. Mrs. Parsons, weary and prematurely aged, "fiddling helplessly with a blocked wastepipe,"[13] is for Winston a distillation of all the dreariness and hardship of postrevolution London, much as Orwell saw the hopelessness of life on the dole summed up in a young woman on the outskirts of Wigan, "kneeling in the bitter cold, on the slimy stones of a slum backyard, poking a stick up a foul drain-pipe."[14] He has only sympathy for women stuck with doing dishes: "Like sweeping, scrubbing and dusting, it is of its nature an uncreative and time-wasting job."[15] He does not doubt that children—perhaps especially boys—are, once beyond early childhood, troublesome and ungrateful creatures who never fully return the mother love so freely given. He even recognizes, with a certain horror, the stultifying quality of unrelieved domesticity, where "nothing ever happens except the yearly childbirth," as he writes in his essay on Dickens.[16] (His conclusion in this same essay is revealing: "No modern man could combine such purposelessness with so much vitality.") And few contemporary authors have described in grimmer terms the limited choices actually open to women who have neither extraordinary talents nor independent fortunes. Warburton speaks to Dorothy Hare at the conclusion of *A Clergyman's Daughter*.

> Every year your life will be a little bleaker, a little fuller of those deadly little jobs that are shoved off onto lonely women. And remember that you won't always be twenty-eight. All the while you will be fading, withering, until one morning you will look in the glass and realise that you aren't a girl any longer, only a skinny old maid. You'll fight against it, of course. You'll keep your physical energy and your girlish mannerisms—you'll keep them

just a little too long. Do you know that type of bright—too bright—spinster who says "topping" and "ripping" and "right-ho," and prides herself on being such a good sport that she makes everyone feel a little unwell? And she's so splendidly hearty at tennis and so handy at amateur theatricals, and she throws herself with a kind of desperation into her Girl Guide work and her parish visiting, and she's the life and soul of Church socials, and always, year after year, she thinks of herself as a young girl still and never realises that behind her back everyone laughs at her for a poor, disappointed old maid? That's what you'll become, what you must become, however much you foresee and try to avoid it. There's no other future possible to you unless you marry. Women who don't marry wither up—they wither up like aspidistras in back-parlour windows. [17]

Nor is work an answer: even a middle-class woman with a better than average education cannot support herself in anything but genteel poverty. "A nursery governess, for instance, or companion to some diseased hag who will occupy herself in thinking of ways to humiliate you. Or you will go back to school-teaching; English-mistress in some grisly girls' school, seventy-five pounds a year and your keep, and a fortnight in a seaside boarding house every August." [18]

Orwell possesses, then, some sense that woman's lot is hard, that her life means sacrifice without appreciable reward. But he is not led to embrace feminism. Indeed, even as he sees in the women of Wigan the most pathetic victims of poverty, he recognizes that distinct gender roles help give form and meaning to life when chronic unemployment threatens to destroy both individual identity and family integrity. Whatever injustice women suffer, their sacrifice is necessary because it helps keep a fragile world intact.

We had an argument one evening in the Searles' house because I helped Mrs. S. with the washing-up. Both of the men disapproved of this, of course. Mrs. S. seemed doubtful. She said that in the North working-class men never offered any courtesies to women (women are allowed to do all the housework unaided, even when the man is unemployed, and it is always the man who sits in the comfortable chair), and she took this state of things for granted, but did not see why it should not be changed. She said that she thought the women now-a-days, especially the younger women, would like it if men opened doors for them, etc. The position now-a-days is anomalous. The man is practically always out of work, whereas the woman occasionally is working. Yet the woman continues to do all the housework and the man not a hand's-turn, except carpentering and gardening.

Yet I think it is instinctively felt by both sexes that the man would lose his manhood if, merely because he was out of work, he became a "Mary Ann."[19]

Orwell divided the world into distinct male and female spheres, I think, for both personal and political reasons. His own life, as recent biographers have interpreted it, was characterized by tension and ambivalence with regard to women—greater tension and ambivalence, perhaps, than was the case for many of his contemporaries. The absence of his father during the first eight years of Orwell's life was not a usual experience, though the pattern of female control in his family may have been quite common in the middle class. His early schooling, which he claimed to remember as a quasi nightmare, was largely in the charge of a capricious and dominant woman. During his early years of apprenticeship as a writer he was resentfully dependent for financial support on women—on his mother, his older sister, his maternal aunt, and a family friend. His biographers believe that he was as a young man unusually shy with women and that his sexual initiation may have been relatively late. And more than one female friend recalls that while George was undoubtedly fond of her, he didn't appear to like women generally or to think much of their intellectual abilities. An echo of this brash and prickly young man is heard in a 1934 letter to a female friend.

> I had lunch yesterday with Dr. Ede. He is a bit of a feminist and thinks that if a woman was brought up exactly like a man she would be able to throw a stone, construct a syllogism, keep a secret, etc. He tells me that my anti-feminist views are probably due to Sadism! I have never read the Marquis de Sade's novels—they are unfortunately very hard to get hold of.[20]

None of this can, of course, do more than suggest that Orwell's understanding of women may have incorporated rather more than the usual measure of resentment of female control and fear of female rejection. His antifeminism also stems from the guilt he seeems always to have felt about his own reasonably comfortable childhood and essentially upper-class education. Orwell regarded feminism in large part as an effort of the well-to-do to be free of the burdens life necessarily imposed on women, as an ideology intended to make life more pleasant for an already overprivileged group. And indeed, to an ever greater extent than in the United States, English feminism was a largely upper-middle-class movement. Orwell's association of feminism with the middle classes—and, predictably, with hostility to men—is evident in his brief sketch of a bookshop patron in *Keep the Aspidistra Flying*.

A lean, straight-nosed, brisk woman, with sensible clothes and gold-rimmed pince nez—school marm possibly, feminist certainly—came in and demanded Mrs. Wharton-Beverley's history of the suffrage movement. With secret joy Gordon told her that they hadn't got it. She stabbed his male incompetence with gimlet eyes and went out again.[21]

Orwell's views on women, men, and the family, however, are concerned with considerably more than the wounds his ego sustained as he negotiated his dealings with the opposite sex. Orwell is a remarkable left-wing thinker in his generation largely because he possessed a conservative's sense of the fragility of the social fabric, and understood that respect for tradition and a strong ethic of mutual obligation are as essential to a humane society as liberty and economic justice. The path to the good society, as *Nineteen Eighty-Four* makes clear, can never be blazed by a cadre of party elite; the good society is created—slowly perhaps—out of the values and experiences that reflect the best and most generous impulses of ordinary life. Just as Winston Smith is moved to political consciousness by his memories of family love and family loyalty, so too will political leaders worth trusting ground their pursuit of justice in the ethic of mutual obligation that animates family life at its best. The family, then, creates the moral man; it is in the family that true mutual dependence and responsibility make human animals into human beings. And the family attains its moral dimensions because men and women, but especially women, give up a degree of individual freedom to care for one another and for children. It is this sacrifice that makes possible not only the continuation of the human race but the values of loyalty and responsibility that give life meaning and order. (Since Orwell assumed that religion was no longer a significant social force in the developed world—this is evident in *Nineteen Eighty-Four*—the importance of the family as the molder of moral behavior has become more and not less great in the twentieth century.)

What feminism does, in Orwell's view, is challenge the tradition of mutual dependence that sex roles within the family foster. Feminism argues against woman's limiting role with no thought to the social consequences of undermining that role. Feminism is premised on an abstraction wholly unconnected with reality—it is, ultimately, dangerous as well as frivolous politics. This was, I think, a part of the message Orwell wished to convey when he described the happy working-class family in *The Road to Wigan Pier*. He is celebrating working-class culture, of course, but that culture was largely defined by strict gender roles, by strong family loyalties, and by a sense of both the inevitability and the indissolubility of marriage. These are not values with which most left-wing intellectuals would be comfortable, and yet, according to Orwell, the traditional working-class family was both "saner" and "happier" than the small, relatively egalitarian and easily dissolved families advocated by much of the left.

> I would say that a manual worker, if he is in steady work and drawing good wages—an "if" which gets bigger and bigger—has a better chance of being happy than an "educated" man. His home life seems to fall more naturally into a sane and comely shape. I have often been struck by the peculiar easy completeness, the perfect symmetry, as it were, of a working-class interior at its best. Especially on winter evenings after tea, when the fire glows in the open range and dances mirrored in the steel fender, when Father, in shirtsleeves, sits in the rocking chair at one side of the fire reading the racing finals, and Mother sits on the other side with her sewing, and the children are happy with a pennorth of mint humbugs and the dog lolls roasting himself on the rag mat—it is a good place to be in.[22]

We are to understand, I think, that the values which undergird this family life make an important contribution to whatever sanity English political life can be said to possess. And if these values are greatly weakened, the political future of England will dim accordingly.

We see much the same sentiment in Orwell's fondness for the domestic literature of mid-nineteenth-century America, for *Little Women* and other less-known books like *Helen's Babies*. Orwell admired the world these books evoke because it was politically and economically free—or so he believed—and because it was, despite its individualistic values, a world that cohered, where family loyalties were strong and social life was usefully regulated by an elaborate but freely accepted code of etiquette.[23] Orwell thought that the pervasive Protestantism of the period was largely responsible for this odd conjunction of freedom and sedate domesticity, and he was at least partly right. But mid-nineteenth-century American culture achieved its delicate balance between social cohesion and individual liberty largely because women were expected to repress their own individualistic impulses in order to create the homes which temper the individualistic selfishness of men. Ministers preached this gospel, but popular literature did too, especially novels like *Little Women*. Whatever inequities women's sacrifice might entail, however, did not for Orwell mar the health of this nineteenth-century world.

> the civilization of nineteenth-century America was capitalist civilization at its best. Soon after the civil war the inevitable deterioration started. But for some decades, at least, life in America

was much better fun than life in Europe—there was more happening, more colour, more variety, more opportunity—and the books and songs of that period had a sort of bloom, a childlike quality.[24]

Orwell was quite right to recognize the genuine charm that characterized many "good bad books" produced in nineteenth-century America. But it is worth emphasizing that the sunlit novels he admired were books in which the message of female subordination to men and of a thoroughly domestic female sphere is central. And they are books in which female subordination is assumed to be essential to maintaining social order.

The feminist's response to this kind of thinking is obvious. Orwell's assumptions about women's intellectual inferiority and their natural inclination to domesticity are both false and deeply offensive to women. Orwell's analysis of the family rests on the almost certainly erroneous assumption that the gender roles of the nineteenth-century middle class are the only sure source of family stability and the citizenly virtues he rightly prized. And he evidently never thought seriously about the moral and political implications of consigning half the population to circumscribed lives in order to ensure an elusive social stability. His celebrated passion for liberty and equality, in short, is from a woman's perspective a curiously limited one.

But an honest feminist cannot, I think, dismiss as silly or irrelevant the issues with which Orwell was dealing when he wrote about gender roles and family. His fears about the alienating quality of modern life were legitimate, and so was his concern that politics be fundamentally a moral enterprise. He was right to see the family as a crucial source of social cohesion and individual identity. And he was wise to worry that a weakening of family bonds would intensify anomie and erode an already fragile but essential ethic of mutual dependence. Indeed, when feminist thinking today is shallow or irresponsible, as it sometimes is, it is largely the result of failure to deal seriously with these concerns, to consider the effects of changing gender roles on the family and society, to consider ways in which greater freedom for women can be reconciled with the obvious needs of society for reasonably stable families and for a social ethic that accords protection to the weak and validates the networks of mutual dependence which most people need in order to survive. Feminism, as Orwell himself argued, has too often tended toward an ethic of unrelieved individualism, speaking largely to the interests of the young and affluent. This is not to deny that feminism is fundamentally an expression and extension of the humane egalitarian tradition in which Orwell, ironically, stands. But it helps to explain the peculiar vulnerability of American feminism to assaults by the New Right, for the attack on feminism as excessive—even amoral—individualism is at the heart of much neoconservative thinking in America today. Orwell was neither the first nor the last social critic to try to glue society together with women.

That Orwell can in any way be associated with the New Right suggests the point much earlier raised—that Orwell's conservatism on issues of gender roles and family may divide him in an important way from many present-day and future readers. He will surely not cease to be read, and *Nineteen Eighty-Four* especially will retain its capacity to horrify. But will Orwell's work be increasingly seen as dated— raising important questions, but in terms that are not our own? In some sense this is the fate that waits for every writer. I suggest only that the first fissure has appeared in the landscape, that many of us gaze across that divide at a man whose sexual politics were almost Victorian, but whose ultimate political concerns are still our own.

Notes

1. George Orwell, "Review of *The Reilly Plan* by Lawrence Wolfe," in *The Collected Essays, Journalism and Letters of George Orwell*, ed. Sonia Orwell and Ian Angus, 4 vols. (New York: Harcourt Brace Jovanovich, 1968), 4:91. Cited hereafter as *CEJL*. See also "The Art of Donald McGill," *CEJL* 2:159–65.

2. George Orwell, *Keep the Aspidistra Flying* (New York: Harcourt, Brace, 1956). Orwell, "The Art of Donald McGill," *CEJL* 2:160–61. Orwell, "The English People," *CEJL* 3:4, 11, 30–33. Orwell, "London Letter to *Partisan Review*," *CEJL* 3:192–93. Orwell, "Review of *The Reilly Plan*," *CEJL* 4:88–92. Orwell, "*Tribune*, 22 March 1946," *CEJL* 4:123–24. George Woodcock, *The Crystal Spirit: A Study of George Orwell* (Boston: Little, Brown, 1966), 263, 284.

3. George Orwell, *Burmese Days* (London: Secker and Warburg, 1949), 89–90.

4. George Orwell, "George Gissing," *CEJL* 4:443. Bernard Crick, *George Orwell: A Life* (Boston: Little, Brown, 1980), 251.

5. Richard Rees, *George Orwell: Fugitive From the Camp of Victory* (London: Secker and Warburg, 1961), 107–8.

6. George Orwell, *Nineteen Eighty-Four* (New York: Harcourt, Brace, 1949), 127, 129.

7. Orwell, *Keep the Aspidistra Flying*, 195.

8. George Orwell, *The Road to Wigan Pier* Diary, 31 January–25 March 1936," *CEJL* 1:173.
9. Crick, *Orwell*, 12–13.
10. George Orwell, *Coming Up for Air* (London: Secker and Warburg, 1948), 105.
11. Orwell, *Nineteen Eighty-Four*, 111.
12. Orwell, *Nineteen Eighty-Four*, 136.
13. Orwell, *Nineteen Eighty-Four*, 64.
14. George Orwell, *The Road to Wigan Pier* (New York: Berkley Publishing Corp., 1961), 29.
15. George Orwell, "As I Please *(Tribune*, 9 February 1945)," *CEJL* 3:329–30.
16. George Orwell, "Charles Dickens," *CEJL* 1:447–48.
17. George Orwell, *A Clergyman's Daughter* (New York: Harper, 1935), 303.
18. Orwell, *A Clergyman's Daughter*, 304.
19. Orwell, "*Wigan Pier* Diary," *CEJL* 1:195.
20. George Orwell, letter to Brenda Salkeld, *CEJL* 1:136. Peter Stansky and William Abrahams, *The Unknown Orwell* (London: Constable, 1972), 32–33, 71, 227–32, 245–46. Stansky and Abrahams, *Orwell: The Transformation* (London: Granada Enland, 1981), 43, 75. Crick, *Orwell*, 12–13, 25.
21. Orwell, *Keep the Aspidistra Flying*, 18.
22. Orwell, *The Road to Wigan Pier*, 105.
23. George Orwell, "Inside the Whale," *CEJL* 1:499.
24. George Orwell, "Riding Down from Bangor," *CEJL* 4:247.

From Bingo to Big Brother:
Orwell on Power and Sadism

Gorman Beauchamp

> *. . . hence we shall see*
> *If power change purpose, what our seemers be.*
> *Measure for Measure*

After their first meeting, at Potsdam, President Truman commented
that Stalin bore an eerie resemblance to Boss Pendergast, the Kansas
City politico and Truman's erstwhile mentor. I have seen this remark
cited as evidence of Truman's typically American naivete, a failure to
grasp that the evil incarnated in Stalin exceeded by orders of magnitude anything to be encountered in American political experience.
This failure of perception is, in turn, held to account for the inability
of pragmatic politicians like Truman to deal adequately with the fath-
omless malignity of probably the most monstrous figure of our century.
Simple-minded Truman—runs the inference—could not see that vast,
unbridgeable gulf that separated a Stalin from a glorified ward heeler
like Pendergast. But Truman had the advantage over such critics of
knowing first hand both parties in his comparison, so that instead of
dismissing his comparison as prima facie fatuous, we should consider
the possibility that it was in fact accurate: that the totalitarian tyrant
and the Missouri machine boss *were* essentially, "eerily" alike. To
find the comparison inherently implausible assumes that there is a
difference in kind, not just in degree—a radical discontinuity—between the kinds of political personalities to be found operating in
Kansas City and the Kremlin.

A difficulty with this assumption involves explaining how the "totalitarian personality" arises at all if not as an evolution from a more
common or, if you will, a more "normal" personality type, the power
seeker. Put most simply, if Truman's observation is correct, then the
resemblance between a Pendergast and a Stalin results from their
belonging to the same psychopolitical genus, the latter merely a more
extreme—indeed, a psychopathic—exemplar of the familiar type. What
differs is not the personality but the circumstance. A character in
Aldous Huxley's *Chrome Yellow*, Mr. Scogins, plays a thought game.

> When I meet someone for the first time, I ask myself this ques-
> tion: Given the Caesarean environment, which of the Caesars
> would this person resemble—Julius, Augustus, Tiberius, Cali-
> gula, Claudius, Nero? I take each trait of character, each mental

65

and emotional bias, each little oddity, and magnify them a thou-
sand times. The resulting image gives me the Caesarean formula.
. . . The Caesarean environment makes the Caesar.[1]

So the Caesarean environment—the virtually limitless exercise of
power—made Stalin Stalin: a matter of the degree of opportunity to
do evil, not of personality type. Had history situated Josef Vissarion-
ovich in Kansas City circa 1930 instead of Moscow he would have had
to settle for stuffing ballot boxes instead of liquidating Kulaks. Given
the dynamics of the power-seeking personality as a constant, only
opportunity separates the big-league Caesars from the bush-league
bosses.

Orwell's view of power seekers—generally one of repugnance—is
well known, embodied probably most clearly in the pigs of *Animal
Farm*.[2] In addition, however, he seemed to hold to something like
Mr. Scogins's idea of the importance of the Caesarean environment,
with the corollary that one finds little Caesars in all stations of life,
exercising such petty tyrannies as their circumstances allow. Consider,
for instance, Orwell's claim that "it was only *after* the Soviet regime
became unmistakably totalitarian that English intellectuals, in large
numbers, began to show interest in it": for the "secret wish" of the
Russophile intelligentsia is "to destroy the old, equalitarian version of
Socialism and usher in a hierarchical society where the intellectual can
at last get his hands on the whip."[3] If I read this passage aright, Orwell
sees ranks of incipient Caesars—Caligulas and Neroes especially—
itching to become real ones, to get their hands historically on the
whip. The sadistic motive that Orwell saw underlying this will to
power I shall return to presently, but for now I want to stress that he
views the power seekers as differing not in kind but only in degree of
opportunity: they occupy a single psychological spectrum extending—
as my title puts it—from Bingo to Big Brother.

Bingo is the nickname given to the wife of the headmaster at Crossgates (really St. Cyprian's) in Orwell's autobiographical essay "Such,
Such Were the Joys." Since the publication of Anthony West's attack
in the *New Yorker* (1957) on Orwell's political thought, this essay has
become a crux in interpreting his critique of totalitarianism generally
and *Nineteen Eighty-Four* in particular. The deepest understanding
of totalitarianism at which Orwell could arrive, West contends, was to
imagine it resembling a very bad boys' school. "Whether he knew it
or not, what he did in *Nineteen Eighty-Four* was to send everybody
to Crossgates to be as miserable as he had been." Since most of his
misery at Crossgates emanated from the cruel caprice of Bingo, she
became, West asserts, Orwell's model of the totalitarian tyrant of his

novel. "Big Brother, the feared dictator whom everyone pretends to love, is really Bingo."[4]

Most critics have dismissed West's essay as fatuous psychological reductionism, a response with which I have much sympathy. But leaving aside its parlor Freudianism, I want here to accept its basic premise and argue for a different conclusion: not West's own conclusion that the identification of Crossgates with Oceania and Bingo with Big Brother trivializes and thus undermines Orwell's depiction of totalitarian tyranny but, rather, the conclusion that this identification extends and universalizes the sadistic power drives that crystallize in the Caesarean environment of totalitarianism. Put most simply, Crossgates *is* a microcosm of Oceania, Bingo *is* a Big Brother in miniature: only the scale, not the essence, differs. There is nothing inherently implausible in Orwell's identification of Crossgates as Oceania writ small, nothing preposterous about presenting Bingo as a prototype of Big Brother: for, unless such personalities exist in "everyday life," whence do they appear at the Caesarean moment? *Ex nihilo nihil fit*, and both Dr. Goebbels and Il Duce began their careers as schoolmasters.

Orwell is not suggesting, of course, that all schools are microcosms of despotism nor that all schoolmasters—or their wives—are crypto-totalitarian, but he does seem to suggest that a place like Crossgates offers an image of pointless persecution of the weak by the strong, of a cruelly arbitrary exercise of dictatorial power, that, much magnified, reflects the modus operandi of the totalitarian state. According to Orwell's friend T. R. Fyvel, "he was convinced that for people who had grown up among the safe conventions of democratic England—and the intelligentsia above all—the only English parallel for the nightmare of totalitarianism was the experience of a misfit boy in an English boarding school."[5] He is, then, not so much imposing his schoolboy experience on totalitarianism as he is imposing totalitarianism on his schoolboy experience.[6]

Thus, given that the essay is a far slighter work than *Nineteen Eighty-Four*, one finds adumbrated in it a number of the motifs developed more fully in Orwell's final novel. Even though a school for upperclass students, Orwell's Crossgates is marked by an atmosphere of deliberate dirtiness, dinginess, and deprivation—exactly the atmosphere that permeates Oceania.

> It is curious, the degree—I will not say of actual hardship, but of squalor and neglect—that was taken for granted in upper-class schools of that period. . . . Since this was an expensive school, I took a social step upwards in attending it, and yet the standard of comfort was in every way far lower than in my own home, or, indeed, than it would have been in a prosperous working class

home. One only had a hot bath once a week, for instance. The food was not only bad, it was also insufficient. Never before or since have I seen butter or jam scraped on bread so thinly. . . . A maxim often repeated to us at Crossgates was that it is healthy to get up from a meal feeling as hungry as when you sat down. . . .

I should be falsifying my own memories if I did not record that [those of Crossgates] are largely memories of disgust. The overcrowded, underfed, underwashed life that we led *was* disgusting. . . . It is not easy for me to think of my schooldays without seeming to breathe in a whiff of something cold and evil-smelling—a sort of compound of sweaty stockings, dirty towels, faecal smells blowing along corridors, forks with old food between the prongs, neck-of-mutton stew, and the banging doors of the lavatories.[7]

The many critics who have viewed the sordidness of Airstrip One in 1984 only as a reflection of the actual and unavoidable conditions of wartime London have not paid sufficient attention to this sort of description of an environment kept *intentionally* harsh and dismal. As explained in Goldstein's *Theory and Practice of Oligarchical Collectivism,* the ends of the totalitarian state, which depends on hierarchical differentiation, are served by keeping all but a small elite in a state of constant deprivation. The endless warfare of the three superstates is waged in order to demand sacrifices of their citizens; the sacrifices are not demanded in order to wage war.

The primary aim of modern warfare . . . is to use up the products of the machine without raising the general standard of living. . . . The world of today is a bare, hungry, dilapidated place compared with the world that existed before 1914, and still more so if compared with the imaginary future to which people in that period looked forward.

Such a future was deliberately prevented since "an all-round increase in wealth threatened the destruction—indeed, in some sense was the destruction—of a hierarchical society."

In a world in which everyone worked short hours, had enough to eat, lived in a house with a bathroom and a refrigerator, and possessed a motorcar or even an airplane, the most obvious and perhaps the most important form of inequality would already have disappeared. If it once became general, wealth would confer no distinction. . . . [Furthermore] if leisure and security were enjoyed by all alike, the great mass of human beings who are normally stupefied by poverty would become literate and would learn to think for themselves; and when once they had done this, they would sooner or later realize that the privileged minority had no function, and they would sweep it away. In the long run, a hierarchical society was only possible on a basis of poverty and ignorance.[8]

Thus Oceania is marked by shortages, shoddiness, a pervasive grimness and grime: the atmosphere of Crossgates—something cold and evil-smelling—encompassing a whole world. Bingo and Sim (Mr. Wilkes) justify their parsimony on the grounds that deprivation builds character, while their true motive is greed; likewise Big Brother imposes a regime of permanent austerity, ostensibly for national defense but really to ensure the inequality on which the power of the Party rests.

Though there are no laws in Oceania, everyone lives with a constant sense of guilt; the same atmosphere permeates Crossgates. "Guilt seemed to hang in the air," Orwell wrote, "like a pall of smoke" (p. 36). Bingo repressed the erotic instincts of her charges with all the rigor exhibited by the Party's Junior Anti-Sex League. She anticipates one of the tactics of Oceania's Thought Police in accusing the boys of *facecrime,* an appearance that reveals one's guilt.

> "Have you looked in the glass lately, Beacham?" said Bingo. "Aren't you ashamed to go about with a face like that? Do you think everyone doesn't know what it means when a boy has black rings around his eyes?"
>
> Once again the load of guilt and fear seemed to settle down upon me. . . . And many times . . . I have gazed anxiously into the glass, looking for the first hint of that dreaded stigma, the confession which the secret sinner writes upon his own face. (P. 37)

Indeed, the boys at Crossgates—and I must reemphasize that we are concerned with Orwell's perception and not necessarily the literal reality of St. Cyprian's—live, like their counterparts in Oceania, with the sense of being under constant surveillance, under the eye of their own Big Brother. Orwell tells of a time when, sent on an errand, he slips into a shop to buy some forbidden chocolates (the shop perhaps the prototype of Mr. Charrington's in *Nineteen Eighty-Four,* and the chocolates the equivalent of the contraband diary).

> As I came out of the shop I saw on the opposite pavement a small sharp-faced man who seemed to be staring very hard at my school cap. Instantly a horrible fear went through me. There could be no doubt as to who the man was. He was a spy placed there by Sim! . . . It did not seem to me strange that the head-

master of a private school should dispose of an army of informers, and I did not even imagine that he would have to pay them. I assumed that any adult, inside the school or outside, would collaborate voluntarily in preventing us from breaking the rules. Sim was all-powerful, and it was natural that his agents should be everywhere. (P. 23)

Such conditions of life at Crossgates conspire to create in the Orwell persona an intense ambivalence toward Sim and Bingo: a feeling of hatred compounded by the guilt experienced in hating them, his "benefactors."

Sim and Bingo had chosen to befriend me, and their friendship included canings, reproaches and humiliations, which were good for me. . . . That was their version, and I believed in it. It was therefore clear that I owed them a vast debt of gratitude. But I was *not* grateful, as I very well knew. On the contrary, I hated both of them. . . . But it is wicked, is it not, to hate your benefactors? So I was taught and so I believed. (P. 32)

It is this guilt-ridden ambivalence that West identifies as the origin of Winston Smith's hate-love relationship with Big Brother—or, more precisely, with the Big Brother surrogate, O'Brien.

How difficult it is for a child to have any real independence of attitude could be seen in our behavior toward Bingo. I think it would be true to say that every boy in the school hated and feared her. Yet we all fawned on her in the most abject way, and the top layer of our feelings toward her was a sort of guilt-stricken loyalty. Bingo . . . hardly pretended to dispense justice. She was frankly capricious. An act which might get you a caning one day, might next day be laughed off as a boyish prank. . . . [A]lthough my memories of Bingo are mostly hostile, I also remember considerable periods when I basked under her smiles, when she called me "old chap" and used my Christian name, and allowed me to frequent her private library. . . . Whenever one had the chance to suck up, one did suck up, and at the first smile one's hatred turned into a sort of cringing love. (Pp. 32–33)

While the pre-echoes here of Winston's tortured psychomachia are palpable,[9] the Orwell persona nevertheless triumphs over Bingo by leaving Crossgates with his hatred for her still intact. She had damaged but had not destroyed him, and writing ill of her (as Winston wants to of Big Brother) proved the best revenge. But then Crossgates lacked, of course, the true terror tactics of Oceania, which succeed in violating even "the few cubic centimeters inside your skull" that Winston thought inviolable and in converting his hatred of Big Brother into "love."

In reading "Such, Such Were the Joys" as a prolegomenon to *Nineteen Eighty-Four*, the danger lies in distorting the scale, making small affairs loom too large to bear comparability with great ones. Still, it seems to me undeniable that the essay provides—if not a secret code that explains away *Nineteen Eighty-Four* as residual adolescent animus, as West claims—a microcosm in quotidian life of *l'univers concentrationnaire* of totalitarianism. As Alex Zwerdling writes, "Although 'Such, Such Were the Joys' is in no obvious sense of the word political, it has the same elements as [Orwell's] political pieces—victims, oppressors, a highly systematized form of tyranny."[10] If we recall Orwell's concentration on political subjects in his writing after 1936, and particularly his obsession with totalitarianism, then his using even the relatively trivial and peculiarly English genre of schoolday reminiscences to show the cryptototalitarian personality functioning in spaces outside the walls of the Reichstag or the Kremlin will not surprise us.

My point thus far has been not to represent Bingo as exceptional, but rather as all too typical of that particular personality that can be called the power seeker. As already noted, Orwell was at once fascinated and repelled by this type, which he saw as increasingly dominating the ideological life of the modern world. "From Carlyle onwards, but especially in the last generation," he wrote in *The English People*,

> the British intelligentsia have tended to take their ideas from Europe and have been infected by habits of thought that derive ultimately from Machiavelli. All the cults that have been fashionable in the last dozen years, Communism, Fascism, and pacifism, are in the last analysis forms of power worship.[11]

This worship of power, the desire to get one's hand on the whip, fatally vitiated, Orwell thought, even the most benevolently intended attempts at social amelioration.

> Throughout history, one revolution after another—although usually producing a temporary relief, such as a sick man gets by turning over in bed—has simply led to a change of masters, because no serious effort has been made to eliminate the power instinct. . . . In the minds of active revolutionaries, at any rate the ones who "got there," the longing for a just society has always been fatally mixed up with the intention to secure power for themselves.[12]

This motive, Orwell feared, was not absent even among adherents of his own political faith, Socialism. To his friend Richard Rees, he confided, "I notice people always say '*under* Socialism.' They look forward to being on top—with all the others underneath, being told what is good for them."[13] Indeed, as Orwell asserted in his review of Bertrand Russell's *Power*, "Bully-worship, under various disguises, has become a universal religion,"[14] particularly, he believed, among intellectuals who at once genuflected before their political Bingos and longed to do some bullying themselves. The Germans, aptly enough, have a term for this type—*Radfahrernaturen*, the bicyclist character: above he bows, below he kicks.

In *Nineteen Eighty-Four* Orwell provides, of course, the apotheosis of bully worship, a scenario of the future where brute power provides the only social bond and thus where the power-seeking personality, incarnated in the mythical figure of Big Brother and the mundane one of O'Brien, rules without any of the traditional restraints on power. Oceania serves as Orwell's ultimate Caesarean environment and allows for a degree of tyranny that the cruelest of Roman emperors would have envied.

In this context, Orwell advances a motive for the exercise of power that has proven the most controversial crux of *Nineteen Eighty-Four*. "I understand HOW" Winston Smith writes in his thoughtcriminal diary, "I do not understand WHY" (p. 68): why, that is, the Party has deliberately constructed a world hard, ugly, and brutal. In a famous passage, O'Brien, a member of the Inner Party, explains WHY.

> The Party seeks power entirely for its own sake. We are not interested in the good of others; we are interested solely in power. Not wealth or luxury or long life or happiness; only power, pure power. The German Nazis and the Russian Communists came very close to us in their methods, but they never had the courage to recognize their own motives. They pretended, perhaps they even believed, that they had seized power unwillingly and for a limited time, and that just around the corner lay a paradise where human beings would be free and equal. We are not like that. We know that no one ever seizes power with the intention of relinquishing it. Power is not a means; it is an end. One does not establish a dictatorship in order to safeguard a revolution; one makes the revolution in order to establish the dictatorship. The object of persecution is persecution. The object of torture is torture. The object of power is power. Now do you begin to understand me? (P. 217)

Tutored in the torture chambers of the Ministry of Love, Winston does begin to understand O'Brien's message: that one asserts power over another by making him suffer.

> Obedience is not enough. Unless he is suffering [O'Brien continues], how can you be sure that he is obeying your will and

not his own? Power is in inflicting pain and humiliation. Power is in tearing human minds to pieces and putting them together again in shapes of your own choosing. Do you begin to see, then, what kind of world we are creating? . . . A world of fear and treachery and torment, a world of trampling and being trampled upon, a world which will grow not less but *more* merciless as it refines itself. . . . If you want a picture of the future, imagine a boot stamping on a human face—forever. (P. 220)

This terrible image epitomizes what, for Orwell, was the real, if often disguised, motive force that underlay the exercise of power—sadism. Men seek power in order to dominate, humiliate, and torture others.

Clearly, this is an appalling conclusion, one that, if true—or to the degree that it is true—would undermine the legitimacy of any form of rule of some men over others. Isaac Deutscher, who characterizes this pessimistic conclusion as "the mysticism of cruelty," claimed that "at heart Orwell was a simple-minded anarchist" in whose eyes "any political movement forfeited its *raison d'être* the moment it acquired a *raison d'état*."[15] There is, without doubt, an unmistakable streak of the Prudhon-Bakunin mentality in much of Orwell's political thought; and, if O'Brien's credo truly reveals the motive for the gaining and deploying of power, then anarchism, in some degree or other, would indeed seem the only possible antidote—a conclusion that should come as no surprise to any reader who recalls Orwell's praise in *Homage to Catalonia* of the anarchism in Barcelona in the early days of the Spanish Civil War.[16] But it is not any imagined alternative to, but rather the indictment of power that stands at the center of *Nineteen Eighty-Four*, and the indictment demands consideration.

In "Raffles and Miss Blandish," Orwell declares, "The interconnection between sadism, masochism, success worship, power worship, nationalism and totalitarianism is a huge subject whose edges have barely been scratched, and even to mention it is considered somewhat indelicate." He continues,

Fascism is often loosely equated with sadism, but nearly always by people who see nothing wrong in the most slavish worship of Stalin. The truth is, of course, that the countless intellectuals who kiss the arse of Stalin are not different from the minority who give their allegiance to Hitler or Mussolini . . . nor from the older generation of intellectuals . . . who bowed down before German militarism. All of them are worshipping power and successful cruelty. It is important to notice that the cult of power tends to be mixed up with a love of cruelty and wickedness *for their own sakes*. (Emphasis in original.)[17]

Obviously Orwell saw that the most persuasive evidence for O'Brien's credo of power-as-sadism was provided by the twin totalitarianisms of the 1930s and 1940s—Fascism and Communism. Some of the investigations into the psychological substructures of these phenomena— for instance, Erich Fromm's *Escape from Freedom*—indeed bear out much of Orwell's analysis of the totalitarian mentality; and inhabitants of Eastern Europe, Czeslaw Milosz testifies in *The Captive Mind,* "are amazed that a writer who never lived in Russia should have so keen a perception into its life."[18] But Orwell's point in "Raffles and Miss Blandish" is that the cult of power, with its love of cruelty for its own sake, is in no wise peculiar to totalitarian regimes—though most obvious there, since its manifestations are writ so large—but had become a pervasive feature of twentieth-century life. The essay, after all, specifically examines a Western pop-cult phenomenon—the detective story—that Orwell found increasingly brutal in its contents and its appeal. That the English reading public had made a best-seller of a work of "intellectual sadism" like *No Orchids for Miss Blandish*— "Carlyle for the masses," he called it—Orwell saw as symptomatic of the times, symptomatic of the power worship that seemed universal.

> People worship power in the form in which they are able to understand it. A twelve-year-old boy worships Jack Dempsey. An adolescent in a Glasgow slum worships Al Capone. An aspiring pupil at a business college worships Lord Nuffield. A *New Statesman* reader worships Stalin. There is a difference in intellectual maturity, but none in moral outlook.[19]

Thus, as Bingo prefigures Big Brother and Crossgates Oceania, so the ethos of power that eventuates in O'Brien's declaration of sadism appears in less virulent forms, Orwell believed, at all levels of life: in England and America, for instance, no less than in Russia or Germany. "In the old-style English novel you knocked your man down and then chivalrously waited for him to get up before knocking him down again; in the modern version he is no sooner down than you take the opportunity of jumping on his face."[20] The stamping boot knows no politics.

The proposition that a sadistic desire to dominate and degrade underlies *all* exercise of power, however, evokes strong resistance. Isaac Deutscher argues in "The Mysticism of Cruelty" that this view indicates Orwell's tendency to judge the world in terms of simplistic, ahistorical generalizations. And George Kateb, to cite just one other example, levels much the same criticism.

> Common sense prevents acceptance of sadism as a constant and sufficient source of action. . . . There is no historical experience

that would bear Orwell out. The worst Nazi lived on something besides cruelty. In so far as one can deal with the question of political motivation in the abstract, one must conclude that the heart of *1984* is unsound.[21]

While such criticisms are not without merit, several things should be said in Orwell's defense. First, *Nineteen Eighty-Four* belongs to the literary genre called the anti-utopia or dystopia, an extrapolation of certain negative features of the author's own day into the future. The dystopia functions as a *Gedankenversuch* or "what if" novelistic formula that allows for the spinning out of speculative possibilities to their ultimate conclusion. Of *Nineteen Eighty-Four* Orwell wrote,

> I do not believe that the kind of society I describe necessarily *will* arrive, but I believe (allowing of course for the fact that the book is a satire) that something like it *could* arrive. I also believe that totalitarian ideas have taken root in the minds of intellectuals everywhere, and I have tried to draw these ideas out to their logical consequences.[22]

Like all dystopias, then, *Nineteen Eighty-Four* is an admonitory satire, warning of dangers that lie ahead. And the warning consists precisely in drawing out totalitarian ideas "to their logical consequences." Put another way, Oceania is the logical consequence, the pure idea, of the totalitarian mentality—the truly Caesarean environment where power operates without constraint—and not an attempt at historical mimesis. David Riesman has contended that "the grandiose fantasies at the bottom of the fears of people like Orwell" reflect "the deeply repressed fantasies of human omnipotence such as [have been] traced in the totalitarians themselves." In other words, Orwell (Riesman argues) accepts the totalitarians' own estimate of their power to manipulate and remake personalities to fit their ideology.[23] Riesman is correct, of course, in stressing the discrepancy between totalitarian aims and real-world results; he is also correct in viewing *Nineteen Eighty-Four* as a reflection of the totalitarians' fantasy of complete omnipotence; but he fails to see that embodying this fantasy was Orwell's conscious strategy. Orwell offers a negative Platonic ideal—an archetype of the unjust state which, in its pure evil, corresponds to no known historical reality. In the *Republic* Plato writes,

> when we set out to discover the essential nature of justice and injustice and what a perfectly just and a perfectly unjust man [and state] would be like, supposing them to exist, our purpose was to use them as ideal patterns. . . . We did not set out to show that these ideals could exist in fact.[24]

In this sense, Oceania can be seen as the perfection of totalitarianism, an ahistorical *idolum* in which all other motives for power except its essentially sadistic one are purged away by imagination: it is the *ideally unjust* state. Or, as another writer recently put it,

> Is absolute . . . control conceivable? Perhaps it is as unattainable as absolute zero on Lord Kelvin's scale. . . . Something like absolute zero is illustrated by Orwell in *1984*. But perhaps Orwell's book is as utopian as the books of the Renaissance thinkers or the Fourierists, who depicted the ideal state of society, the brave new world with ideal people. Perhaps a hopeless hell on earth is just as impossible as a hopeless heaven.[25]

If *Nineteen Eighty-Four* is a dystopian extrapolation of totalitarian potentialities carried to their logical extreme and not an analysis of historical totalitarianism, still the extrapolation, to have ideological significance, must be based on some perceived truth about the real-world phenomenon. But the problem is that we do not know the truth—or even if there *is* a truth—about the motives of totalitarianism. Indeed, some scholars even question whether there is such a thing as totalitarianism, a set of characteristics that delimit a precise phenomenon; "totalitarianism is to modern political science," claims one, "what reason was to Luther: a conceptional harlot of uncertain parentage, belonging to no one but at the service of all."[26]

In short, no consensus exists on any feature of totalitarianism, particularly on so controversial a subject as the psychological motives of its adherents. But this very uncertainty means that Orwell's theory of power-as-sadism, insofar as it is drawn from the historical phenomenon, cannot be dismissed as a distortion of *the* truth, for it is just such a fixed truth about totalitarianism that we lack. Indeed, as Irving Howe notes, none of Orwell's critics "has yet been able to provide a satisfactory explanation for that systematic excess in destroying human values which is a central trait of totalitarianism."[27] Deutscher, Kateb, and like-minded critics notwithstanding, sadism offers as logical an explanation of the motives of totalitarian rulers as any other that has been advanced.

Furthermore, Orwell is by no means alone in proposing it as the power motive of the real-world O'Briens. In his essay in this volume, Alex Zwerdling skillfully surveys Orwell's relation to the literature on totalitarianism, and I will not duplicate his effort here. But I want to adduce at least one instance of an analysis of the totalitarian mentality—Fromm's *Escape from Freedom*—that, in its essentials, accords remarkably with that found in *Nineteen Eighty-Four*. Fromm's is a complex argument, but basically he sees the relationship that obtains between rulers and ruled in totalitarian systems as a "symbiotic" sadomasochistic one. Fromm agrees with Orwell in discovering "the wish for power" as "the most significant expression of sadism."

> What is the essence of the sadistic drives? . . . All the different forms of sadism which we can observe go back to one essential impulse, namely, to have complete mastery over another person, to make of him a helpless object of our will, to become the absolute ruler over him, to become his God, to do with him as one pleases. To humiliate him, to enslave him, are means to this end and the most radical aim is to make him suffer, since there is no greater power over another person than that of inflicting pain on him, to force him to undergo suffering without his being able to defend himself. The pleasure in the complete domination over another person . . . is the very essence of the sadistic drive.[28]

This, of course, could be O'Brien speaking; and, indeed, Fromm sums up the essence of "the authoritarian character" in what is a perfect description of O'Brien's philosophy: "Power fascinates him not for any values for which a specific power may stand, but just because it is power."

In summary, then, these two things can be said about Orwell's theory of sadism as it relates to historical totalitarianism. First, that it is intended as a deliberate exaggeration—a dystopian extrapolation— of totalitarian practice into a "pure" or ideal form. As Howe puts it, "the world of 1984 is *not* totalitarianism as we know it, but totalitarianism after its world triumph. Strictly speaking, the society of Oceania might be called post-totalitarian."[29] Second, that while so little agreement obtains about the nature of the real-world phenomenon, Orwell's imputation of sadism as the power motive in totalitarianism seems as reasonable as any other and finds support in the analytical literature on the subject. The extrapolation of *Nineteen Eighty-Four*, then, is an extrapolation of the brute reality that in our century (as Orwell wrote in 1940) "human types supposedly extinct for centuries . . . have suddenly reappeared, not as the inmates of lunatic asylums, but as the masters of the world"—a world of "slave populations toiling behind barbed wire, women dragged shrieking to the block, cork-lined cellars where the executioner blows your brains out from behind."[30] O'Brien's credo of sadism is thus merely the logical extension of the experience of Auschwitz and Buchenwald, his boot stamping on a human face forever the ideal of the totalitarian modus operandi perfected and extended into the future, crushing the whole world beneath it.[31]

I argued earlier that for Orwell the Big Brothers are merely exaggerations of the Bingos, that the Caesarean tyrant represents the ordinary power seeker magnified by the Caesarean environment. Concomitantly, the impulse that motivates the totalitarian Caesars—

sadism—must be the same impulse that motivates all power seekers, however limited their sphere of action. In other words, the underlying motive of all power is the desire to dominate as an end in itself, making others suffer serving as the purest sign of one's dominance. All other rationales for power, then, are simply so much camouflage disguising the essentially sadistic motive. This would seem to be the implicit corollary of Orwell's position in *Nineteen Eighty-Four*, the corollary of the power worship that he saw as "a universal religion" of our age. If the Bingos are all incipient Big Brothers, then their basic drive is the same, differing only in the degree of opportunity it has to manifest itself. Again, unless one makes this assumption, then sadism, when it unmistakably appears, must seem wholly aberrant rather than an intensification of a commonplace drive operative in everyday situations. Which is it?

The question admits probably of no conclusive answer, but Orwell at any rate seemed keenly sensitive to the role not only of power worship in everyday life but of sadism in everyday life, evidence for which he discovered in the most mundane manifestations—in, for instance, the detective story, as we have already seen, and in pulp magazines. In his famous 1939 essay "Boys' Weeklies," examining the popular "penny dreadfuls," he notes the postwar emergence of "bully worship and the cult of violence." The young readers of such fantasies are encouraged to identify "with some single all-powerful character who dominates everyone about him and whose usual method of solving any problem is a sock on the jaw. This character is intended as a superman, and as physical strength is the form of power that boys can best understand, he is usually a sort of human gorilla." As was usual with Orwell, he saw Americans in advance of the English in glorifying violence.

> In the Yank Mags you get real blood-lust, really gory descriptions of the all-in, jump-on-his-testicles style of fighting, written in a jargon that has been perfected by people who brood endlessly on violence. A paper like *Fight Stories*, for instance, would have little appeal except to sadists and masochists.[32]

Even in the "anti-fascist" fantasies of America at war with the Nazis, "there is the frankest appeal to sadism, scenes in which the Nazis tie bombs to women's backs and fling them off heights to watch them blown to pieces in mid-air" and so on. But the same sort of crypto-sadistic appeal could be found as well in highbrow literature: in, for instance, Huxley's *Ape and Essence*. To Richard Rees, Orwell wrote,

> the more holy he gets, the more his books stink with sex. He cannot get off the subject of flagellating women. Possibly, if he had the courage to come out & say so, that is the solution to the

problem of war. If we took it out in a little private sadism, which after all doesn't do much harm, perhaps we wouldn't want to drop bombs etc.[33]

Ironically, just this sort of criticism has been leveled against *Nineteen Eighty-Four*—that its concentration on sadism reveals a distinct streak of perversity in its author's own personality—but whatever the truth about Orwell's own psyche, the perception he tosses off here remains to be evaluated: the relation, that is, between "public" and "private" sadism. Orwell seems to suggest that the aggressive and destructive manifestations of power politics (dropping bombs, etc.) are the large-scale displacements of individual desires to hurt others—drives that, rather than exceptional, are commonplace and found all around us.

In the best early review of *Nineteen Eighty-Four*, Philip Rahv compared Orwell's analysis of power favorably with that of Dostoevsky in *The Brothers Karamazov*.

> The dialectic of power is embodied in the figure of O'Brien, who simultaneously recalls and refutes the ideas of Dostoevsky's Grand Inquisitor. For a long time we thought the legend of the Grand Inquisitor contained the innermost secrets of the power-mongering human mind. But no, modern experience has taught us that the last word is by no means to be found in Dostoevsky. . . . There are elements of the idealistic rationalization of power in the ideology of the Grand Inquisitor that we must overcome if we are to become fully aware of what the politics of totalitarianism come to in the end.[34]

The Grand Inquisitor offers the classic statement of totalitarian paternalism: that a ruling elite justifiably monopolizes power to benefit, not itself, but weak, helpless subjects incapable of determining their own social destiny and willing to sacrifice freedom in exchange for a child-like security. Winston assumes that O'Brien, too, will offer such a justification for the Party's exercise of power. In response to O'Brien's catechistic question, "Why should we want power?" Winston gives what he thinks is the Party line: "You are ruling over us for our own good. . . . You believe that human beings are not fit to govern themselves, and therefore—" (p. 216). At this point O'Brien increases the voltage of torture: "That was stupid, Winston, stupid!" O'Brien rejects, that is, the self-serving, self-deluding apology of the Grand Inquisitor as naive—the rationalization of a seeker after total power unwilling to face the truth about his own motives—and offers instead the explanation quoted above: "Power is not a means; it is an end. . . . The object of power is power." Rahv—and I agree with him—finds O'Brien's explanation more truthful than that of the Grand Inquisitor,[35] but he seems to restrict its applicability to totalitarian regimes alone. "That, precisely, is the lesson the West must learn if it is to comprehend the meaning of Communism. Otherwise we shall go on playing Winston Smith, falling sooner or later into the hands of the O'Brien's of the East, who shall break our bones until we scream with love for Big Brother."[36] But the difficulty with drawing Rahv's moral is that it excepts all power except totalitarian power from O'Brien's characterization, when, in fact, what O'Brien is saying is that *all* power functions as an end in itself (and thus sadistically)—a far more sweeping claim than Rahv allows for and far more difficult proposition to accept.

The temptation is to see what is revealed by the analyses of totalitarianism as inapplicable to other, more moderate systems. Let me take a final example, again from Erich Fromm but this time from his instructive essay printed as an afterword to *Nineteen Eighty-Four*. Here Fromm several times makes the salutary point that "it would be most unfortunate if the reader smugly interpreted *1984* as [only] another description of Stalinist barbarism, and if he does not see that it means us, too."[37] Fromm notes a number of significant parallels between the "predictions" of Orwell and the actual developments in the West since 1948: the growth of militarism, of doublethink, of mind control. All of this, surely, "means us, too." But O'Brien's revelation about the universal motive for power—does that mean us, too? Fromm does not say.

When the wielder of power is a Hitler or a Stalin, even an Andropov or a Lyndon Johnson, perhaps we can accept O'Brien as their unacknowledged spokesman; but when power is wielded by the more or less innocuous likes of a Jimmy Carter, a Margaret Thatcher or a Mitterrand, can we really believe that he has revealed the hidden truth about *them*? It strains the imagination to the breaking point to think so. In its indictment of *all* exercise of power as sadistic, rather than in any attribution of sadism solely to totalitarian functionaries, *Nineteen Eighty-Four* renders its most problematic, most improbable judgment. If the heart of the novel is, as Kateb claims, unsound, surely here lies the source of its ideational weakness. And what credence can we accord a book with "an unsound heart"?

Interestingly enough, Orwell asked almost exactly this question about Swift's *Gulliver's Travels*, a work that figures in eighteenth-century English literature very much as *Nineteen Eighty-Four* will most likely figure in twentieth-century English literature. "In a political and moral sense I am against him," Orwell writes of Swift.

Yet curiously enough he is one of the writers I admire with least reserve, and *Gulliver's Travels*, in particular, is a book which it seems impossible for me to grow tired of. . . . Its fascination seems inexhaustible. If I had to make a list of six books which were to be preserved when all others were destroyed, I would certainly put *Gulliver's Travels* among them. This raises the question: what is the relationship between agreement with a writer's opinions, and enjoyment of his work?[38]

Orwell found Swift's politics retrograde (as many critics have found his own) and considered his world view antihuman and life-denying, rooted in a deep disgust with man's animal nature. Yet, he asks, "why is it that we don't mind being called Yahoos, although firmly convinced that we are *not* Yahoos?" To turn his question back on Orwell, we might ask why we esteem—enjoy is not, I suppose, quite the right word—a work that contends that all our rulers are secret sadists, when we are convinced that they are not so.

His answer about *Gulliver's Travels* could serve as our answer about *Nineteen Eighty-Four*.

The explanation must be that Swift's world-view is felt to be *not* altogether false—or it would probably be more accurate to say, not false all the time. . . . Swift falsified his picture of the world by refusing to see anything in human life except dirt, folly and wickedness, but the part which he abstracts from the whole does exist, and it is something which we all know about while shrinking from mentioning it. . . . In his endless harping on disease, dirt and deformity, Swift is not actually inventing anything, he is merely leaving something out. Human behavior, too, especially in politics, is as he describes it, although it contains other more important factors which he refuses to admit.[39]

For *Nineteen Eighty-Four* to make the indelible impression that it does, we must feel that its power-as-sadism premise is not altogether false, or not false all the time; that the part Orwell abstracts from the whole does exist, though we shrink from mentioning it; that political behavior *is* often as he describes it, although he refuses to admit more important factors. All in all, this seems like a fair and accurate assessment of *Nineteen Eighty-Four*. Like the political cartoonist—and like Swift—Orwell draws a caricature that is an exaggeration, no doubt a gross exaggeration, but there is a truth to it—not the *whole* truth, but *a* truth—and we confront it with the shock of recognition. In an unwitting self-characterization, Orwell concludes, "Swift did not possess ordinary wisdom, but he did possess a terrible intensity of vision, capable of picking out a single hidden truth and then magnifying it and distorting it." Orwell's presentation of power and sadism as inextricably linked is just such an instance of that terrible intensity of vision, magnifying and distorting a single hidden truth.

No one would, I suppose, be tempted to rank *Nineteen Eighty-Four* as highly as Orwell ranks *Gulliver's Travels,* as one of a half dozen to be preserved if all others perished. Yet it surely ranks as one of the half dozen most important books of this century, arguably—for all its artistic and ideological limitations—the most influential one. Kateb, for instance, despite the reservations he expresses, declares it "a *tour de force,* one of the most successful acts of political imagination ever made."[40] Our perception of politics has been permanently altered by it—perhaps, as Warren Wagar argues in his essay in this volume, not always and in every instance to salutary effect. But if the brooding image of a fictional Big Brother or the inquisitorial doctrine of O'Brien, entering our collective consciousness, has restrained the practices of their real-life avatars or alerted us to resist the dangers, then Orwell will have succeeded in his purpose even if he had to exaggerate a single truth about the hidden nature of power in order to do it.

Notes

1. *Chrome Yellow* (1922; reprint, New York: Harper and Row, 1974), 75–76.
2. See, for example, Alex Zwerdling, *Orwell and the Left* (New Haven: Yale University Press, 1974), for an excellent discussion of Orwell's political thought. For other useful discussions, see Carlyle King, "The Politics of George Orwell," *University of Toronto Quarterly* 26 (1956):79–91; Sir Richard Rees, "George Orwell," in *The Politics of Twentieth-Century Novelists,* ed. George A. Panichas (New York: Hawthorn Books, 1971), 85–99; S. J. Ingle, "The Politics of George Orwell: A Reappraisal," *Queens Quarterly* 80 (1973):22–33; and David Lowenthal, "Orwell: Ethics and Politics in the Pre–*Nineteen Eighty-Four* Writings," in *The Artist and Political Vision,* ed. Benjamin R. Barber and Michael J. G. McGrath (New Brunswick, N.J.: Transaction Books, 1982), 335–61.
3. "James Burnham and the Managerial Revolution," in *The Collected Essays, Journalism and Letters of George Orwell,* ed. Sonia Orwell and Ian Angus, 4 vols. (New York: Harcourt Brace Jovanovich, 1968), 4:179. Subsequent references will be given as *CEJL.*
4. Anthony West, "George Orwell," in his *Principles and Persuasions: The Literary Essays of Anthony West* (New York: Harcourt, Brace, 1957), 164–76. For a more elaborate, better supported development of this thesis, see Gerald Fiderer, "Masochism as Literary Strategy: Orwell's Psychological Novels," *Literature and Psychology* 20 (1970):3–21. But for

defenses of Orwell against this sort of attack, see, e.g., George Woodcock, *The Crystal Spirit: A Study of George Orwell* (Boston: Little, Brown, 1966), 198–203; and Richard J. Voorhees, *The Paradox of George Orwell* (Lafayette, Ind.: Purdue University Studies, 1961), 27–37.

5. "George Orwell and Eric Blair: Glimpses of a Dual Life," *Encounter* 13 (July, 1959):60.

6. For the most thorough and discriminating discussion of what is "fact" and what is "fiction" in this essay, see Bernard Crick, *George Orwell: A Life* (New York: Penguin, 1982), 58–99. See also his appendix B on the dating of "Such, Such Were the Joys."

7. "Such, Such Were the Joys," in George Orwell, *A Collection of Essays* (Garden City, N.Y.: Doubleday, 1954), 27–30. Subsequent page references appear parenthetically in the text. This essay appears in *CEJL*, but in a somewhat different form from its original publication: St. Cyprian's is called such, not Crossgates; Sim is called Sambo and Bingo, Flip. I use the earlier version, however, because it is the one referred to in previous criticism—and because Bingo alliterates with Big Brother, while Flip does not. Besides, I *see* Mrs. Wilkes as a Bingo.

8. *1984* (1949; reprint, New York: Signet Classics, 1961), 156. In *Pentagonism: A Substitute for Imperialism* (New York: Grove Press, 1968), Juan Bosch, the former president of the Dominican Republic who was deposed in a CIA-directed coup, advances an explanation for the enormous growth in American military spending that is straight Goldstein.

> Pentagonism . . . differs from imperialism in that it does not share its most characteristic feature, military conquest of colonial territories and their subsequent economic exploitation. . . . To succeed in the exploitation of its own people, pentagonism colonizes the mother country; but since the colonization of the mother country must be achieved through the same military process as was used to conquer a colony and since it cannot wage war against its own people, the mother country sends its armies out to make war on other countries. . . . The fact is that the use of military power has not changed; what has changed is the purpose for which it is used. The military forces of a pentagonist country are not sent out to conquer colonial territories. War has another purpose; war is waged to conquer positions of power in the pentagonist country, not in some far-off land. What is being sought is not a place to invest surplus capital for profit; what is being sought is access to the generous economic resources being mobilized for industrial war productions. (Pp. 21–22)

Although Bosch nowhere mentions Orwell, he nevertheless provides provocative evidence for Orwell's prescience as a prophet of megamilitarism.

9. I have dealt with some of this ambivalence, particularly the erotic displacement involved in leader worship, in my essay "Of Man's Last Disobedience: Zamiatin's *We* and Orwell's *1984*," *Comparative Literature Studies* 10 (1973):285–301.

10. Zwerdling, *Orwell and the Left*, 137.

11. *CEJL* 3:7.

12. "Catastrophic Gradualism," *CEJL* 4:18.

13. Richard Rees, *George Orwell: Fugitive From the Camp of Victory* (London: Secker and Warburg, 1961), 153.

14. *CEJL* 1:375.

15. "*1984*—The Mysticism of Cruelty," in Isaac Deutscher, *Heretics and Renegades and Other Essays* (London: Hamish Hamilton, 1955), 47.

16. But for Orwell's reservations about anarchism, see Ruth Ann Lief, *Homage to Oceania: The Prophetic Vision of George Orwell* (Columbus: Ohio State University Press, 1969), 74–75.

17. *CEJL* 3:222.

18. Czeslaw Milosz, *The Captive Mind*, trans. Jane Zielonko (1953; reprint, New York: Vintage, 1981), 42.

19. *CEJL* 3:223–24.

20. Review, *CEJL* 1:220.

21. George Kateb, "The Road to *1984*," *Political Science Quarterly* 81 (1966):566.

22. *CEJL*, 4:502.

23. "Some Observations on the Limits of Totalitarian Power," in David Riesman, *Individualism Reconsidered and Other Essays* (Glencoe, Ill.: Free Press, 1954), 424.

24. *The Republic*, trans. Francis M. Cornford (New York: Oxford University Press, 1941), 177. Max Weber employed a similar methodology as a tool of modern sociology. His "much discussed 'ideal type,' " write H. H. Gerth and C. Wright Mills,

> refers to the construction of certain elements of reality into a logically precise conception. The term "ideal" has nothing to do with evaluation of any sort. For analytical purposes, one may construct ideal types of prostitution as well as of religious leaders. The term does not mean that either prophets or harlots are exemplary or should be imitated as representatives of an ideal way of life. By using the term, Weber . . . merely intended to bring to full awareness what social scientists and historians had been doing when they used words like "the economic man," "feudalism," "Gothic *versus* Romantic architecture," or "kingship." He felt that social scientists had the choice of using logically controlled and unambiguous conceptions, which are thus moved from historic reality, or of using less precise concepts, which are more closely geared to the empirical world. (Introduction, *From Max Weber: Essays in Sociology* [New York: Oxford University Press, 1946], 59.)

25. Tomas Venclova, "The Game of the Soviet Censor," *New York Review of Books*, March 31, 1983, p. 34.

26. Benjamin R. Barber, "Conceptual Foundations of Totalitarianism," in *Totalitarianism in Perspective: Three Views*, ed. Carl J. Friedrich et al. (New York: Praeger, 1969), 19. Barber further asserts:

The realities the term was originally introduced to describe have been metamorphosized by time. . . . Yet both the concept of totalitarianism and the ideological perspective out of which it grew linger on—despite increasing dissatisfaction among many students of comparative politics with its definitional ambiguities and despite an almost complete absence of consensus on the specific regimes to which the term can be appropriately applied. (P. 4)

27. Irving Howe, *Politics and the Novel* (New York: Horizon, 1957), 250.
28. Erich Fromm, *Escape From Freedom* (1941; reprint, New York: Avon, 1965), 183, 177–78, 190.
29. Howe, *Politics and the Novel*, 250.
30. "Notes on the Way," *CEJL* 2:15–16.
31. See Melvyn New, "Orwell and Antisemitism: Toward *1984*," *Modern Fiction Studies* 21 (1975):81–105.
32. *CEJL* 1:476–78.
33. *CEJL* 4:479.
34. Philip Rahv, "The Unfuture of Utopia," *Partisan Review* 16 (July, 1949): 747.
35. I believe, however, that Dostoevsky's own understanding of the motive of power is superior to that of his Grand Inquisitor, whom he sees as self-deluded. I have developed this idea—and Dostoevsky's agreement with Orwell—in a paper, " 'The Legend of the Grand Inquisitor': The Utopian as Sadist," presented at the Seventh Annual Conference on Utopian Studies, University of New Brunswick (Canada), Sept. 10, 1982. For a perceptive recent commentary on Rahv's analysis, see Irving Howe, "*1984*: Was Orwell Right?," *New Republic*, Special Year-End Issue, 1982, p. 30.
36. Rahv, "The Unfuture of Utopia," 748.
37. Erich Fromm, "Afterword" to *1984* (New York: Signet, 1961), 267.
38. Orwell, "Politics vs. Literature: an Examination of *Gulliver's Travels*," *CEJL* 4:220–23.
39. *CEJL* 4:221–22.
40. Kateb, "The Road to *1984*," 579.

Orwell's Psychopolitics

Alex Zwerdling

A helpless man is being tortured. He is a prisoner of the state, without hope of rescue. His tormentors use the weapons of terror and coercion: the fist, the boot, the truncheon, electric shock, mental torture, isolation, humiliation, degradation. His body is broken; his mind invaded; his self-respect virtually annihilated. How does he respond to his torturers? In Orwell's *Nineteen Eighty-Four*, the classic formula of melodrama is suddenly abandoned at this point. For Winston Smith regards O'Brien, the agent of the Thought Police responsible for his pain, not with defiant hatred but with love: "For a moment he clung to O'Brien like a baby, curiously comforted by the heavy arm round his shoulders. He had the feeling that O'Brien was his protector, that the pain was something that came from outside, from some other source, and that it was O'Brien who would save him from it."[1] And as the pain is renewed and intensified, Winston gazes at O'Brien with increasing devotion: "At sight of the heavy, lined face, so ugly and so intelligent, his heart seemed to turn over. If he could have moved he would have stretched out a hand and laid it on O'Brien's arm. He had never loved him so deeply as at this moment" (p. 208).

The torture scenes in *Nineteen Eighty-Four* have disturbed Orwell's readers from the first, and for good reason. What can account for this shocking betrayal of expectation? Is the political world of the novel being encroached upon by the neurotic aberrations of Orwell's psyche? Is the triumphant totalitarian regime it depicts more properly understood as a sadomasochistic fantasy imperfectly controlled by the author's conscious intentions? At least two influential readers of Orwell's novel have taken this line. Isaac Deutscher argues that *Nineteen Eighty-Four* is the product not of rational observation but of "the mysticism of cruelty" and that Orwell's obsession with conspiracies is "a Freudian sublimation of persecution mania."[2] Anthony West sees the novel as a working out of its author's "infantile" terror, the warped "paranoid" product of Orwell's unconscious mind. And he concludes, "Only the existence of a hidden wound can account for such a remorseless pessimism."[3]

The need to defend Orwell's novel, and Orwell himself, from such charges has dominated commentary on his work for the last two decades and has produced a distinct split among the defenders. We are asked to choose between a sociopolitical and a psychological interpretation of *Nineteen Eighty-Four*: the terms are strictly either-or. So Bernard Crick, Orwell's official biographer, insists that the "hidden wound" theory merely explains away what is after all "a rational work of political reflection," and that Orwell had an essentially "sociological rather than a psychological imagination."[4] He treats Orwell as a shrewd observer of modern politics who is fundamentally indifferent to the pyschological elements in his fiction. The opposing viewpoint should be apparent merely from the titles of some recent books or essays: "The Wall of Blackness: A Psychological Approach to *1984*"; "Masochism as Literary Strategy: Orwell's Psychological Novels"; *Primal Dream and Primal Crime: Orwell's Development as a Psychological Novelist.*[5] The line of defense in such interpretations is to treat Orwell's novel not as the product of his own morbidity but as the work of a penetrating psychological observer, even if this is done at the price of his political insight. Winston Smith becomes an interesting case study. His "obsessions" are taken to be under Orwell's clinical scrutiny; and the author's psychological penetration is given primacy over what is seen as the more superficial political subject matter of his book. To quote one such reading of the novel, "That Orwell is treating here with the pyschology of the impotent neurotic rather than social criticism of the body politic is clear."[6]

Psychology *rather than* social criticism; political observation *rather than* psychological insight: these apparently are the choices available to us in reading *Nineteen Eighty-Four*. Both are ways of domesticating the uneasiness we are likely to feel in reading the book, an uneasiness that seems to me to overflow both the political and psychological containers we are offered. The novel reverberates with an intensity that challenges the vision of Orwell as a detached observer, carefully describing certain interesting political or psychological phenomena unconnected to his own experience. The torture scenes transgress the limits of commonsense plausibility more surely than do Newspeak, the telescreens, and the other characteristics of the future Orwell allows himself to invent. It is important to ask both what the deepest sources in Orwell's experience for these scenes are and whether they connect with his conscious intentions in writing *Nineteen Eighty-Four*.

By this point we know enough about Orwell's life (from his autobiographical writings as well as from memoirs and biographies) to answer the first question. There is little doubt that there was a sadomasochistic streak in Orwell's nature, which he generally managed to keep under control, but which sometimes erupted into action. In *The Road to Wigan Pier*, he confessed that he was haunted by the memory of "servants and coolies I had hit with my fist in moments of rage" during his years as an imperial policeman in Burma.[7] Rayner Heppenstall has described Orwell's brutal attack on him with a shooting stick when Heppenstall returned home drunk one night to the flat they shared.[8] And Orwell himself records an altercation with a disgruntled Paris taxi driver and admits that he threatened the driver with the words "You think you're too old for me to smash your face in. Don't be too sure!"[9] The parallels between such incidents and some of Winston's sadistic fantasies about Julia are striking: "Vivid, beautiful hallucinations flashed through his mind. He would flog her to death with a rubber truncheon"; and when he is convinced she is following him, he determines to "smash her skull in with a cobblestone" (pp. 16, 85–86).

I do not think Orwell would have been outraged to see such connections between his life and work. He was trying to understand and account for the brutal, irrational strain in totalitarianism, and he knew that only a writer with a touch of the disease could describe it persuasively. As he wrote in 1941, "The people who have shown the best understanding of Fascism are either those who have suffered under it or those who have a Fascist streak in themselves" (*CEJL* 2:144). His favorite example of a writer in the second category was Jack London, whose novel *The Iron Heel* Orwell took to be the first accurate prophecy of modern totalitarianism. "London could foresee Fascism," Orwell insists, "because he had a Fascist streak in himself: or at any rate a marked strain of brutality and an almost unconquerable preference for the strong man as against the weak man" (*CEJL* 4:25). The whole strange world "created by secret-police forces, censorship of opinion, torture and frame-up trials" was so unfamiliar to those living in a different orbit like England's that only a writer whose psyche produced a responsive chord could hope to interpret it. As Orwell puts it in his essay on Arthur Koestler, "To understand such things one has to be able to imagine oneself as the victim" (*CEJL* 3:235) or, one might add, as the victimizer. Like many a courageous investigator of dangerous maladies, Orwell was ready to use himself as a guinea pig.

By the time he came to write *Nineteen Eighty-Four*, he was conscious of an unprecedented irrational streak in modern politics that could not be understood in classic terms: economic first causes, class warfare, progress and reaction, international competition, *Realpolitik* and all the other rational explanations of what went on in public life. By comparison, his earlier political allegory, *Animal Farm*, was built on a more familiar foundation: class distinctions, the permanence of privilege, the predictable stages of a revolution, and so on. Perhaps it was the intellectual conservatism of the book's conceptual framework that allowed Orwell to write such a spare, elegant, perfectly controlled parable. All the forces in *Animal Farm*, including that of the author's vision, are essentially rational.

Only a few years later, such a foundation would no longer strike him as sound. He had come to feel that political explanations would have to use the vocabulary of mental illness, religious zealotry, and primal emotions. "We shall get nowhere," he wrote in 1946, "unless we start by recognising that political behaviour is largely non-rational, that the world is suffering from some kind of mental disease which must be diagnosed before it can be cured" (*CEJL* 4:249). The writers who interested him most had grasped this essential point. His model for the world of the future was not to be the utopias of Wells or Huxley but the darker vision embodied in Zamyatin's *We*. For "Wells is too sane to understand the modern world"; and Huxley also suffers in the comparison: "It is this intuitive grasp of the irrational side of totalitarianism—human sacrifice, cruelty as an end in itself, the worship of a Leader who is credited with divine attributes—that makes Zamyatin's book superior to Huxley's" (*CEJL* 2:145; 4:75). Orwell's most sustained attempt to analyze this vision of modern political life is the essay "Notes on Nationalism," written in 1945 as he was thinking out his last novel. It consistently uses the descriptive terminology of mental illness: *obsession, fixation, schizophrenia* are all words applied to modern political behavior. Politics has become a realm in which free-floating fantasy and urgent emotion are in control—"fear, hatred, jealousy and power worship are involved," he writes, and as a result "the sense of reality becomes unhinged" (*CEJL* 3:379).

This sense of a subterranean, deeply irrational current in public affairs is part of Orwell's legacy. He was not of course alone in detecting its presence and his vision was shaped by the events of his time. In 1939, Peter Drucker published his book *The End of Economic Man: A Study of the New Totalitarianism*, a work Orwell knew well and referred to frequently. Drucker argued that neither the fascist nor Russian communist regime could be understood in rational terms. Their adherents had come to believe in a world ruled by demonic forces from which only a quasi-mystical leader could protect them. In Drucker's words,

> It is not in spite of its being contrary to reason and in spite of its rejecting everything of the past without exception, but because of it, that the masses flocked to fascism and Nazism and that they abandoned themselves to Mussolini and Hitler. The sorcerer is a sorcerer because he does supernatural things in a supernatural way unknown to all reasonable tradition and contrary to all laws of logic. And it is a sorcerer able to work powerful miracles that the masses in Europe demand and need to allay their intolerable terror of a world which the demons have reconquered.[10]

The primitive fears and exaltations such a view of the world releases are not calculated or strategic, at least in the minds of the adherents.

They relate rather to the deepest level of fantasy, often evoked in nightmare, in which our rational faculties are not in control. In that world nothing is implausible; everything is possible.

"Normal men do not know that everything is possible." This is a sentence from David Rousset's ground-breaking study of the concentration camps, *L'Univers concentrationnaire* (1946) which Hannah Arendt uses as an epigraph in her book *The Origins of Totalitarianism* (1951). Rousset's work, which Orwell also knew well, is one of the first attempts to describe the nightmare world fascism had created in the camps, and it is based on his sense of an unbridgeable gap between the knowledge of the internees and the world of "normal men." For the inmates "have experienced anxiety as an ever present obsession. . . . They have lived through long years in the fantastic setting of degraded human dignities. They are separated from other people by an experience which it is impossible to communicate."[11] Yet it is precisely in fantasy that the two worlds meet, and this is why Orwell's novel is so heavily reliant on it. Modern political terror is essentially reified nightmare. In Hannah Arendt's words,

> Everything that was done in the camps is known to us from the world of perverse, malignant fantasies. The difficult thing to understand is that, like such fantasies, these gruesome crimes took place in a phantom world, which, however, has materialized, as it were, into a world which is complete with all sensual data of reality but lacks that structure of consequence and responsibility without which reality remains for us a mass of incomprehensible data.[12]

Nineteen Eighty-Four attempts to evoke this realm of perverse, malignant fantasy. Its historical roots seem to me to lie as much in the first postwar descriptions of what went on in the concentration camps as in the earlier reports of the Soviet purges, though of course the two are related. But the seedtime of Orwell's novel—the mid-1940s in which he was planning the book and composing the first draft—coincided with the first widespread publicity about just what had happened in Dachau and Buchenwald, in Belsen and Treblinka and Auschwitz. Those names were carved in the Western memory as one camp after another was liberated by the Allied armies in 1945.[13] The spring 1945 volume of *The Official Index to* The Times (London) had a new subheading under Germany: "atrocities." The list of relevant pieces in the *Times* for this three-month period alone fills four columns. To read through these articles, editorials, and letters is to get a sense of how shocking those first reports were to a world prepared to think only about what might be called normal warfare. The photographs of the neatly stacked naked corpses at Belsen, of the human skeletons who had somehow managed to survive, of the crematoria; the tale of Ilse Koch's lampshades; the description of the hills of human teeth from which the gold fillings had been extracted; the story of the band at Maidanek that played tangos as the victims were marched to the gas chamber: all these monstrous details, which have by now taken on the status of myth or legend, were presented to a large readership for the first time. A parliamentary delegation sent to visit Buchenwald a few days after it was liberated concluded its report by saying that "such camps marked the lowest point of degradation to which humanity had yet descended."[14]

These journalistic descriptions were followed in the next two or three years by many important book-length studies, including those written by survivors like David Rousset. It is clear that Orwell was deeply interested in such works, that he read many of them, and that he took the camps to be symptomatic of the pervasive irrationalism of modern political life. As he writes to Rousset's English translator, "The point is that these forced-labour camps are part of the pattern of our time, & are a very interesting though horrible pheonomenon" (*CEJL* 4:421). They illustrated better than any other fact of contemporary history that the images of nightmare—of monstrously powerful opponents, helpless victims incomprehensibly assaulted, prisons without doors, purposeless torture, sadomasochistic pain and pleasure—were more useful to an understanding of what was going on in the real world than the ordinary waking observation of "normal men."

This is why dreams and fantasies are so pervasive in *Nineteen Eighty-Four*. The boundary between reality and imagination is consistently blurred in the novel, and we are often left uncertain about whether something actually happened. A voice murmurs, "Don't worry, Winston; you are in my keeping. For seven years I have watched over you. Now the turning-point has come. I shall save you, I shall make you perfect." But Winston cannot remember if the voice is O'Brien's or whether he heard it "in drugged sleep, or in normal sleep, or even in a moment of wakefulness" (p. 201). Winston's dreams are recurrent and always revelatory. The dream of the voice that tells him "We shall meet in the place where there is no darkness" (p. 25), of his mother in a sinking ship cradling his baby sister, the recurrent dream of the "Golden Country" and that of "standing in front of a wall of darkness," on the other side of which "there was something unendurable, something too dreadful to be faced" (p. 120): all are significant and illuminate his actual situation and experience. Orwell consistently emphasizes the vital importance of these unwilled excursions into fantasy, and he draws attention to the links between them and reality: "It was one of those dreams which, while retaining the characteristic dream scenery, are a continuation of one's intellectual life, and in which one becomes aware of facts and ideas which still seem new and valuable after one is awake" (p. 28).

Nineteen Eighty-Four also uses the world of childhood fantasy to stretch the limits of "normal" adult consciousness and tap the world of the irrational. The seemingly innocent nursery rhyme that begins "Oranges and lemons, say the bells of St. Clement's" is gradually recalled in the course of the book; O'Brien himself ominously provides the last line. And when Winston and Julia are arrested, the voice of the "friendly" antique dealer, Mr. Charrington, who had recited for Winston the rhymes "about four and twenty blackbirds, and another about a cow with a crumpled horn, and another about the death of poor Cock Robin" (p. 125), now mocks him with a final message from the nursery: "Here comes a candle to light you to bed, here comes a chopper to chop off your head!" (p. 183). The anarchic, incomprehensible violence of childhood fantasy meshed all too easily with the bizarre and frightening reality of the modern police state.

Such connections between the imagination of children and the experience of adults have been used to question the credibility of Orwell's vision of totalitarianism. Anthony West's attack on *Nineteen Eighty-Four* tries to demolish the book by finding a whole network of parallels between it and Orwell's brilliantly evocative essay about his preparatory school, "Such, Such Were the Joys." For West, *Nineteen Eighty-Four* is an implausible adult recasting of the panic of Orwell's childhood experience at the school, in which "the masters seem, by some kind of magical omniscience, to know what every boy does and even what he thinks."[15] He sees the novel as a kind of allegory in which the central characters can be identified with prototypes from Orwell's schooldays. Mechanical as is West's application of this thesis, there must be something about it that is right. Otherwise it would have sunk into oblivion rather than producing so many impassioned rebuttals over the years. But the connection between essay and novel is not so much in the cast of characters as in the mental atmosphere both try to convey.

Orwell's deepest interest in "Such, Such Were the Joys" lies not in describing his school as it actually was but in conveying the nature of a child's imagination. The arguments by various biographers over whether his picture of St. Cyprian's is accurate or not seem to miss the point. Again and again in the essay, Orwell emphasizes that he is trying to recapture the child's subjective, inevitably distorted perception of the adult world. One narrative passage begins, "And here there occurred one of those wild, almost lunatic misunderstandings which are part of the daily experience of childhood." He goes on to describe "a deeper grief which is peculiar to childhood and not easy to convey: a sense of desolate loneliness and helplessness, of being locked up not only in a hostile world but in a world of good and evil where the rules were such that it was actually not possible for me to keep them." And he concludes, "Only by resurrecting our own memories can we realise how incredibly distorted is the child's vision of the world" (*CEJL* 4:332, 334, 367).

Ironically, however, the sense of distortion and improbability in a child's imagination, which is said to give way gradually to an adult sense of reality, turned out to be remarkably useful to an understanding of one adult creation: the modern totalitarian state. This was *not* merely a peculiar notion of Orwell's but an insight other victims and analysts of totalitarianism came to endorse. They argued that such regimes deliberately set out to reduce the competent, independent adult to a state of childish helplessness and fear. Bruno Bettelheim's important book on the concentration camps, *The Informed Heart*, offers the best description of this sinister process. His whole section on "Childlike Behavior" emphasizes the analogy between prisoner and helpless child. He concludes, "There seems no doubt that the tasks they [the prisoners] were given, as well as the mistreatment they had to endure, contributed to the disintegration of their self respect and made it impossible to see themselves and each other as fully adult persons any more."[16] Bettelheim goes on to apply this theory to the ordinary subjects of totalitarian regimes outside the concentration camps. "Only in infancy did other persons, our parents, have the power to throw us into desperate inner turmoil if our wishes conflicted with theirs. . . . This power for creating unmanageable inner conflicts in the child must be compared with the power of the total state to create similar conflicts in the minds of its subjects."[17] Totalitarian regimes adopted a deliberate policy of infantilizing their citizens as a way of giving the ruler uncontested power over their lives.

The politics of such regimes were the politics of family life. This analogy is at the heart of *Nineteen Eighty-Four*. Orwell describes a world in which familial loyalty is deliberately undermined so that the displaced emotions can be appropriated by the state. The solidarity of the family is treated as a threat to party loyalty and is therefore systematically weakened. Children are encouraged to betray their parents. They are organized into single-generation, transfamilial groups (the Spies, the Youth League). Constant obligatory adult activities at the Community Centre take up evenings and weekends that might otherwise have been spent with the family. Marriages are subject to Party approval and prevented if the partners betray too much affection. Sex is discouraged except as a means of procreation. The home is not a sanctuary but a goldfish bowl.

The parallels with the practices of totalitarian regimes are obvious. Bettelheim describes Nazi Germany on the eve of World War II as a society in which "state control of individual behavior invaded the privacy of the home." Children were encouraged to spy on their parents and report all questionable conversations to the authorities. As a result, "no German could feel safe in his private life any more."[18] And Hannah Arendt has argued that this deliberate isolation of the individual, the shattering of all important connections between people and the resulting atomization of society, is "the psychological basis for total domination." For total loyalty "can be expected only from the completely isolated human being who, without any other social ties to family, friends, comrades, or even mere acquaintances, derives his sense of having a place in the world only from his belonging to a movement, his membership in the party."[19] The intention is to transfer the primal emotion between husband and wife, parent and child, between lovers or intimate friends, over to the state.

In *Nineteen Eighty-Four*, the regime strives to become the heir of the moribund family and systematically appropriates the emotional capital of that institution. Its leader, Big Brother, combines the qualities of disciplinarian father and loyal sibling. Even the invented conspiracy against him is called "the Brotherhood." What Winston Smith at first misses from this world is the sense of maternal protection. He dreams ceaselessly about his mother: "His mother's memory tore at his heart because she had died loving him, when he was too young and selfish to love her in return, and because somehow, he did not remember how, she had sacrificed herself to a conception of loyalty that was private and unalterable" (p. 28). Her love was unconditional and uncoercive, and there are really no substitutes for such affection in the public world Winston inhabits.

His task is to transform this need for maternal sponsorship into one of the emotions licensed by the state. The pressure for him to do just this is relentless, and eventually he succumbs. His disturbing response to O'Brien's torture is a stage in this process: "For a moment he clung to O'Brien like a baby, curiously comforted by the heavy arm round his shoulders" (p. 207). There are only two characters in the novel who address Winston by his first name—his mother, and O'Brien. Others refer to him as "comrade" or "Smith"; Julia calls him "dear" or "love" but never uses his name; the voice on the telescreen barks "6079 Smith W." Only O'Brien persistently uses the intimate, familiar, endearing form of address associated with childhood. It is not entirely ironic that the building in which Winston Smith is being tortured is called the Ministry of Love. By the last paragraph of the novel, when all his other bonds—including the loving bond to Julia—have been cut, he finally twists the strands of his need for mother, father, sibling, and lover into a single emotion.

O stubborn, self-willed exile from the loving breast! Two gin-scented tears trickled down the sides of his nose. But it was all right, everything was all right, the struggle was finished. He had won the victory over himself. He loved Big Brother. (P. 245)[20]

The emotions recorded in such passages echo the feelings described in the psychoanalytic literature on sadomasochism and reopen the question of whether Orwell's vision of totalitarianism is not fundamentally skewed by some neurotic aberration. In Freud's two important papers on the subject, " 'A Child Is Being Beaten' " (1919) and "The Economic Problem in Masochism" (1924), punishment is always linked to parental figures or substitutes for them and is a form of love. The earlier piece, an analysis of the beating fantasy in patients, concludes: "So the original form of the unconscious male phantasy was not the provisional one that we have hitherto given: 'I am being beaten by my father,' but rather: *'I am loved by my father.'* "[21] In the later essay, Freud shows how this sadomasochistic response is eventually taken out of the parental sphere. "In the course of development through childhood which brings about an ever-increasing severance from the parents, their personal significance for the super-ego recedes. To the imagos they leave behind are then linked on the influences of teachers, authorities, of self-chosen models and heroes venerated by society."[22]

These classic studies of masochism treat the condition as a problem in individual psychology and as a primarily sexual aberration. The subtitle of Freud's earlier paper is "A Contribution to the Study of the Origin of Sexual Perversion," and he categorizes most of the actual patients on whom the study was based as "true masochists in the sense of being sexual perverts."[23] In the course of time, however, sadomasochism came to be seen as a universal *tendency* in human nature, neither primarily sexual nor entirely aberrant. Freud himself broadened the term by inventing the category "moral masochism," a psychological state defined by a persistent "need for punishment," whether administered by a loved person or not, and not necessarily having consequences in sexual life.[24]

Post-Freudian psychologists broadened the category further. In Erich Fromm's *The Fear of Freedom* (published in England in 1942; American title *Escape from Freedom*, 1941), he renames the sadomasochistic tendency in so-called normal persons the "authoritarian character."[25] People dominated by this tendency see the world in terms of power relationships and are intensely interested in issues of authority. They forge strong bonds with others in which power and dependence, coercion and humiliation, predominate. In Theodor Reik's *Masochism in Modern Man* (1941), Freud's "moral masochism" is renamed "social masochism" in order to stress its wide currency. Reik too divorces the term from sexual deviance and focuses on a more general personality trait—the conscious or unconscious tendency to seek out suffering and dependence rather than trying to avoid them. The sexual perversion originally identified by the clinical term *sado-masochism* has dissolved, in Reik's words, "but dissolved like a lump of salt in water. It is everywhere, has become an attitude of life."[26]

It is no accident that these influential post-Freudian studies should have been published during World War II. Both were attempts to understand the mass psychology of fascism by extending the insights of individual psychology, in order to discover—as Auden puts it in "September 1, 1939"—"What huge imago made /A psychopathic god." The worship of a strong figure associated with brutality and violence, the eagerness to submit to rigid discipline, to surrender autonomy and be ruled, could scarcely be treated as an individual aberration in the era of totalitarian dictatorships. It had become a mass phenomenon. Fromm begins his work by raising these issues directly.

> It is the purpose of this book to analyse those dynamic factors in the character structure of modern man, which made him want to give up freedom in Fascist countries and which so widely prevail in millions of our own people. These are the outstanding questions that arise when we look at the human aspect of freedom, the longing for submission, and the lust for power.[27]

And Reik concludes that such docile political behavior can be understood psychologically as a form of exercising power by proxy.

> The tyrannic will of a dictator may ask privations and sacrifices from the masses hardly bearable otherwise than if they consider him their own idealized image. Here the phenomenon of mass-masochism or its predecessors becomes psychologically understandable.[28]

That Orwell was thinking along the same lines is suggested in his 1940 review of *Mein Kampf*, in which he argues that fascism and Stalinism "are psychologically far sounder than any hedonistic conception of life. . . . All three of the great dictators have enhanced their power by imposing intolerable burdens on their peoples" (*CEJL* 2:14).

What interested all of these writers was the way in which certain insights about psychosexual life helped to explain modern leadership cults. In effect, the totalitarian state translates into group behavior forces that were traditionally considered private. In Fromm's formulation, the fundamental biological antithesis between male and female is restructured to produce a vision of two new sexes, "the powerful ones and the powerless ones"; and the regime tries to reshape the responses of the ordinary citizen until "his love, admiration and readiness for submission are automatically aroused by power, whether of a person or of an institution."[29]

Orwell's description of the crowd emotions during the daily Two Minutes Hate sessions and in Hate Week suggest a similar manipulation of group response. These scenes are orgies of sadomasochistic feeling, designed to attach a blocked erotic energy to the central figures in the regime's public fiction: the contest between Big Brother and the hated enemy Goldstein. As Winston comes to understand, "There was a direct intimate connection between chastity and political orthodoxy. For how could the fear, the hatred and the lunatic credulity which the Party needed in its members be kept at the right pitch, except by bottling down some powerful instinct and using it as a driving force? The sex impulse was dangerous to the Party, and the Party had turned it to account" (p. 111). The beastlike roar that emerges from the crowd during Hate Week, or "the deep, slow, rhythmical chant of 'B-B! . . . B-B! . . . B-B!' " that comes unwilled from their throats as Big Brother's powerful face, with its penetrating gaze and hypnotic eyes, flashes onto the screen (p. 17), are examples of the successful channeling of primal emotions to serve the needs of the state. Orwell was trying to convey the atmosphere of a society in which mass psychology, the systematic study and manipulation of crowd response, had become a major force in public life. "Mass-suggestion," he wrote in 1939, "is a science of the last twenty years, and we do not yet know how successful it will be." It seemed to him conceivable that such forces might alter human nature in fundamental ways. "It may be just as possible to produce a breed of men who do not wish for liberty as to produce a breed of hornless cows" (*CEJL* 1:380–81).

Such speculations about the effect of social and political pressures on the human psyche were a hallmark of the intellectual life of Orwell's time. They were the province of a relatively new field of study called "social psychology" that emerged in the period 1930–50. As its name implies, investigators in this field tried to fuse the insights of individual psychology with those of sociopolitical investigation. These years produced works like Harold Lasswell's *Psychopathology and Politics* (1930), Hadley Cantril's *The Psychology of Social Movements* (1941), Theodore Newcomb's *Personality and Social Change* (1943), Wilhelm Reich's *The Mass Psychology of Fascism* (1933; English trans., 1946), and finally *The Authoritarian Personality* by T. W. Adorno and others (1950). The impetus for such studies grew out of a sense that the separation of psychology, sociology, and politics into relatively independent disciplines was responsible for the failure to understand certain vitally important forces in modern life. Psychoanalytic thinking, at least in the early years of the movement, had focused on the shaping power of one's own family and largely ignored the effect of broader societal forces. Adult political behavior had been treated as unrelated to deep psychic needs, despite the new direction suggested in pioneering works like Le Bon's *The Crowd* (1895) and Freud's *Group Psychology and the Analysis of the Ego* (1921).

People trained to think in such watertight compartments could make no sense of some of the major events of their time, let alone of their own experience. Bruno Bettelheim's explanation of how he came to write *The Informed Heart* suggests that the shock of his imprisonment in Dachau and Buchenwald quickly brought about a revolution in his intellectual assumptions.

> I was imprisoned in the camps at about the time when my convictions derived from psychoanalysis were at their height: that the personality shaping influence of the immediate family is all important, and that society in the broader sense is relatively negligible by comparison. . . . My experience in the camps taught me, almost within days, that I had gone much too far in believing that only changes in man could create changes in society. I had to accept that the environment could, as it were, turn personality upside down, and not just in the small child, but in the mature adult too.[30]

As a result of his own experience and his close observation of other prisoners, he came to understand just how malleable the adult personality could still be when subjected to intense societal pressure. And he concluded that "we should never again be satisfied to see personality change as proceeding independent from the social context."[31]

This way of looking at the problem weights the forces unequally: society is the agent, the psyche merely the reagent. And of course since Bettelheim is studying the behavior of involuntary inmates this makes sense. But not all works of social psychology worked with such a simple notion of cause and effect. *The Authoritarian Personality*, for example, is an attempt to understand the personality forces that favored the voluntary acceptance of fascism. Adorno and his associates were trying to explain why modern dictators often had tremendous popular support. To what elements in the psyche were they appealing? What sort of person would be likely to become an enthusiastic follower of such a leader? They tried to describe and account for the prevalence in modern society of what they called "the *potentially fascistic* individual." Such individuals, they concluded, showed "a general disposition to glorify, to be subservient to and remain uncritical toward authoritative figures of the ingroup and to take an attitude of punishing outgroup figures in the name of some moral authority."[32] The study served to show that such personality characteristics were extremely widespread, that they crossed the boundaries of class, age, and sex, and that they were often unconscious.

In social psychology, the individual psyche becomes a microcosm of society itself and a way of studying public life at the cellular level. The kinds of questions that social psychologists try to answer are attempts to explain sociopolitical behavior by linking it to fundamental human needs and fears. "Can freedom become a burden, too heavy for man to bear, something he tries to escape from?" Erich Fromm asks. "Is there not also, perhaps, besides an innate desire for freedom, an instinctive wish for submission? . . . Is there a hidden satisfaction in submitting, and what is its essence? What is it that creates in men an insatiable lust for power?"[33]

Any reader of *Nineteen Eighty-Four* will recognize these questions. Orwell was a writer of fiction, not a social psychologist. But his deep interest in totalitarianism led him to think about issues of freedom and submission, power and impotence in similar terms. Winston Smith has many of the characteristics described in some of the works of social psychology written in the decade that produced Orwell's novel. He is of course a rebel on the surface and thinks he is joining a conspiracy to bring down a despotic regime. But Orwell makes it clear that at a deeper level Winston wills his own degradation because of his wish to submit. He knows he will be caught, has no chance of escape, yet deliberately chooses a path that can only lead him to a place where he will be—in his own words—"utterly without power of any kind" (p. 137). And when O'Brien stands revealed not as a fellow conspirator but as an agent of the regime, he says to Winston in words that ring true, "You knew this. . . . Don't deceive yourself. You did know it— you have always known it" (p. 197).

O'Brien is the instrument of Winston's reformation, the force that will allow him to shed his painful, undesired isolation, the confessor who will understand and save him from himself. Winston reflects that "at bottom it did not matter whether O'Brien was a friend or an enemy. . . . O'Brien was a person who could be talked to. Perhaps one did not want to be loved so much as to be understood. . . . In some sense that went deeper than friendship, they were intimates" (p. 208). This is why he freely surrenders his last secret, the core of his resistance to the state. When O'Brien asks him "Can you think of a single degradation that has not happened to you?" Winston helpfully answers, "I have not betrayed Julia" (p. 225). He thus initiates the final torture with the cage of rats in which he surrenders that last, rival loyalty. "Do it to Julia! Do it to Julia!" he screams, "Not me! Julia!" (p. 236).

Orwell's novel depicts a world in which societal pressure has become so relentless that the isolated individual no longer even wishes to hold out against it. The psychic price is too high. Orwell understood the emotional appeal of Hitler's slogan, "Better an end with horror than a horror without end" (quoted in *CEJL* 2:14). In *Nineteen Eighty-Four* he imagined his way into the mind and heart of an unheroic character whose sense of isolation has become unbearable enough to make him want to get rid of the independent self that is creating it. The forces that can lead to such a surrender are analyzed in Bettel-heim's *The Informed Heart*.

> The more absolute the tyranny, the more debilitated the subject, the more tempting to him to "regain" strength by becoming part of the tyranny and thus enjoy its power. In accepting all this one can attain, or reattain, some inner integration through conformity. But the price one must pay is to identify with the tyranny without reservation; in brief, to give up autonomy.[34]

This, one might say, is what happens at the end of *Nineteen Eighty-Four*. Winston's final, agonized surrender is his attempt to follow O'Brien's prescription and promise of relief. If only he will submit completely and merge his will in that of the Party, the intolerable burden of his independence will be lifted.

All this may help us to understand the psychology of the victim, of the follower. But what can account for the actions of the leader, of the victimizer? The two questions interested Orwell equally, and he did his best to grasp what he called "the special quality in modern life that makes a major human motive out of the impulse to bully others" (*CEJL* 4:249). In his long essay on James Burnham, Orwell protests "that in all his talk about the struggle for power, Burnham never stops to ask *why* people want power. He seems to assume that power hunger, although only dominant in comparatively few people, is a natural instinct that does not have to be explained, like the desire for food." Orwell, on the other hand, is eager to find "some psychological cause which Burnham makes no attempt to discover" (*CEJL* 4:177–78). This question of motive haunts *Nineteen Eighty-Four*. "*I understand HOW: I do not understand WHY*" (p. 68) Winston Smith writes in his diary. And the last passage in Emmanuel Goldstein's book that he manages to read before his arrest directly addresses this question.

> Here we reach the central secret. As we have seen, the mystique of the Party, and above all of the Inner Party, depends upon *doublethink*. But deeper than this lies the original motive, the never-questioned instinct that first led to the seizure of power and brought *doublethink*, the Thought Police, continuous warfare and all the other necessary paraphernalia into existence afterwards. This motive really consists. . . . (Pp. 178–79)

Winston never gets the chance to read on, and the promised explanation is teasingly withheld.

It is withheld, that is, until O'Brien delivers his speech on the subject during the torture scenes. His explanation goes on for five pages (with interruptions from Winston), but it is curiously unsatisfactory for anyone trying to understand "motive" in the traditional sense of the word, as a concept associated with cause, purpose, and reason. O'Brien's speech is tautological; and it has an incantatory quality that baffles rational understanding. "The Party seeks power entirely for its own sake. We are not interested in the good of others; we are interested solely in power. Not wealth or luxury or long life or happiness: only power, pure power. . . . The object of persecution is persecution. The object of torture is torture. The object of power is power" (p. 217). Coleridge complained that Iago's soliloquies in *Othello* were "the motive-hunting of a motiveless malignity."[35] O'Brien's speech has some of the same quality and is equally baffling. But Shakespeare was writing in a time and for an audience that still believed in "demi-devils," which is what Iago is called. Orwell's skeptical consciousness, his need for explanations, would not be satisfied by writing such people out of the human race.

And indeed he was not satisfied with his own understanding of the question. He was convinced only that the explanation, when it was forthcoming, would be psychopolitical and involve apparently disparate areas of contemporary experience that seemed to him related in some obscure way. "The interconnection between sadism, masochism, success worship, power worship, nationalism and totalitarianism is a huge subject whose edges have barely been scratched, and even to mention it is considered somewhat indelicate" (*CEJL* 3:222). He wrote those words toward the end of the war, and it is hardly surprising that the impulse to *understand* the aggressor would have met with little encouragement at the time, or even in the years immediately following, when the human casualties of fascism were still being counted. Contemporary attempts by political theorists to explain the motives of totalitarian leaders were equally unhelpful. Hermann Rauschning's study of Nazi Germany, which Orwell often cited, "explains" the interest in power in the same circular fashion: "the new élite makes use of their power and resources mainly in order to maintain themselves in power and to extend their power"; "The ultimate aim is the maximum of power and dominion."[36] And for Peter Drucker, totalitarianism's most radical innovation is the ridicule of the need to provide an alibi for seizing power: " 'Power is its own justification' is regarded as self-evident."[37]

It was only some years after the war that students of totalitarianism could begin to think seriously about what might account for these attitudes. Hannah Arendt, in *The Origins of Totalitarianism* (1951), saw the cult of power as a logical development of imperialist expansionism after the remote corners of the earth had been conquered. Once set in motion, the motor will not stop running even when it only destroys.

> This contradiction, inherent in all ensuing power politics . . . takes on an appearance of sense if one understands it in the context of a supposedly permanent process which has no end or aim but itself. Then the test of achievement can indeed become meaningless and power can be thought of as the never-ending, self-feeding motor of all political action that corresponds to the legendary unending accumulation of money that begets money.[38]

Hannah Arendt too eventually wrote a probing and highly controversial assessment of a figure who might well be considered a modern Iago—Adolf Eichmann. She calls the text of his eight-month-long interrogation by the Israeli authorities "a veritable gold mine for a psychologist." And she concludes, in her *Eichmann in Jerusalem: A Report on the Banality of Evil* (1963), that "Eichmann was not Iago and not Macbeth, and nothing would have been farther from his mind than to determine with Richard III 'to prove a villain.' Except for an extraordinary diligence in looking out for his personal advancement, he had not motives at all. . . . He *merely*, to put the matter colloquially, *never realized what he was doing.*"[39]

Such attempts to understand the victimizer as well as the victim are a luxury of a later historical stage, when the conflict has begun to recede into the past. It was really too early for Orwell, as he was writing his book in the mid-1940s, to look at the issues with this kind of detachment or understanding. And so, in *Nineteen Eighty-Four*, we never enter the mind of O'Brien: we only hear his speeches. And we do not know whether Big Brother even exists or is merely a psychologically necessary fiction of the regime. To go further is to imperil the more horatory elements in Orwell's book, his need to expose totalitarianism without generating sympathy for its leaders. The relative opacity of O'Brien and the Inner Party is the product both of Orwell's own bafflement and of his urgent political purpose.

Yet he was not by temperament a propagandistic or melodramatic writer: quite the opposite. The absolute distinction between victim and victimizer that the times demanded struck him as an unacceptable simplification. Though *Nineteen Eighty-Four* has its melodramatic moments, it also regularly challenges the neat categories of that genre. Julia is not an idealistic rebel but a hedonist intent on her own pleasure and largely indifferent to others. Winston Smith betrays her, he is not cast in the heroic mold, and some of his reactions suggest that he is capable of committing his own "atrocities." As he looks at the "silly blond face" of a foolish colleague who unintentionally prevents him from talking to Julia, he "had a hallucination of himself smashing a pick-axe right into the middle of it" (p. 93). And he readily agrees "to throw sulphuric acid in a child's face" if it would serve the interests of the revolutionary Brotherhood (p. 142). The connections between these impulses and O'Brien's vision of the future— "a boot stamping on a human face—for ever" (p. 220)—are obvious. And O'Brien is far from being a stock villain. He is (if his speeches can be trusted) a fanatical idealist, a true believer. His is also incomparably the most powerful intelligence in the book, as Winston repeatedly feels: "There was no idea that he had ever had, or could have, that O'Brien had not long ago known, examined, and rejected. His mind contained Winston's mind" (p. 211).

All these passages reveal that victim and victimizer inhabit a common mental landscape. This insight, like so many others in Orwell's work, finds echoes both in the early psychoanalytic studies and in the contemporary analyses of totalitarianism. The psychological predisposition involved, after all, is called sadomasochism. The term itself insists on linking the roles of victim and victimizer and indeed of treating them as interchangeable—different parts played on different occasions, as great actors have sometimes alternated the roles of Othello and Iago in successive performances. Freud claimed that it was impossible to decide "whether the pleasure attaching to the beating-phantasy was to be described as sadistic or masochistic."[40] Otto Fenichel's *Psychoanalytic Theory of Neurosis* describes the sadomasochist in a passage that illuminates Winston's cry "Do it to Julia!" "If a person is able to do to others what he fears may be done to him, he no longer has to be afraid. . . . What might happen to the subject passively is done actively by him, in anticipation of attack, to others."[41] And Fromm saw the bond between victim and aggressor as fundamentally symbiotic, a state of mutual dependence between persons cut from the same cloth. "People are not sadistic *or* masochistic, but there is a constant oscillation between the active and the passive side of the symbiotic complex, so that it is often difficult to determine which side of it is operating at a given moment."[42]

What might once have seemed highly speculative flights of psychoanalytic imagination proved all too real in the world of the concentration camps. The most shocking revelation in David Rousset's book concerned not the brutality of the SS but the imitation of their sadistic behavior by internees given any kind of authority within the camp hierarchy. There was Franz, for example, "pleasant, full of smiles, always had a kind word to say, and never struck anyone." Once elevated to a position of power, "his attitude changed completely. . . . He became a terror to the men such as few had been. The black jack never left his hand. He would hurl himself on the mass of prisoners

with an ardour and a blind fury which intoxicated him."[43] And according to Bruno Bettelheim, prisoners who had been in the camps
a long time often came to identify with the SS, even to hero-worship
some of them, because the persistent "aggressions against the self
weakened the prisoner's personality to such a degree that he was
forced to borrow strength from figures of prestige. The only persons
who met the description were the SS."[44] In such extreme situations,
the morally reassuring distinction between the persecutor and his object breaks down. As Hannah Arendt put it, "What totalitarian rule
needs to guide the behavior of its subjects is a preparation to fit each
of them equally well for the role of executioner and the role of victim."[45]

These repugnant ideas undermine the foundation of traditional moral
thought. Orwell was fully aware of their disruptive power but determined to incorporate them in his vision of totalitarianism. Yet the
decision to do so created a major challenge for him as an artist: how
to overcome the reader's inevitable resistance to such revelations. This
resistance was strong, despite the powerful response to the reports
about the concentration camps toward the end of the war. Bettelheim
claims that the first wave of outrage in the Allied countries "was soon
followed by a general repression of the discovery." He explains this
as a kind of psychological self-defense. "To have to accept that one's
personality may be changed against one's will is the greatest threat to
one's self-respect."[46] In addition, the fundamental incomprehensibility
of the camps made those who had no personal knowledge of them
refuse to take them in. "The atmosphere of madness and unreality,
created by an apparent lack of purpose," Hannah Arendt argues, "is
the real iron curtain which hides all forms of concentration camps from
the eyes of the world."[47]

In Britain there were two other reasons for this reluctance to accept
what had been revealed. The first was that many people remembered
the fraudulent atrocity tales manufactured by both sides in World
War I and came to think of all such stories as propaganda. Fed during
the earlier war on a diet of "preposterous lies about crucified Belgian
babies," the ordinary British citizen had developed a skeptical attitude
toward such tales. " 'Atrocities' had come to be looked on as synony-
mous with 'lies,' " Orwell wrote in 1944. "But the stories about the
German concentration camps were atrocity stories: therefore they were
lies—so reasoned the average man" (*CEJL* 3:117). In addition, Britain
was a country without totalitarian experience, as Orwell often pointed
out. The English had "a highly original quality," a "habit of *not killing
one another*." It was one of the few countries "where armed men do
not prowl the streets and no one is frightened of the secret police"
(*CEJL* 3:30). Desirable as such conditions obviously are, they created
a real obstacle to the understanding of contemporary world politics.

There was a great deal of complacency in the first English reactions to the reports about the camps, a conviction that such things could only happen "abroad."[48]

Despite his deep affection for England, Orwell disliked this mood of national self-congratulation. It ignored Britain's tragic experience in its own empire—in Ireland, in India, in South Africa (where concentration camps were first used during the Boer War). And it created a hopeless impediment to grasping issues of great importance. He was convinced that to understand the darker side of modern politics one could not make simple distinctions between "them" and "us." So he concludes, for instance, that "the starting point for any investigation of antisemitism should not be 'Why does this obviously irrational belief appeal to other people?' but 'Why does antisemitism appeal to *me*? What is there about it that I feel to be true?' . . . In that way one might get some clues that would lead to its psychological roots" (*CEJL* 3:341).

The fear of the reader's incredulity, indifference, and complaceny all helped to give *Nineteen Eighty-Four* its particular form and texture. He told his publisher in 1947 that this "novel about the future" was proving exceptionally difficult to write because "it is in a sense a fantasy, but in the form of a naturalistic novel" (*CEJL* 4:329–30). The imaginative excursions in the book—essential as we have seen them to be—were kept in check by a more pervasive circumstantiality of detail, an almost photographic realism. The decaying block of flats where Winston lives, with its smell of boiled cabbage, its lift that seldom works, its blocked drainpipes; the seedy antique shop in a slum quarter where he and Julia find temporary shelter; the Sunday outing to the country that begins at Paddington Station—all would have struck a British reader of the 1940s as the familiar scenery of his own world.

Virginia Woolf complained in her essay "Mr. Bennett and Mrs. Brown" that Edwardian novelists had unnecessarily "laid an enormous stress upon the fabric of things" and thus inhibited their psychological penetration.[49] Her precepts helped to produce a style of modernist fiction in which the internal world took precedence over the external. Orwell, however, faced with the problem of trying to convey a bizarre psychological state to a potentially skeptical audience, needed a dense and instantly recognizable external reality to lend it credence. That his strategy was successful is suggested in the *Times Literary Supplement* review of *Nineteen Eighty-Four*.

By creating a world in which the "proles" still have their sentimental songs and their beer, and the privileged consume their

Victory gin, Mr. Orwell involves us most skilfully and uncomfortably in his story, and obtains more readily our belief in the fantasy of thought-domination that occupies the foreground of his book.[50]

The same logic demanded that the story be set in England, and in a time that most readers in 1949 could easily imagine as part of their own lives—not in Utopia or in Erewhon, not in some science fiction future that bore no resemblance to the present day. It also dictated that his hero should have a quintessentially English name. All these choices were determined by Orwell's fear that readers would dismiss his imagined future as something having to do with "them," not with "us." For this reason too his protagonist is a kind of everyman. He matters because he might be any one of us if we had the misfortune to find ourselves in his situation. He is not idealized but neither is he perverse. The disturbing violence of his fantasy life, his rapid shifts between resistance and cowardice, his final breakdown are all consequences of the irrational political world in which he finds himself, and which has its roots in the possible, the actual, though it speaks the language of bad dreams. It would be reassuring to think that the world Orwell created in his fiction really *was* only the product of his paranoid imagination. But by this point in the century in which he and we grew up we know that it was not.

His reconceptualization of political life may well prove to be the most enduring aspect of *Nineteen Eighty-Four*. The year itself will come and go. As a piece of prophecy Orwell's novel is not remarkable for its detailed accuracy. Its predictions have more the flavor of 1948 than 1984. But the core of the vision has not really dated, because Orwell's understanding of irrational politics seems increasingly persuasive. Terrorism, fanatical dedication to a cause, religious wars, resurgent nationalisms, political incarceration and torture, the manipulation of public response through fraud, the spreading network of surveillance: who would not instantly recognize these characteristics of the political world of our time? There is of course an important countertradition in democratic countries that might be called rational politics. Our duly elected representatives enact legislation. Guilt and innocence are determined in courts of law. Our leaders make promises, negotiate treaties, try to persuade us of the value of their programs. But though these public events are often taken seriously and are not unreal, the sense of them as masking more anarchic impulses has grown. There is an increasing cynicism—by this time widely felt—about political appearances and a shared sense that what really matters goes on behind the scenes or beyond the confines of normal political life and is largely beyond our control. The vision is not attractive. Orwell was one of the first writers with the courage to face it and the talent to give it unforgettable fictional life. He produced a fantasy in the shape of a naturalistic novel. The naturalism was on the surface, the fantasy at the core. But the fantasy was a nightmare, and the nightmare was the history of his time from which—like Joyce's Stephen Dedalus—he was trying in vain to awake.

Notes

1. George Orwell, *Nineteen Eighty-Four* (New York: New American Library, 1981), 207. Subsequent page references to this edition are incorporated in the text.

2. Isaac Deutscher, "*1984*—The Mysticism of Cruelty," reprinted in *Twentieth Century Interpretations of 1984: A Collection of Critical Essays*, ed. Samuel Hynes (Englewood Cliffs, N.J.: Prentice-Hall, 1971), 38.

3. Anthony West, "George Orwell," in his *Principles and Persuasions: The Literary Essays of Anthony West* (New York: Harcourt, Brace, 1957), 172, 175, 176.

4. Bernard Crick, *George Orwell: A Life* (London: Secker and Warburg, 1980), 365, 397.

5. Marcus Smith, "The Wall of Blackness: A Psychological Approach to *1984*," *Modern Fiction Studies* 14 (1968–69):423–33; Gerald Fiderer, "Masochism as Literary Strategy: Orwell's Psychological Novels," *Literature and Psychology* 20 (1970):3–21; Richard I. Smyer, *Primal Dream and Primal Crime: Orwell's Development as a Psychological Novelist* (Columbia: University of Missouri Press, 1979).

6. Fiderer, "Masochism as Literary Strategy," 17.

7. George Orwell, *The Road to Wigan Pier* (London: Secker and Warburg, 1959), 149.

8. The account is quoted in Crick, *Orwell*, 178. See also the description of Orwell's barbarous evisceration of an adder, which Crick takes as another example of "this sadistic streak in Orwell's character—which usually he mastered" (p. 364).

9. *The Collected Essays, Journalism and Letters of George Orwell*, ed. Sonia Orwell and Ian Angus, 4 vols. (London: Secker and Warburg, 1968), 3:231. Subsequent references to this edition are incorporated in the text using the abbreviation *CEJL*.

10. Peter F. Drucker, *The End of Economic Man: A Study of the New Totalitarianism* (London: William Heinemann, 1939), 79–80.

11. David Rousset, *A World Apart*, trans. Yvonne Moyse and Roger Senhouse

of *L'Univers concentrationnaire* (London: Secker and Warburg, 1951), 109. For Orwell's familiarity with Rousset's work, see his letters to Senhouse, *CEJL* 4:419–21.

12. Hannah Arendt, *The Origins of Totalitarianism*, 2d enl. ed. (London: George Allen and Unwin, 1958), 445.

13. Two critics have noted the connection between *Nineteen Eighty-Four* and the liberation of the camps: Jeffrey Meyers, "The Evolution of *1984*," *English Miscellany* 23 (1972):259; William Steinhoff, *George Orwell and the Origins of* 1984 (Ann Arbor: University of Michigan Press, 1975), 188.

14. "The Horrors of Buchenwald: M. P. Deputation's Report," *Times* (London), 28 April 1945, 2.

15. West, "George Orwell," 172.

16. Bruno Bettelheim, *The Informed Heart: The Human Condition in Modern Mass Society* (London: Thames and Hudson, 1961), 134.

17. Bettelheim, *The Informed Heart*, 296.

18. Bettelheim, *The Informed Heart*, 279–80.

19. Arendt, *Origins of Totalitarianism*, 323–24.

20. This final resolution of Winston's need for maternal protection is also noted by Smith, "The Wall of Blackness," 426, and Smyer, *Primal Dream and Primal Crime*, 159.

21. Sigmund Freud, " 'A Child Is Being Beaten': A Contribution to the Study of the Origin of Sexual Perversion," in his *Collected Papers*, trans. Alix Strachey and James Strachey (New York: Basic Books, 1959), 2:195.

22. Sigmund Freud, "The Economic Problem in Masochism," trans. Joan Riviere, in *Collected Papers* 2:263.

23. Freud, " 'A Child Is Being Beaten,' " *Collected Papers* 2:192.

24. Freud, "Economic Problem in Masochism," *Collected Papers* 2:262–63.

25. Erich Fromm, *The Fear of Freedom* (London: Kegan Paul, Trench, Trubner, 1942), 141.

26. Theodor Reik, *Masochism in Modern Man*, trans. Margaret H. Beigel and Gertrud M. Kurth (New York: Grove Press, 1941), 303.

27. Fromm, *Fear of Freedom*, 3.

28. Reik, *Masochism in Modern Man*, 184.

29. Fromm, *Fear of Freedom*, 145.

30. Bettelheim, *The Informed Heart*, 134.

31. Bettelheim, *The Informed Heart*, 37.

32. T. W. Adorno, et al., *The Authoritarian Personality* (New York: Harper and Brothers, 1950), 1, 228.

33. Fromm, *Fear of Freedom*, 4. It is worth noting that Fromm's ideas on this subject are highly controversial. For a critique, see John H. Schaar, *Escape from Authority: The Perspectives of Erich Fromm* (New York: Basic Books, 1961).

34. Bettelheim, *The Informed Heart*, 294.

35. S. T. Coleridge, *Notes and Lectures upon Shakespeare*, in *The Complete Works of Samuel Taylor Coleridge*, ed. W. G. T. Shedd (New York: Harper and Brothers, 1884), 181.

36. Hermann Rauschning, *Germany's Revolution of Destruction*, trans. E. W. Dickes (London: Heinemann, 1939), 34, 281.

37. Drucker, *The End of Economic Man*, 13.
38. Arendt, *Origins of Totalitarianism*, 137.
39. Hannah Arendt, *Eichmann in Jerusalem: A Report on the Banality of Evil*, rev. and enl. ed. (Harmondsworth, Eng.: Penguin, 1979), 48, 287.
40. Freud, " 'A Child Is Being Beaten,' " *Collected Papers* 2:175.
41. Otto Fenichel, *The Psychoanalytic Theory of Neurosis* (New York: W. W. Norton, 1945), 354.
42. Fromm, *Fear of Freedom*, 136.
43. Rousset, *A World Apart*, 51–52.
44. Bettelheim, *The Informed Heart*, 294.
45. Arendt, *Origins of Totalitarianism*, 445.
46. Bettelheim, *The Informed Heart*, 252.
47. Arendt, *Origins of Totalitarianism*, 445.
48. One correspondent to the *Times* writes that when the newsreel films about the camps were shown in British theaters, they brought home "to the general public the bestialities of which Germans are capable" (letter from Cecil G. Bernstein, *Times* [London], 19 May 1945, 5). In a debate in the House of Lords in 1945, one speaker proposed "that there was some sort of sadism in the Germans which encouraged them to like the kind of thing which was carried on at Buchenwald"; he was challenged by another who ventured to suggest that other countries had committed atrocities in their time; and that speaker in turn was sharply reproved by the Lord Chancellor for allowing anyone to suppose that British soldiers might do such things. "Cheers" greeted this last patriotic speech ("Buchenwald and Weimar," *Times* [London], 2 May 1945, 8).
49. Virginia Woolf, "Mr. Bennett and Mrs. Brown," in her *Collected Essays* (London: Hogarth Press, 1971), 332.
50. "Power and Corruption," *Times Literary Supplement*, 10 June 1949, 380. Orwell guessed that the review was by Julian Symons and wrote to thank him (*CEJL* 4:502–3).

The Self and Memory
in *Nineteen Eighty-Four*

Joseph Adelson

We do not think of George Orwell as a psychological novelist, and on the whole we are correct in that judgment. Orwell does not take us deeply into the inner life of his characters, nor does he deal with exotic psychological types, nor does he spend much time linking personal history to later behavior. At times he could be dismissive toward those who were in his view inappropriately "psychological." In his discussion of Arthur Koestler's *Arrival and Departure* he comes down hard on the novel's major idea, "that revolutionary activity is the result of personal maladjustment."[1] That may be so, Orwell says, indeed it probably is so, but so what? "Actions have results irrespective of their motives." To be sure, he would sometimes use similar explanations when it suited his purposes—but most of the time he kept psychology firmly in its place. In his essay on P. G. Wodehouse,[2] writing on what it is that led him to broadcast for the Germans during the war, he seems to eschew any speculation on Wodehouse's personal motives, speaking instead of his "mentality," by which he means the author's limited and antiquated understanding of reality. It is a cognitive view of Wodehouse, rather than a psychodynamic one. And in his many, many acerbic and disgusted observations of the perfidy of intellectuals, their appetite for the totalitarian state, I cannot recall a single comment having to do with their inner motivations, individually or collectively. Perhaps there are some we can find in that vast body of work, but it is fair to say that these are occasional. If Mr. Jones, who was once a Mosley Fascist, and later a member of the Communist party, and later still a convert to the Roman Catholic church, now announces that he has given up politics and religion to become a vegetarian, Orwell may make note of that history, but only for what it reveals about the man's habits of mind—that is, his way of thinking—rather than for what it may say about his inner conflicts or his mental health. That reticence is refreshing, living as we do in a time and place simply besotted with psychology and psychologizing—much of it gratuitous, superficial, and vulgar.

So I did not think there would be much to say, even on a close rereading, about Orwell as a psychological writer. His work would prove to be interesting politically and morally, but would provide little

111

nourishment for those interested in the complications of mind. In *Sincerity and Authenticity*, Lionel Trilling speaks of the common nine-teenth-century judgment of the English, that their unique moral type was marked by "probity and candour."[3] He quotes Emerson's *English Traits*, pointing to sincerity as the basis of their moral style—they "are blunt in expressing what they think and they expect others to be no less so."[4] Probity, sincerity, candor—that summed up Orwell per-fectly, as a man and as a writer: a quintessentially nineteenth-century English personality, honest, open, a bit innocent.

It is not a type much given to an agitated speculation on motives. But now imagine that personality cast adrift in another time and place, one marked in its politics by lies, dissimulation, contradiction, hypoc-risy, duplicity. Imagine it to be this kind of place: something that is said to have happened did not happen; something that did happen is said not to have happened. Someone who was there at the time, and saw that it took place, now says with complete conviction that it never did take place. He will swear to it. We must imagine what our nine-teenth-century personality might ask himself. How is one persuaded to overcome memory? How is self-deception engineered, and once engineered, what are its consequences for the self? Conversely, what allows someone to resist falsehood? How is probity achieved, and what are its consequences?

Let me anticipate my argument. These questions haunt Orwell's writing from 1937, following his return from Spain, to the end of his life, and the publication of *Nineteen Eighty-Four*, somewhat over ten years later. These questions begin from the shocked recognition of political lying, and what is worse, lying by the presumably progressive and humane elements in society. In pondering those questions he was led—almost against his will, certainly against his native bent—to treat in his fiction many of the issues that torment modern psychology.

We are now so accustomed to political lying, it is so much a part of the climate of politics, that we find it hard to credit its traumatic effect upon Orwell. He went to Spain to fight a good clean fight against the Fascists, as so many other innocents did, and once there found that the Communist forces were far more eager to eliminate their rivals on the left than they were to win the war. The word "eliminate" is to be taken literally here, since the Communists meant to do more than win a political victory; they meant to get rid of their rivals by treachery and murder. That was bad enough. What made it worse for Orwell was his discovery upon returning from Spain that the story was not being told, that the slogans of revolution were being used to con-ceal a bloodbath directed against the revolution itself, that the liberal and left journals in England were quite deliberately telling their read-ers a pack of lies, which this audience was quite content to believe.

Confronting this state of affairs—the lies told abroad, the lies told at home—enraged Orwell, and ultimately made him a changed man. The first article he wrote on his return was entitled "Spilling the Spanish Beans,"[5] the first line reading, "The Spanish war has probably produced a richer crop of lies than any event since the Great War . . . ,"[6] then going on to say that it was the "left wing papers . . . with their far subtler methods of distortion, that have prevented the British public from grasping the real nature of the struggle."[7] Orwell then goes on to specify the tactics through which allies are discredited, and are turned into political enemies, enemies so vicious indeed as to require elimination. "The logical end is a regime in which every opposition party and newspaper is suppressed and every dissenter of any importance is in jail."[8] Quite clearly the ideas that were to find their way into *Animal Farm* and *Nineteen Eighty-Four* were already evident in 1937. Orwell found himself isolated in much the way he described, his journalism rejected for taking the wrong political line, as was his book on Spain, the great *Homage to Catalonia,* which was turned down by Orwell's publisher even before it was written, for the same reason. We begin to see Orwell's writing haunted by the theme of falsehood. In the year after he returned from Spain, almost every letter and review we have available adverts to it.

The war provided another experience which was to influence Orwell's thinking. It brought him into touch with the internecine rivalries of the international left—much more savage than the British variety—and above all, it brought home to him the importance of the Moscow show trials, which exposed an entirely new dimension of political lying, the confession of error and treason by the losing side of the revolutionary party. Here were the revered figures of the revolution, the Old Bolsheviks, the apostles, confessing abjectly to having betrayed that revolution, to having conspired with its enemies, and to having done so almost from the beginning. Here they were confessing to crimes which had not taken place, which were impossible psychologically, but beyond that, could not have been carried out because the historical record proved otherwise—Comrade X, confessing to a secret meeting with capitalist agents in, let us say Berlin, was in fact at that very moment at a party meeting in Leningrad, as official documents would show.

Show trials were later to become commonplace—routine rituals in totalitarian regimes—so we may find it difficult to appreciate the shock of their first appearance—that is, among those immersed in the politics of the left. Of course, many believers kept on believing, blinded by faith or stupidity; and many believers did not believe, but pretended to because that was the progressive thing to do; but there were some deeply of the left, like Orwell and Koestler, who understood quickly that the trials were a malevolent charade, the defendants having been coerced into false confessions. You then found yourself struggling with unexpected and perplexing psychological questions. How were the confessions induced? By physical means such as torture and privation? By psychological means, and if so, which ones? New drugs, perhaps, or new methods of hypnosis, or more conventional means of persuasion? Those broken creatures on the stand, telling lies about themselves—did they now believe what they were saying or did they keep one part of their minds clear and in touch with the truth, or were they too confused or indifferent to know the difference between truth and untruth? What had happened to these men, as total human beings? These questions led in turn to others. Why did the regime feel it vital to have these men confess publicly? Why did it not merely murder them, secretly or openly, slowly or swiftly, as it was doing with hundreds of others? Did Stalin, in his paranoia, believe the lies he was forcing his opponents to confess to, thus making untruth into truth? Or was he inducing the confession of what he knew to be lies, as a display of consummate power?

So the Spanish war provided Orwell with a theme which was to inspirit his writing for the rest of his life: the political lie—its origins, its vicissitudes, its functions, its aims, its effects. Some of his most powerful essays examine its consequences for thinking and writing: the famous "Politics and the English Language"[9] and "The Prevention of Literature."[10] In "Writers and Leviathan,"[11] one of the last full-scale essays he wrote—on the relation of politics and writing—one finds, in a seven-page article, fourteen separate references to falsehood or self-deception. Even in his minor writing, the casual newspaper columns, we find him contemplating the lie, and its effects on the mind. Indeed, in one of these brief pieces, he offers some examples of what was later to be called "doublethink." Orwell is obsessed by the lie, and I do not use the term pejoratively, since the obsession is rational. Everywhere he looks, he finds that politics, and especially the high-minded politics of the intellectual, consists of people being lied to, and lying to others, and lying to themselves. As you read through the four magnificent volumes of his essays, journalism, and letters, you watch this calm, sardonic man overcome by exasperation—and perhaps some despair, and perhaps some smoldering rage—as he witnesses the triumph of falsehood in world politics. The obsession recedes only in the very last year of his life, when he was writing *Nineteen Eighty-Four*, and which we will imagine was absorbing all he had left to say on those questions.

Through his preoccupation with the lie, Orwell was led in unwitting prescience to issues which were about to overtake psychology and psychiatry—the idea of the self, and its division into true and false sides. To deceive oneself, or to allow oneself to be deceived, without inner protest, is to divide oneself. In dealing with a divided self, as he does in *Nineteen Eighty-Four*, Orwell was looking ahead to psychologies not yet written. He was also—again I suspect unwittingly—looking back to the birth of modern pyschology, in the latter part of the nineteenth century, when such writers as William James and Pierre Janet were trying to fashion a theory of the self, and a theory of inner division. That direction of thought, though never quite forgotten, had been put aside by the triumph and continuing hegemony of Freud's doctrine. Not that psychoanalysis was uninterested in the problem of how we deceive ourselves—to the contrary—but it was hostile to the concept of the self. It was, and in many ways it still is, for the self-concept is seen as a sly way of bringing back to life a moribund, discredited psychology of mere consciousness. Hence those psychologies which posited a self, or even implied it, came to be seen as anti-Freudian, in intention or effect—that is, as nondynamic, superficial, simple-minded, retrogressive. The history of Freudian polemics is for the most part a history of denunciations of those who tried to reintroduce the idea of the self, that is, the self not merely as a derivative of more fundamental processes, but as an active, autonomous agent striving to fulfill aims of its own. So the self-theorists were slain, one after another, decade after decade—Adler, Horney, Fromm, Sullivan, all of the existentialists, most of the English school, such as Fairbairn and Winnicott, most recently Heinz Kohut—each slain, yet each arising again, in a new, generally improved version. In a way, it is a return of the repressed.

These theories rose again because they were willing to address a number of questions psychoanalysis would consider only late in its history, and even then uneasily. "What is the nature and source of the self, and of personal identity?" "How do we achieve and sustain the sense of self-worth?" "How do we understand and treat the divided self?" I have suggested that these questions have been with us from the beginning, that they were present at the creation of modern psychology, in the second half of the nineteenth century. William James's work is of particular interest to us here, in part because his writings on the self have remained amazingly contemporary, though nearly a century old, and in part because in his masterwork, *The Varieties of Religious Experience*,[12] he sets forth an analysis of the sick soul in search of its cure which provides, through ironic juxtaposition, some remarkable commentary on the failed voyage toward redemption recounted in *Nineteen Eighty-Four*.

At the very heart of James's book we come upon a cluster of chapters entitled "The Sick Soul," "The Divided Self and the Process of Its

Unification," and "Conversion." In the first sentence of the first of the
two chapters on conversion, James writes as follows:

> To be converted, to be regenerated, to receive grace, to expe-
> rience religion, to gain an assurance, are so many phrases which
> denote the process, gradual or sudden, by which a self hitherto
> divided, and consciously wrong, inferior, and unhappy, becomes
> unified and consciously right, superior, and happy, in conse-
> quence of its firmer hold upon religious realities.[13]

That sentence may serve us as a text for one understanding of *Nineteen
Eighty-Four*.

When the novel opens, Winston Smith is a soul sick and divided,
wrong, inferior, and unhappy, who seeks to be unified, to become
right, superior, and happy. In James's language, he seeks "a process
of remedying inner completeness and reducing inner discord."[14] He
is in a state of anhedonia, a term James brought to general awareness,
and which he defined as "passive joylessness and dreariness, discour-
agement, dejection, lack of taste and zest and spring."[15] He comes to
life through his love for Julia, and then seeks to heal his sickness and
inner division through a symbiosis with O'Brien. The faith he seeks
eludes him; indeed his very seeking is turned against him, cruelly so,
for in asking to be replenished, healed, and unified, he is at the end
of his journey emptied and destroyed.

Orwell takes the traditional idea of conversion, as we find it in
James, and turns it upside down. In its true religious meaning, conversion is a moment of epiphany, in which grace, insight, and conviction arise from within, unbidden, unforced, miraculous. In the brutal,
climactic moments of *Nineteen Eighty-Four*, in the chilling dialogue
with Winston, O'Brien uses the term twice, first to tell Winston that
Julia has betrayed him, and that she did so quickly. "I have seldom
seen anyone come over to us so promptly. . . . It was a perfect conversion, a textbook case."[16] At another point in the interrogation,
O'Brien tells Winston that he is not content "with the most abject
submission. . . . We do not destroy the heretic because he resists us;
so long as he resists us, we never destroy him. We convert him; we
capture his inner mind; we reshape him. We burn all evil and all
illusion out of him; we bring him over to our side, not in appearance,
but genuinely, heart and soul."[17] You may want to remember James's
words on the outcome of conversion—"To be regenerated, to receive
grace, to experience religion, to gain an assurance"—and then listen
to O'Brien's counterpoint. "Never again will you be capable of love,
or friendship, or joy of living, or laughter, or curiosity, or integrity.
You will be hollow. We shall squeeze you empty, and we shall fill you
with ourselves."[18] Throughout these terrible passages Orwell plays

brilliantly upon traditional religious language. O'Brien tells Winston that "everyone is washed clean," and at another point, "always we shall have the heretic at our mercy, screaming with pain, broken up, contemptible—and in the end utterly penitent, saved from himself, crawling to our feet of his own accord."[19]

The destruction of personality O'Brien proposes, undertakes, and achieves has already been prepared by the erosion of personal identity in Oceania, an erosion accomplished by the steady chipping away of memory by its institutions, by doublethink and the memory hole and the Ministry of Truth. The questions which had been nagging at Orwell since his return from Spain, as he witnessed the unchecked spread of deceit in politics, are at last answered in *Nineteen Eighty-Four*: to lie, to be lied to, to accept being lied to, or to rationalize and defend lying for the sake of a better world—all of that, taken to its extreme, will produce a sick and divided soul. The rewriting of history destroys any sense of the past, and with it the sense of personal continuity. That is by no means a surreptitious theme in *Nineteen Eighty-Four*. At the thematic climax of the book, O'Brien asks Winston whether he believes that the past has real existence. He replies that it does, that it can be found in the records, in the mind, and in human memories. O'Brien counters that the Party controls all records and all memories, indeed controls the nature of reality, and to drive the point home undertakes the torture of Winston, forcing him to confess to a false reality, that two and two equal five.

Winston yields, but he has already been weakened, as we learn from his struggle throughout the book to remember his own past. From beginning to end, *Nineteen Eighty-Four* is taken up with Winston's efforts at recollection. At the beginning, "He tried to squeeze out some childhood memory that should tell him whether London had always been quite like this."[20] We soon learn that he has bought a diary, so as to preserve a record of the past for the future, and he fills it with scattered recollections of his own past. Throughout the book he is tormented by a vain attempt to recover memories of his mother and sister, who had disappeared suddenly and without explanation, and at the end we have Winston recalling, unexpectedly, a happy childhood memory, one of reconciliation with his mother—a memory he dismisses as false, saying to himself, "Some things have happened, others have not happened."[21] If that sentence has a familiar ring to it, it is because it repeats Orwell's bitter complaints about the journalism of the Spanish war, that things happened which were not reported, and things did not happen which were.

Winston Smith's argument is Cartesian: "I remember, therefore I exist." To which O'Brien replies, "I control memory, and therefore your existence." As a number of commentators have pointed out, Winston can be understood as a last remnant of Western individualism, now about to be crushed by the megastate. He believes that he is unique and thus precious in possessing a store of personal memory which defines him, and which cannot be taken away from him. It is a claim O'Brien dismisses contemptuously, telling him that men are malleable, and infinitely so. The debate between them is between two views of human nature, both of which can be said to underlie contemporary liberalism, and which account for much of the confusion and contradiction in current democratic thinking. Winston is a Pelagian, in that he believes man to have an intrinsic moral sense and thus an inherent moral dignity. O'Brien is the ultimate Lockean, believing that man is nothing beyond what the social order chooses to instill. As he tells Winston, "We shall squeeze you empty, and we shall fill you with ourselves."

Notes

1. George Orwell, "Arthur Koestler," in *The Collected Essays, Journalism and Letters of George Orwell*, ed. Sonia Orwell and Ian Angus, 4 vols. (New York: Harcourt Brace Jovanovich, 1968), 3:241. Cited hereafter as *CEJL*.
2. George Orwell, "In Defense of P. G. Wodehouse," *CEJL* 3:341–55.
3. Lionel Trilling, *Sincerity and Authenticity* (Cambridge, Mass.: Harvard University Press, 1972), 112.
4. Trilling, *Sincerity and Authenticity*, 112.
5. George Orwell, "Spilling the Spanish Beans," *CEJL* 1:269–76.
6. Orwell, "Spilling the Spanish Beans," *CEJL* 1:269.
7. Orwell, "Spilling the Spanish Beans," *CEJL* 1:269.
8. Orwell, "Spilling the Spanish Beans," *CEJL* 1:275.
9. George Orwell, "Politics and the English Language," *CEJL* 4:127–40.
10. George Orwell, "The Prevention of Literature," *CEJL* 4:59–72.
11. George Orwell, "Writers and Leviathan," *CEJL* 4:407–14.
12. William James, *The Varieties of Religious Experience* (1902; reprint, New York: Macmillan, 1961).
13. James, *Varieties of Religious Experience*, 160.
14. James, *Varieties of Religious Experience*, 150.
15. James, *Varieties of Religious Experience*, 127.

16. George Orwell, *Nineteen Eighty-Four* (New York: Harcourt, Brace, 1949), 214.

17. Orwell, *Nineteen Eighty-Four*, 210.

18. Orwell, *Nineteen Eighty-Four*, 211.

19. Orwell, *Nineteen Eighty-Four*, 221.

20. Orwell, *Nineteen Eighty-Four*, 7.

21. Orwell, *Nineteen Eighty-Four*, 243.

The Political Theory of Pessimism:
George Orwell and Herbert Marcuse

Alfred G. Meyer

The prevalent religion in the Western world during the nineteenth century was the religion of progress. Two world wars, Stalin and Hitler, Auschwitz and Gulag, major depressions, colonial wars, and a host of other shocking events in the twentieth century have shattered this faith, and confidence has been replaced by fear. Many people today look into the future with vague apprehension, and the very idea of progress is being questioned widely.[1]

Let me begin my discussion with a sketchy summary of some of the persistent worries stalking America today; and then I will examine two seminal works which anticipated this gloomy outlook, namely George Orwell's *Nineteen Eighty-Four* and Herbert Marcuse's *One-Dimensional Man: Studies in the Ideology of Advanced Industrial Society.*

This is 1984; so let us provide a hasty blueprint of the United States, say, in 2038. Let us assume a deepening of the energy and resource shortages now predicted by many ecologists. Let us posit further that, by 2038, the United States will no longer be able to monopolize the same large share of the world's resources which it consumes today. One can thus foresee an America living on a greatly reduced level of material comfort, with much of its natural beauty despoiled, much of its fertile soils exhausted, its polluted streams and lakes depleted of fish, with city water and sewer systems decaying, the nation's highway network crumbling, and gross deterioration in the people's nutrition and health.

With resources depleted, and inflation rampant, lingering economic disaster will plague the business community, so that competition and the struggle for mere survival will have become lethal: only those people best equipped for cutthroat competition will survive, i.e., those ready to cut throats. What seems to be happening already in a few branches of business and labor, namely, the rise to leadership of professional criminals and their syndicates, may well become a standard pattern. Fierce fights for control will rage between monopolies and within them; success means survival and possible affluence, failure means powerlessness and material want.

Let us therefore assume that the contrast between rich and poor will have grown sharper. The rich will become a small embattled minority, ever on their guard against the resentful mob of the poor. Violent crime will stalk the society far more than today; life and property rights will have become cheap. Rich and poor alike will live in walled ghettos. The police will be ubiquitous. Penology will have turned harshly punitive. But, given the precarious situation within a revolutionary world, the United States will be security-minded abroad as well; hence we can project a growth in the nation's intelligence and military establishments, their increasing independence from citizens' control, and their growing influence over national politics. Within this repressive system, of course, permissiveness might still reign in certain areas. Victimless crimes now on the statute books might have been decriminalized; prostitution, gambling, and the sale and use of various substances now forbidden may have become branches of business as respectable and law-abiding as Lockheed Aircraft or the Teamsters Union are today. To some people, it may look like a really free society.

Citizens' control will be eroded further by the growing bureaucratization of life, i.e., by the subjection of the chaos of human interaction in a nation of 250 million or more to the control of social engineers. Bureaucracy is the imposition of rationality on human affairs through complex organization and scientific management. It is the application of engineering principles to human relations, and it has the consequence of eliminating much of what is human from these relations. Bureaucratic thinking is instrumental thinking; to the manager, human beings are resources, to be treated strictly in accordance with their utility to the system. It is essentially heartless.

I am tempted to develop this nightmare in greater detail by speculating about the framework of seemingly democratic institutions within which such a society could function, about the doubletalk with which it might seek to legitimize itself, and about the variety of ways by which people might try to assuage their anxieties and escape from their misery. However, let me summarize this projection by suggesting that it is based on the assumption that the very same cultural and personal character traits by which people often explain the promise, the attractiveness, the power, and accomplishments of the United States could turn from virtues and strengths into weakness and vices— individualism and autonomy into snarling selfishness; generosity into wastefulness, healthy irreverence for authorities into cynicism; community spirit into intolerance, patriotism into chauvinism. Such a transvaluation could be triggered by decline in the nation's power and influence. Once the tide of ever-increasing wealth and might has turned, once further expansion has become impossible, the system may turn into a caricature of its former self, its democratic traditions twisted into hollow forms. There are, of course, a lot of people who argue that all this has already taken place, and the two books I propose to discuss have contributed to this pessimistic mood. Both George Orwell's *Nineteen Eighty-Four* and Herbert Marcuse's *One-Dimensional Man: Studies in the Ideology of Advanced Industrial Society* convey gloomy prophecies of encroaching totalitarianism which go against the religion of progress, a faith in which both authors must have been raised and which, when they were younger, led them both to identify with socialism in one form or another.[2]

Both books deal with the United States, Marcuse's unequivocally, Orwell's by implication. While the scene of his novel is London, he emphasizes that England, in his 1984, is but the transatlantic outpost of a totalitarian state comprising all the Americas. Both authors make clear, however, that they are talking about *all* highly developed countries, capitalist and communist. In Marcuse's work this identification of the USA with the USSR is qualified by some cautious reservations, but Orwell makes clear that all the superstates of 1984 are identical structurally, culturally, and ideologically.

Before beginning with Orwell's Oceania, let me first explain that this paper was written, not by an Orwell specialist, but by a political theorist who looks at the world of politics not only through his own eyes, but also through the eyes of others, through literature. And while I am aware that there are those who regard *Nineteen Eighty-Four* as literature, and therefore not open to political analysis, or as satire, and therefore not open to interpretation as an anxious look into the future, this makes no sense to me. There is tradition for both; and as for the latter term, satire, even of the Swiftian kind, requires a goodly dash of humor. Orwell's novel is conspicuously deficient in even the slightest trace of a sense of humor; hence the work is as different from Swiftian satire as the English temper is from the Irish one. From this understanding, I will analyze both Orwell's and Marcuse's nightmare systems summarizing not only the way that they function, but also the political theories offered by the authors to explain why they work that way.

In the Western world in 1984, nothing works. The simplest necessities of life—razor blades, shoelaces—are scarce. Whatever is available is of poor quality and ugly form; London is rotting and crumbling and rat-infested; grey faces and smelly armpits characterize the people; life is "bare, dingy, and listless" (paraphrased from p. 63). The people have ugly personalities. The culture of London in 1984 is decidedly sadistic; life has become a horror movie. Indeed, hatred and love of cruelty are the only emotions still permitted, so that all human kindness has disappeared from human relations. Conjugal and filial love, warmth, affection, and every kind of fun have disappeared. Pleasure has been removed from sex. Total repression reigns. As a result, people are gripped by an inner rage, a perpetual hysteria, which the regime aims at carefully selected targets inside and outside the country.

In Oceania this deep hatred expresses itself as militarism and fear of foreigners, as witchhunting for subversives, and as macho rage against women. The misogyny and sadism of Oceania are aptly demonstrated through the characterizations of Julia and Winston. When Julia is first mentioned, we learn that Winston "dislikes nearly all women" (p. 12). Winston gives two reasons for this "dislike": (1) women are "the most bigoted adherents of the Party," and (2) he does not have access to their bodies for sex (pp. 12–13). A few pages later, during the Two Minutes Hate, Winston *willingly* transfers his hatred from the face of Goldstein to a female stranger, who is later identified as Julia. Although it is a long quotation, it serves its purpose.

> Winston succeeded in transferring his hatred . . . to the dark-haired girl behind him. Vivid, beautiful hallucinations flashed through his mind. He would flog her to death with a rubber truncheon. He would tie her naked to a stake and shoot her full of arrows like Saint Sebastian. He would ravage her and cut her throat at the moment of climax. . . . He hated her because she was young and pretty and sexless, because he wanted to go to bed with her and would never do so. (P. 16)

The woman-hatred and sadism are blatant and prevalent in Winston's character and in Oceania itself.

This generalization must be qualified. Even while sadism, militant chauvinism, and fear of subversives pervade the entire population, even while scarcities and drabness are all-pervasive, the puritanic spirit of repression is imposed only on the upper- and middle-level elites, especially the latter class—the white-collar bureaucrats of the system. Within the slums, where the large masses of the working people live, permissiveness reigns according to the Party slogan "Proles and animals are free" (p. 62).

It is important to note the reasons Orwell gives for the persistent scarcities, drabness, and decay. It is not a lack of resources or of scientific and technological know-how (although a good deal of science has been destroyed deliberately). To be sure, there was a brief episode of atomic warfare some decades ago, which left part of London (and, presumably, other cities in Oceania) ruined; and since there is now perpetual war, conventional, nonatomic bombs occasionally still fall into the city. But with all resources at the disposal of the state, all this could be repaired, and a more comfortable life could be provided. Why is this not done? We expect the answer to be that the demands of military preparedness crowd out all other economic considerations; but Orwell makes clear that the continual warfare is but a charade, a marginal phenomenon actually requiring only modest resources. This charade is practiced, not only to perpetuate the mood of hysteria in the population, but also to serve as the pretext for the real cause of the material drabness, which is deliberate and systematic waste of available resources. Surpluses in Oceania must be used up without raising living standards, except those of the topmost elite. Orwell stresses this several times, to make sure the reader understands it. What is his explanation of this systematic waste? The reader may think at first that here we have Orwell reviving neo-Marxist theories of imperialism, according to which capitalism can remain profitable only by getting rid of accumulated surpluses. Indeed there are several passages in the book arguing that systematic waste alone keeps the economy going. But that must be dismissed as a mindless echoing of socialist theories the author has absorbed, because he makes it clear that private property has been abolished in Oceania, so that profitability no longer is a possible motive (p. 170). Instead, we learn that the rulers of Oceania keep living standards depressed because they are convinced that general affluence and scientific knowledge suggest the obsolescence of all hierarchic relationships; affluence and knowledge undermine authority. Where wealth is generally distributed, the idea can easily arise that power also should be distributed evenly, and "that the privileged minority had no function." The class structure can be preserved only by preventing affluence; "in the long run, a hierarchical society was only possible on a basis of poverty and ignorance" (p. 175). Leninism here has been given a strange twist.

Capitalism has been abolished, but Oceania is a class society, with a thin top elite, a middle class comprising about 15 percent of the population, and the working masses, the proles, forming the bulk of the nation. Underneath them are the lowest of the low, the prisoners of war who are doing slave labor. Orwell seems to assume that all societies, past and present, contain such a structure.

Given his ideals, that is a gloomy assessment of human history and achievements. Orwell clearly writes as a socialist who believes in the possibility and desirability of creating a society of equals who share power, affluence, and comforts, and govern themselves without ruling classes or bureaucrats. He also believes that our aim should be for a society in which we can behave decently toward each other, while cultivating the life of the soul and the emotions, and acquiring a taste for the aesthetic enjoyment of nature, art, and sexual relations. His socialism is decidedly British, both in that it is based on a philosophy of common sense and because it is highly individualistic. Orwell distrusts elaborate philosophic schemes and pretentious language; that is the meaning of his stress on objectivity and rationalism, which alone will save us from the delusions of ideology. At the same time, he has convinced himself that people are easily deluded, and, like John Stuart Mill, he steadfastly defends the autonomous individual who constitutes a minority of one—the solitary sane individual in a world gone crazy (p. 179).

So here is Orwell's nightmare of the United States in 1984. Political and economic equality are now possible but, since it would spell the end of power for the top elite, must be averted. What then are the motives of this elite? Here Orwell's answer is clear: lust for power and delight in ruling. "The Party seeks power entirely for its sake. . . . Power is not a means; it is an end" (p. 217). And what is power, according to Orwell's spokesman, O'Brien? It is the ability to reshape other human beings, to dehumanize and destroy them. One asserts power over another by inducing suffering.

> Power is in tearing human minds to pieces and putting them together again in new shapes of your own choosing. . . . The old civilizations claimed that they were founded on love and justice. Ours is founded upon hatred. In our world there will be no emotions except fear, rage, triumph, and self-abasement. . . . If you want a picture of the future, imagine a boot stamping on a human face—forever. (P. 220)

In short, the driving force of politics in Oceania is sadism. The most vivid passages in the novel are a nightmare of torture and brutality. Clearly Orwell's mind was shaken by the cruelties he himself had witnessed—in school and in Burma, as a drifter during the Depression and as a soldier in Spain, and finally at the time of World War II. He must have concluded that people are capable of every kind of barbarity; and the horror fascinated him.

Here it is appropriate to note evidence of a related trait in Orwell's characters: all the male figures in *Nineteen Eighty-Four* are chauvinists. His female character, Julia, is depicted as mere sex object, who lacks intellect, is uninterested in politics and philosophy, and falls asleep when her lover talks about them. She is conniving and practical, but without depth, "a rebel only from the waist down" (p. 129). It occurs to me that Orwell does not deal with Julia realistically. For instance, since she is wildly promiscuous, having slept with scores of men, how does she keep from getting pregnant? Her alleged love for Winston Smith is unconvincing, as is her characterization in many other respects. She is a portrait of a woman by a man who does not understand women very well.

Orwell identifies the power-hungry sadists who rule Oceania as bureaucrats, scientists, technicians, union bosses, social scientists, public relations and media people, and professional politicians, in short, the very same people who wield various kinds of authority in the world as we know it (p. 169). He suggests that their lust for power comes from their ability to exercise it; give people some power, he seems to say, and even if they are decent and well-intentioned, it will corrupt them. His depictions of the ruling class of Oceania closely correspond to descriptions of contemporary social and political elites, whether or not he was aware of these resemblances. For instance, he associates Oceania's official double-talk, Newspeak, with the totalitarian countries of the 1930s (p. 252); yet the examples he gives can be easily identified as modern American bureaucratese, whether military, civilian, or corporate. In general, Orwell can be faulted for missing the enormous influence which bureaucratization has had in shaping modern society and in imposing controls and conformity on it.

Orwell's Oceania is immune to revolution. The masses do not even know they are oppressed, they have no standards for comparison of their lot with that of others, and in any event "have no intellect" (pp. 171, 173). Conquest by an outside power is ruled out as impossible. The middle class, historically the fomenter of revolution, is under total control, and so indeed are the members of the top elite. Much of the novel concentrates on how this control works. Essentially, it is based on the rulers' success in dislocating the people's sense of reality through language control. Doublethink, one of the devices in this mind control, obviously is meant to be a caricature of both the Marxist dialectic and the Soviet principle of *partiinost'*: "Reality exists . . . only in the mind of the party. . . . Whatever the Party holds to be truth *is* truth" (p. 205). One might argue that Orwell's model of doublethink and Newspeak might also have come from the world of advertising. Moreover, the practice that seems to horrify him the most, the control of the past by falsifying records and rewriting history, is, of course, as old as historiography itself. In the eyes of Winston Smith, this process of falsifying historic memory is "more terrifying than mere torture and death" (p. 32). Clearly, for Orwell, knowledge of the past provides an anchor of sanity. Without it, human society would be left without meaning. In Oceania, this has disappeared; people exist and do their work, but whatever happens to them or around them is episodic, hence profoundly irrational. Genuine rationality, or something approaching it, resides only in the Third World (p. 177); that world, however, is politically irrelevant. Any spark of rationality arising in a citizen of Oceania will be extinguished with gruesome cruelty.

Herbert Marcuse's *One-Dimensional Man*, written fifteen years after Orwell's novel, differs from it in form, content, and in the author's basic philosophy, but the points of agreement, in the final analysis, are more striking and thought-provoking. What first impresses the reader is the difference in the language of the two works. Orwell writes in his usual clear, crisp, straightforward fashion, while Marcuse's prose is ponderous, pretentious, difficult, and opaque. The book cannot be read quickly; one must work through it. I am tempted to say that Marcuse writes, as he spoke, with a heavy German accent; or, to use different imagery, his language is to that of Orwell as the music of Alban Berg is to that of Eric Coats.

The society he describes is anything but drab and impoverished; Marcuse seems to have been unaware of the possible exhaustion of finite resources and assumed instead that there are no limits to our domination of nature. Hence his America is affluent, efficient, free, permissive, and it cultivates that objective science so dear to Orwell's heart. Indeed, America described by Marcuse seems to conform to many of Orwell's ideals; yet Marcuse denounces it as unjust, oppressive, exploitative, and totalitarian.

To explain this we must look at Marcuse's concept of the ideal society. His goal is the minimization of toil and domination, and the maximization of every potential slumbering in each individual or, as he puts it, the use of available resources "for the optimal development and satisfaction of individual needs and faculties with a minimum of toil and misery" (p. xi). This would include a distributive system granting each individual according to need, a reduction of the work load, broad training and activity in a wide variety of pursuits, and rotation of people to different tasks. While the division of labor would continue, executive and supervisory functions no longer would carry power or privilege (p. 44). In such a happy world, destructive forms of struggle and competition would no longer be necessary; instead, we could bring about cooperation and harmony. He calls this goal "pacification of existence," which he defines as "the development of man's struggle with man and with nature, under conditions where the competing needs, desires, and aspirations are no longer organized by vested interests in domination and scarcity—an organization which perpetuates the destructive forms of this struggle" (p. 16).

Pacification would lead to a democratic culture based on the restoration of the right to privacy, granted to all, and protected for each—privacy not only against the bureaucratic machine but also against public opinion and mass democracy. Like John Stuart Mill, Marcuse in the final analysis opts for the dissenting, eccentric individual. Self-determination, for him, has been achieved when the masses have dissolved into genuine individuals free from all forms of manipulation (pp. 244, 252). In this as well, he is surprisingly similar to Orwell.

Moreover, Marcuse assumes that such a society is well within reach. " 'Pacification,' 'free development of human needs and faculties'—these concepts can be empirically defined in terms of the available intellectual and material resources and capabilities and their systematic use for attenuating the struggle for existence" (p. 220). Yet it is at the same time utterly out of our grasp. The potential is not being fulfilled.

The key to Marcuse's conception of contemporary America is the word *suffering*. We are suffering injustices, indignities, and deprivations of many kinds. We suffer them needlessly; and, what is worst, we do not even know that we are suffering. We are being exploited; we are compelled to perform mindless, tiresome, unnecessary tasks, which let our creative potentials wither. Inequalities in our society are glaring. The competitive struggle makes us all vicious animals. The system eggs us on to waste and to consume, and it gives us many choices, but the choice is only between different kinds of junk. What we can buy satisfies false needs, while our true needs remain unsatisfied. We are dominated and manipulated by self-perpetuating elites. Violence and war are on the increase. We have political rights and freedoms which are phony, because the choices we are offered within the system are meaningless. Just as we buy shoddy things which we do not need, and vote for shoddy politicians who sell us out, so we consume junk entertainment and indulge in stupefying forms of relaxation. Our culture is a manipulated mass culture which anesthetizes us instead of empowering us.

The reason for this is that our society does indeed deliver much of what it promises and, in that sense, is rational. It satisfies us. We are free to indulge in many pleasures that used to be taboo, we are having fun, we are mobile and believe that we have many opportunities for self-advancement. If our system is totalitarian, it is a pleasant totalitarianism; we are no longer alienated (p. 11). Instead, people identify with the society. But that very society robs them of their genuine potential! What Marcuse is saying insistently is that the very comforts which Winston Smith longs for in the London of 1984 are what enslave us to a status quo far short of *the historically attainable*. Marcuse refers to our many freedoms by a Freudian term, *desublimation*, which suggests that the censorious superego has withered away; and he argues that desublimation in a world which still depends on, and reproduces, the injustices, violence, and degradations of our time is repressive desublimation. "Comfort, business, and job security in a society which prepares itself for and against nuclear destruction may serve as a universal example of *enslaving contentment*" (p. 243, emphasis added).

The totalitarianism of Oceania was instituted by a criminal conspiracy of the top elite; Marcuse's America is the product of the historical dialectic of progress. To be sure, he has unkind things to say about those who wield power in the contemporary world, and on occasions he suggests that the villain which prevents our system from serving human interests is the capitalist profit motive, which skews all rationality by continuing

> to link the realization of the general interest to that of particular
> vested interests. In doing so, it continues to face the conflict
> between the growing potential of pacifying the struggle for ex-
> istence, and the need for intensifying this struggle; between the
> progressive "abolition of labor" and the need for preserving labor
> as the source of profit. The conflict perpetuates the inhuman
> existence of those who form the human base of the social pyra-
> mid—the outsiders and the poor, the unemployed and unem-
> ployable, the persecuted colored races, the inmates of prisons
> and mental institutions. (P. 53)

But, ultimately, the totalitarian society is a result of the "rational universe which by the mere weight and capabilities of its apparatus blocks all escape" (p. 71).

The villain for Marcuse is not a conspiratorial elite or class, and he rejects the assumption of an innate drive to power, even though in stating this he comes close to echoing Orwell's thesis.[3] The villain, rather, is the system itself, "the objective order of things," and this system is that of high technology and scientific management—the rule of *rationality*. Through the use of human reason we have raised productivity and the standard of living; we have made freedom and comforts possible. But this same rational enterprise has created "a state of mind and behavior" which justifies the most destructive and oppressive features of the enterprise. The benefits of scientific management lead to a new form of social control (p. 146).

Friedrich Engels, in his work against Dühring, predicted the withering away of the state; the domination of men would give way to the administration of things. But Marcuse obviously believed that the management of things ultimately leads to the domination of people. "When technics becomes the universal form of material production, it circumscribes an entire culture" (p. 154). "The logos of technics," he writes, "has been made into the logos of continued servitude. The liberating force of technology—the instrumentalization of things—turns into a fetter of liberation: the instrumentalization of man" (p. 159). The ultimate conclusion of this is that "the rational society subverts the idea of reason" (p. 167; see also x, xvi, 3, 71). What Marcuse is assailing is the entire bureaucratic mode of life with its human engineering on the basis of rational utility considerations; and he suggests that this "rationalization" of human intercourse makes democracy with all its features—participation, vote, parties, and freedom of expression—meaningless. He talks about the "tyranny of rationality."

The good society thus is within our reach, but it is also out of reach.

What places it within reach is technology; but that same technology also renders it unattainable. Advanced industrial society manifests "a trend toward the consummation of technological rationality" together with "intensive efforts to contain this trend within the established institutions" (p. 17; see also pp. 43, 144–46, 154, 159, 166–67, 221, 226). But, while the weight of the techniques and institutions themselves seems overbearing, what prevents us from transcending them ultimately is delusion, an induced incapacity of our collective minds to think beyond a reality which makes us suffer. Most of the book deals with the many means by which the system structures our minds to enforce conformity, and because of this preoccupation with the corruption of intellect his vision of contemporary totalitarianism seems to come closest to that of Orwell. Yet in actual fact this is the point at which the two books diverge the most.

Earlier I alluded to the difference between Marcuse's and Orwell's language. The difference symbolizes fundamental disagreement between the two authors on the kind of thinking which would *promote* the good society. Orwell believes that we will be saved only if we preserve common sense, precise language, and empiricist inquiry. By implication, he denounces dialectical philosophy. Marcuse says the exact opposite. Among the philosophic traditions which he blames for skewing our minds, he includes empiricism and positivism, and he believes we will escape from totalitarianism only with the help of the dialectic, as conceived in the writings of Plato, Hegel, and Marx.

What the dialectic means to Marcuse can be summarized fairly simply. Human beings exist in a world which is at one and the same time factual and potential, a world of actual relations and a world of possibilities, of "is" and "ought." Both are part of reality; and since they are in conflict with each other, there is tension or contradiction in reality. Hence every description of reality is both true and false; all description is critical; every description is an imperative; all discourse is subversive. "Contradiction belongs to the very nature of the *object* of thought, to reality, where Reason is still Unreason, and the irrational still the rational" (p. 142). Stated differently, morality is a legitimate part of political discourse, and any philosophy which explains morality away is against reason, hence positivism and empiricism are denounced as profoundly irrational. They accept this world as it is and seek to endow it with reasonability. They seek to cure us from our ideals, illusions, dreams, and utopias. They structure language and discourse so as to eliminate past and future. But they are insidious primarily because they tolerate deviant ideas, yet, in tolerating them they relegate them to the realm of play, dream, or fantasy: positivism and empiricism categorically refuse to take dreams seriously (p. 184). But dreams are essential preconditions of the inquiring mind.

Marcuse, like Orwell, accuses the present system of regarding the inquiring mind as subversive and dismissing it as a symptom of sickness or lunacy, but, unlike Orwell, he insists on accepting the subversive label. The inquiring mind will refuse to accept "reality," and, he says in so many words, anyone who remains sane in this insane world has lost his reason. Positive philosophy, he argues, prides itself in its therapeutic character, just as O'Brien in *Nineteen Eighty-Four* sees himself as a healer. Marcuse rejects the treatment: "Who is the patient? Apparently a certain sort of intellectual, whose mind and language do not conform to the terms of ordinary discourse." Again,

> in a sense, according to Freud, the patient's disease is a protest reaction against the sick world in which he lives. But the physician must disregard the "moral" problem. He has to restore the patient's health, to make him capable of functioning normally in his world. (P. 183)

Both Orwell and Marcuse write in praise of the heretic who will not allow himself to be brainwashed. But Orwell's heretic is a man whose anchor of sanity is knowledge of the past, whereas Marcuse's heretic is the person who dreams of a different future; and while Orwell wants us to return to good old plain English, Marcuse advocates a philosophy and a vocabulary of negativism, arguing that it is necessary to break through the boundaries of the established vocabulary. One must call things by their wrong names. "Critical analysis must dissociate itself from that which it strives to comprehend; the philosophic terms must be other than the ordinary ones in order to elucidate the full meaning of the latter" (p. 193). This philosophy requires using language in a manner which would make Orwell shudder in disgust.

Analogous conflicts between the two are apparent in several other areas that touch the human mind. An example would be their attitude toward art. The function of art in Orwell's ideal society is to provide a means for stepping out of the grey world of work and politics, to refresh oneself in aesthetic enjoyment. Art is what adds beauty to our everyday surroundings and thus makes life more gentle, more bearable, more enjoyable. I would trace this commonsense view of art to the writing of William Morris; it is a very appealing view. For Marcuse, in contrast, art is sublimation, i.e., a mode of transforming suffering into enjoyment. Its function is to express inexpressible dreams of *le bonheur*; it is therefore a means of criticizing reality. Romantic art, which he singles out, emphasizes nay-sayers: outlaws, fools, prostitutes, heretics, and neurotics. What then is wrong with contemporary art? What he says, in essence, is that the nay-sayers have become part of the established way of life; further, avant-garde art seems to have become routine; and finally, the enjoyment of art itself has become routine. With this, however, the gap between art and the established order is closing. Once it stood in contradiction to the status quo. Now, with Bach as background music and Plato in the drugstore, the contradiction is flattened out (p. 64). The dream of William Morris, realized in modern society, has turned into a nightmare for Marcuse.

Orwell's Winston Smith seeks in vain to retain his common sense which society declares to be a form of madness. Marcuse argues that what is considered insane in our society is not common sense, but dreaming; and while in Orwell's nightmare the most brutal torture is the means for destroying our humanity, Marcuse laments that what dehumanizes us are the easy satisfactions we are offered; it is the "happy consciousness" which "facilitates acceptance of the misdeeds of this society" (p. 76).

Two or three decades ago, the "end of ideology" school of thought in the United States argued that, having attained a nearly perfect society, we no longer needed dreams but could cope with all remaining problems by applying scientific engineering. To Marcuse that precisely is the danger, and in effect he calls for a revival of what David Bell and others called "ideology." For Orwell all ideologies are lies. His dreams about an alternative take the form of memory of a better past, which he romanticizes (see Orwell, pp. 10, 81). Yet, with all his emphasis on empiricism and common sense, the nightmare he depicts is itself a rather dreamy abstraction, an impossible system in which things seem too perfectly balanced, and whose fundamental principles of operation often seem naive. Marcuse, despite his denunciation of empiricism, at times seems much more realistic in depicting the evils of modern society. They diverge widely also in the faint glimpses of the alternative they provide. Orwell ultimately seems to opt for a return to an egalitarian liberalism. He wants us to remain human, have a family life, private concerns, intimate feelings, loyalties, and strong links to the past (pp. 136, 138). Marcuse, in contrast, looks forward to an as yet dimly outlined future; he wants us to *become* human so we can enjoy freedoms, autonomy, love, creativity, and privacy which we have never had. Orwell's goal is down-to-earth. Marcuse's is utopian: freedom *from* economics, *from* politics and public opinion (p. 4). In positing pacification as an ideal, he places it in contrast to power and argues that it will in fact be the end of power. "Peace and power, freedom and power, eros and power, may well be contraries!" (p. 235). He obviously wants to make love, not war.

While detecting certain macho qualities in Orwell, I am tempted to refer to Marcuse's goal as the feminization of politics, or the feminization of values. We ought to have the courage to be scared, he writes, and among the qualities he would like to see us develop he lists the following:

> refusal of all toughness, togetherness and brutality . . . disobedience to the tyranny of the majority . . . profession of fear and weakness (the most rational rejection to this society!) . . . a sensitive intelligence sickened by what is being perpetrated . . . the commitment to the feeble and ridiculed actions of protest and refusal. (Pp. 242–43)

That two thinkers so different from each other developed nightmares which, despite such obvious differences, nonetheless are profiles of an evil future which bear a striking family resemblance to society today should make us sit up and take notice. Is it really 1984?

The religion of progress is under assault, as it has been for centuries. On the fringes of our society sects have formed which warn about impending doom or about irreversible corruption that has already taken place.[4] The causes for alarm have multiplied far beyond anything either Orwell or Marcuse could have imagined; their works make little or no reference to the risk of mutual nuclear annihilation, ecological disaster, or to the powder kegs of ethnic conflict throughout the globe. But their books can clearly be interpreted as prophecies of the alarm now spreading, themes on which many current predictions of doom are just so many variations. Both can be faulted for their political theories: Orwell for the simple, primitive assumptions of his model depicting the coming totalitarianism, and Marcuse for grossly overestimating the resources at the disposal of American society. I can only hope, however, that the nightmarish projection of my own with which I began this essay is not any more realistic.

Notes

1. See Gabriel A. Almond, Marvin Chodorow, and Roy Harvey Pearce, eds., *Progress and Its Discontents* (Berkeley: University of California Press, 1982).
2. George Orwell, *Nineteen Eighty-Four* (New York: Signet Classic, 1981). Herbert Marcuse, *One-Dimensional Man: Studies in the Ideology of Ad-*

vanced Industrial Society (Boston: Beacon Press, 1964). Further reference to Orwell and Marcuse will appear in the text, in parentheses.

3. He does this in connection with his assessment of trends in the USSR. While on the one hand he lumps it together with the United States as another totalitarian superpower, on the other hand he believes that, the means of production having been nationalized, it is possible for the USSR to become a decent society. To be sure, the ruling elite might want to perpetuate itself (presumably driven by the power urge), but to do so it would have to "arrest material and intellectual growth at a point where domination is still rational and profitable" (p. 45).

4. A recent discussion of contemporary prophets of doom argues that these groups should be regarded as religious sects. See Mary Douglas and Aaron Wildavsky, *Risk and Culture: An Essay on the Selection of Technical and Environmental Dangers* (Berkeley: University of California Press, 1982).

George Orwell: A Prophet
Honored Just after His Time

Eugene J. McCarthy

If I were to pick two authentic, certifiable, prophets (if prophets can be certified) of and for this century, they would be Thorstein Veblen, who recognized the beginnings of the superconsumer, conspicuous waste, conspicuous consumption, planned obsolescence, and conspicuous leisure culture of our time; and George Orwell, who saw the potential for depersonalization and human degradation of the pure and crude forms of totalitarianism historically demonstrated in Nazi Germany and in Communist Russia, and warned of similar danger in more sophisticated, less violent, more subtle forms.

Both prophets were not only farsighted, but bold and brave, for they foretold changes that might well take place, or not take place, within their own lives, thus running the risk of being judged not only in their own countries, and left without honor, but in their own time, unlike some other potential prophets like Robert Heilbronner, who has projected the end of the earth as a habitable planet one hundred and fifty years from now—or from the date of the publication of his book—from population pressure, possible nuclear war, biocarbons in the atmosphere supplemented by residuals from hair spray and other products and conditions. He has now extended the date beyond the one hundred and fifty originally forecast, and well beyond the end of his promised three score years and ten. Both Veblen and Orwell, as often happens to prophets, have gone a little awry in their prophecies, missing a little on time, on degree, on consequences, on awareness; but the judgments of both, as projected into the future, score well within a tolerable margin of error for prophets.

Veblen, dealing with more limited material for prophecy, essentially quantitative and measurable, did not fully anticipate the potential of the people of the United States and of the advanced countries to over-consume and to reach a level of waste unsurpassed in history with two possible exceptions: the Iks, the mountain tribe in Africa reported to gorge themselves on a good day's kill without thought for other people or for their own tomorrow, and the Romans, who provided the vomitorium as an adjunct to the dining room so that the banquet could go on with temporary interruptions. The abandoned car lot in the United States is roughly analogous to the special Roman chamber, serving in our case the concept of planned obsolescence and suggesting that if Karl Marx had known about the potential of the automobile and the automobile culture for waste of money, fuel, materials, space, time, and even life (during the Vietnam War, defenders of that war would occasionally point out that the number of persons killed in the war in a given period was less than the number of persons killed on the United States' highways in the same period), he would have written another chapter, possibly a book, explaining how capitalism could be stimulated even to the point of destruction by either war or the automobile.

Whereas Veblen has been all but forgotten, even, I found recently, on the campus of the University of Wisconsin, we carry on, victims of the the theories that bigger and more are better, even in mice— which are now being crossed, we learn, with rats, thus producing a stronger more virulent strain of mice (the opposite crossing in the hope of getting smaller rats seems to have been overlooked, or postponed). We are victims too of "supply side" economics and of public relations and advertising encouraging "impulse buying" until we find ourselves a people "overbuilt" but not overhoused, overtransported in overpowered cars, overfueled, overheated (some of us), overcooled (many of us), overfed (most of us), and overdefended, or overdefensed (all of us). Veblen, if alive and asked for comment, as he would be asked by some television correspondent, would surely apologize for his hesitancy and for the modest limits of his forecasts.

Orwell is not forgotten as Veblen has been. The fact that he set his ideas in fiction may explain his continued recognition. In any case his continuing status as an accepted social and political prophet is attested to by the fact that persons of somewhat different political and ideological dispositions are claiming him as their own, either for what he was, or thought, when alive, or for what they think he would be, or would be thinking, if alive today. Two recent claims have been filed, one by Norman Podhoretz, in the January 1983 *Harper's*, in which Norman expresses his belief that Orwell would be a neoconservative like Norman.[1] Another claim has been filed by Irving Howe in the *New Republic* issue ending the year 1982. Howe says that it would be foolish to say whether Orwell, had he lived on into the eighties, would have turned to the right, or tried to "refine [his] socialist values toward a greater stress on democracy, . . . [or] abandoned [his] interest in politics entirely."[2] It is clear that Howe would have Orwell on his side. He quotes Orwell in 1940 as writing, "There is [little] question of avoiding collectivism. The only question is whether it is to be founded on willing cooperation or on the machine gun." Howe adds his observation or explanation, "that is—whether it will be democratic or authoritarian." "This," Howe writes, "puts the matter with admirable precision. *1984* shows us what might happen if the machine gun triumphs, but the other choice remains to us."[3]

Howe, I think, misses the significant point. Orwell's concern was not principally over ways and means through which collectivism was to come about, but rather with the reality, which he saw as essentially the same, whether the way was violent and authoritarian, or nonviolent and democratic.

Orwell marked the corruption and abuse of language as a sure warning and sign of loss of integrity and of respect for the person and as a common historically tested instrument for dehumanization, both of the person who was the object of the perverted language and of the person who used it. In his essay "Politics and the English Language," published in 1946, he wrote, "In our time, political speech and writing are largely the defense of the indefensible."[4] Purges and deportations, like later atomic and nuclear bombing were, he noted, too brutal for most people to face, and therefore had to be described, explained, and carried out in a new or unclear language.

In the 1946 essay, Orwell wrote that when "defenseless villages are bombarded from the air, the inhabitants driven out into the countryside, the cattle machine-gunned, the huts set on fire with incendiary bullets, this is called *pacification.*" The same language, almost without change, was used to describe our *pacification* program in Vietnam, reaching its high point in the observation of one officer that a Vietnamese village had to be destroyed in order to save it. When "peasants," he wrote, "are robbed of their farms, sent trudging along the roads with no more than they can carry: this is called *transfer of population* or *rectification of frontiers. . . .* A mass of Latin words falls upon the facts like soft snow, blunting the outlines, and covering up all the details."[5]

Vietnam introduced another measure of war, of progress and failure in application of the symbols and methods of quantification. Kill ratio was the telling indicator. At one point it was held, in and about the Pentagon, that a kill ratio of four to one, four of the Vietnamese, our enemies, and one of us, or of our Vietnamese supporters, was a sign of stalemate. Whereas, if the ratio rose to five to one in our favor, victory was, if not imminent, at least down the road. A ratio of three to one, however, forebode defeat.

In late spring in 1966 infiltration of the North Vietnamese was estimated at between 5,500 and 7,000 a month, a number approximately 50 percent higher than the estimate made early in that year by Secretary McNamara when he said that they (the North Vietnamese) would have the capacity to infiltrate "up to" 4,500 a month with the bombing. Under questioning, the Secretary said that "up to" did not mean a ceiling and that the number they could infiltrate is "less than x, being quite a bit in excess of 4,500 but, in any event, there is some ceiling that would result from the bombing of the lines of communication." Other language used relative to Vietnam was much closer to the Newspeak of Orwell's *Nineteen Eighty-Four*.

My Lai, before the massacre, had been designated a "free-fire zone," by implication one in which it was permitted to fire at anything or even at random. There was a subsequent or supplemental order "not to generate any prisoners," and a final one on the scene, "to take care of these people," consistent with the statement of one American politician that it was "better to kill Vietnamese in the elephant grass of Vietnam, as boys, than to have to kill them, as men, in the rye grass of Western United States."

The language of nonresponsibility was also used and explained by Admiral Moorer, chairman of the Joint Chiefs of Staff under President Nixon, who, when asked whether he had been consulted on the decision to bomb Hanoi, said that he had not been consulted and that there was no need for such consultation, as the standing order was "to bomb," and the president had simply in effect said that the order staying the standing order was no longer in effect. Then the planes took off and the bombs fell.

A major innovation in the language of war was the Nixon administration's description of its military foray into Cambodia as an "incursion"—certainly the first incursion in the history of our nation. Incursions are, more or less, happenings. There is no verb form. One can invade or conduct an invasion. One, or a nation, cannot incurse. The whole proceeding is essentially existential, with no one bearing responsibility.

The development of nuclear weapons has been accompanied by a whole range of language adaptations and innovations. Even classical scholars have been given a role in the naming of weapons—Nike is there and the Trident and the Poseidon. When bombs could no longer be measured in terms of their achieved destruction, as "one Hiroshima," Greek was brought in to measure destruction in kilotons and megatons.

When the neutron bomb was introduced as a part of the mix or "bouquet" of nuclear weapons under the Carter administration, its supporters argued that there was much to be said for it. It would not cause what has come to be called the "collateral damage" of nuclear bombs now in use, or ready for use. Collateral damage is that resulting from blast and fire, rather than radiation. It would not destroy buildings, automobiles, tanks, or other military equipment. After removal of the dead persons and animals (cockroaches, it is believed, will survive), the buildings and equipment could be reoccupied and used within a short time.

The monkeys used in one series of neutron bomb tests were prepared by being taught to run on a treadmill. After being subjected to neutron radiation, those that were not immediately killed were placed back on the treadmill. Evidently their wills were not destroyed, for by report they attempted to run the treadmill.

Some of its advocates said the neutron bomb was more credible than other nuclear weapons presently in stock, now described as "normal nuclear weapons," or "regular nuclear weapons," or "conventional nuclear weapons." They have not quite become "traditional." Moreover, it was pointed out, the neutron bomb is more purely scientific than other instruments of death. The death it causes is "integral"— nothing crude like decapitation, bloodletting, or suffocation. It destroys the cell structure, especially that of the central nervous system. Accepting a more sophisticated and scientific way of bringing about a death has long been a mark of progress in Western civilization. Thus in disposing of enemies of the state during the French Revolution, and after, the guillotine was preferred over the executioner's axe. It was more scientific; it used gravity rather than human strength. It was more accurate; its collateral effects were minimal. Later, the electric chair and the gas chamber were adopted as offering "more humane" ways of execution, and most recently injection has become the preferred method.

With all of these virtues, not surprisingly the new weapon was given the familiar name, "the cookie cutter"; in somewhat the same way, Ronald Reagan has named the MX missile the "peace-keeper." Possibly all weapons should have names, personal ones, or nicknames. History has given us the Bowie knife, the Patton tank, the Sherman tank. We could name atomic and nuclear weapons after presidents associated with their development or deployment, even with their use. We could call the atomic bomb "the Harry," the nuclear bomb "the Ike," the neutron bomb "the Jimmy Carter Cookie Cutter," thus calling up images of mothers, warm kitchens, the smell of baking and cookie forms—diamonds, hearts, clubs, spades, gingerbread boys, Dutch girls, rabbits, and best of all the small, odd-shaped pieces that escaped the cookie cutter. The MX could be called "the Ronnie."

It should be noted that for all of its positive qualities, the neutron bomb is not likely to catch on. Destruction of buildings, visible evidence of conquest, is necessary for victory. One of the reasons, some experts say, that we lost in Vietnam was that people were all we had to destroy. Carthage was razed. General Sherman on the march from Atlanta to the sea did little more than what would now be called collateral damage. Moscow was burned at Napoleon's approach, and so on. Furthermore, the neutron bomb will not do because it does not lend itself to television coverage. For that medium a war without crumbling walls, rubble, flames, fleeing women and children, without blood, will not do.

Newspeak has reached beyond weapons and war itself to the higher levels of strategic thinking and planning. As late as 1960 the word *strategy* and its adjectival form *strategic* carried traditional meanings. A distinction was made between tactics and strategy, in World War II, there was "strategic bombing" and "tactical bombing," the difference being principally one of targets and purpose, not of weapons used. But by 1967 a change had taken place. It was in that year that the Johnson administration approached the Soviet Union on the possibility of holding talks on "Strategic Arms Limitations." The weapons now defined the purposes.

By 1974 the concept of Mutual Assured Destruction (MAD), which had dominated strategic thinking during the sixties and early seventies, was discarded. MAD had never had a very solid footing in history or in the psychology of nations. It seemed to come out of systems analysis during the time that Secretary of Defense Robert McNamara accepted as given or found that if the United States could assure the Russians that our nuclear strike, first, second, or last, would kill approximately 20 percent of the Russians who count and/or destroy 50 percent of Russia's industrial capacity, the Russians would be deterred from launching any nuclear attack and we, the United States, would be deterred by the same prospect or assured result. The strategic goal under this concept was to reach a parity of mutually assured destruction in the 20 to 50 percent range. The introduction of Anti-Ballistic Missiles and the buildup of nuclear arms of various kinds in both countries, to a point at which it was estimated that everyone of importance in each country could be destroyed ·many times over, left MAD, as a strategic theory, far behind.

A new target phrase was introduced: *strategic superiority*, indicating not a better idea, or set of ideas, but a quantitative superiority in nuclear power. In 1974, Harold Brown, secretary of defense in the Carter administration, described it as "meaningful nuclear superiority," as a "disparity in strategic capability" which can be "translated into political effect."

I did not understand what he meant, and was consoled in my lack of comprehension by the fact that in that same year Henry Kissinger, when asked what was meant by "strategic superiority," reponded by saying, "What in God's name is strategic superiority? What can you do with it?"

If Henry didn't know what the terms meant, possibly no one knew, or needed to know. Thus I reassured myself, believing that I shared ignorance with Henry, only to find during the Salt II hearings that I had been living under conditions of false security. For Henry, in his testimony on that treaty in 1979, said that his 1974 words had been spoken under stress, or in a moment of pique, and that he, Henry, did in fact, in 1974, know what constituted "strategic superiority."

Whatever it is, he went on to say, we now had it in 1979 over the Russians, but he added that unless we increased our defense expenditures to take into account inflation, "We must go 5 percent above it," he said. We had indexed—among other things—social security, minimum wages, and congressional salaries, so why not index strategic superiority? With "linkage" to "detente," we would sometime in the early eighties reach a position of "essential strategic equivalence" with the Russians, and after that gradually yield superiority to them.

Henry noted a "perilous momentum" in favor of the Russians, but whether this was a pure momentum or a "momentum of their potential," such as was identified by Melvin Laird when he was secretary of defense in the Nixon administration, Henry did not say. Whatever kind of momentum it was, according to Henry, it was developing ominously against the United States. Other experts in strategic superiority such as James Schlesinger held that unless we spent 4.5 to 5 percent of our gross national product (GNP) on defense, we could come into a "window of peril," by or in 1985. This percentage was established in a year when the American Pickle Institute boasted that approximately 800 million dollars in our GNP came from the pickle industry, giving the nation (the Pickle Institute did not say this, but logic dictates it) an option in the interest of national security of maintaining current levels of defense expenditures, while cutting down on pickle consumption, or continuing, or even increasing pickle consumption, and increasing the defense budget by 5 percent of the pickle factor.

It is obvious that this line of thought and planning has moved us into the realm of the unreal. It is time to take an Orwellian look at the whole process—to turn to a new mode of thought best called "zero-based thinking." Zero-based thinking about nuclear superiority bypasses the concept of Mutual Assured Destruction, and accepts that even the multiple total destruction of strategic superiority, should that strategy become operative, need not destroy all human life. It is positive, and it requires a new strategic concept—MSP or Minimal Survival Potential. Obviously the nation with the Minimal Survival Potential will have strategic superiority. The United States has three principal MSP advantages. The first is in our readiness for evacuation. We evacuate about 30 percent of the population of major urban areas to the suburbs five days a week; about 50 percent leave the cities on weekends, and two thirds on special holidays, leaving in the central cities principally only the lame, the old, and the poor.

In anticipation of a nuclear exchange and so as to upgrade the value of our normal evacuation potential, the president of the United States could be given, in the name of national defense, authority to move holidays. Thus he could advance Memorial Day to the first of April, or the Fourth of July to June 15 with the understanding that when the advanced date was announced, people would accept the announcement as a signal that they should do on the advanced date what they planned to do on the scheduled date. The moveable holiday (the MH) strategically could be a rough equivalent to the Mobile (MX) Missile.

Our second advantage is in our heavily armed citizenry. It is estimated that there are in the possession of U.S. citizens, thanks to the Second Amendment to the Constitution and the National Rifle Association, approximately one hundred million guns of various kinds, together with an adequate supply of ammunition. Russian citizens on the other hand are not so armed. Occupation of the United States even after saturation bombing would be a high-risk venture, as armed survivors, probably only a few million, could come down from the hills and rise from the rubble.

A third advantage, a growing one, which could be pushed faster and further, was pointed out to me by a student—a product of the sixties—who observed that the movement in the United States to provide more and better facilities for the handicapped (such things as ramps, hydraulic lifts for buses and trains, heat-activated elevators, modified automobiles, changed industrial processes, etc.) could, if carried far enough, add greatly to our strategic superiority and our MSP. All of these changes and adaptations, he pointed out, would be helpful when those maimed by the nuclear exchange—those designated in the nuclear war language as "dilatory," or "delayed fatalities," rather than "prompt fatalities"—would be able to launch a final strike and then begin putting civilization back together. He suggested a further step in modifications which was possibly installing a missile system in anticipation of a time when only mutants were left in charge, and our mutants obviously would have a strategic advantage over the Russian mutants.

We must know that we are nearing something when the president of Pakistan, in announcing his intention to build a nuclear bomb, argues for his project on the grounds that among the major religions only Islam is without the bomb. Christians have many nuclear bombs and the atheists do. There is good reason to believe that there is a Judaic bomb or two, a Hindu bomb in India, and what might be called a Buddhist bomb in China. Islam then, to the concern of the president of Pakistan, remains the one religious group protected only by Allah without a nuclear bomb.

The second definable area in which Orwellian progress is evident is that of communications, especially of television. The press has come to think of itself as an institutionalized Estate, with special powers and privileges, a secular substitute, in a country which does not have an established religion, for the medieval First Estate. Without a recognized infallible head, the press claims a comparable power to speak arbitrarily, which is to say "ex cathedra," in press language "from the editor's chair."

The press has its own form of Index according to which it censors news and commentary and gives readers only what it determines is good for them. "All the news that's fit to print," declares the *New York Times* most modestly. One can fairly ask, by whose determination? Fit for whom? Fit for what? The press has taken it upon itself to give the secular equivalents of beatification and canonization. It has its own form of interdict and excommunication, and even condemns, although it does not yet burn people at the stake.

In its insistence on the protection of its sources, the press exercises a version of the seal of the confessional. It also reserves the right to protect its own from scandal, as in the 1978 case of the *New York Times* report on drug use by White House staff members. The *Times* report did not include the fact that at least two *Times* reporters had been present at the pot party—not as reporters, but as participants, it was explained, so as not to cause loss of confidence in the press.

Television communications are of another order. Recently the program director of one network said that the guiding principle in selecting and developing programs is popular response, translated into advertising revenue. The director of news at another network said that Nielsen ratings and revenue were basic in planning and presenting news programs. Hidden persuaders are still forbidden. But liminal, if not subliminal, stimuli are allowed. Spot advertisements of thirty seconds or less are run along with programs and interspersed among news items, which themselves may take no more than thirty seconds. The ads may have little relationship to the news, often distracting from it. For example, at the height of the Three Mile Island crisis, as it was called, CBS News with Walter Cronkite opened with Diane Sawyer standing in the mists of the Susquehanna Valley, evidently in danger of being irradiated. The news story was followed by an antacid ad. The program continued with five or six additional crises of varying intensity and imminence: Mt. St. Helens was threatening, the Iran hostage crisis, the continuing oil shortage, a truckers' strike in progress, and one or two natural catastrophes of limited impact—flood or fire. Among all of these disturbing stories were ads, most of them promising to cure, at least temporarily, and give relief from the pain of minor physical disabilities, or cover up the signs of approaching old age.

There has been change, if not progress, in news promotion and presentation since Walter's time. The old belief that one can lead a horse to water but not make it drink is not accepted by TV news promoters. They believe that listeners, or watchers, can be led to the news and made to watch, or at least leave their television sets on so as to be caught in the Nielsen net. The mastermind of one network laid out the whole scheme in a recent speech to television station owners and operators. What I learned from his speech has greatly complicated my approach to television news, which I was first exposed to under simple black and white conditions, with Edward R. Murrow and no props except his lighted cigarette. Now I know that there are priorities among the various news programs. Evening news is most important. The "finest resources" of at least one network are devoted to evening news. The morning news is becoming something called "infotainment," a cross between information and entertainment, with a slightly different emphasis from "entermation."

It is not enough to trust people to turn on the evening news at the appointed hour—vespers in the ages of faith, and the children's hour, according to Longfellow. People must be prepared for it, and the preparation begins with the morning news and goes on throughout the day. There is "on air" promotion, hints as to what may be in the evening news, implications that one may never make it through the day unless one keeps in mind the need to watch the evening news. Promotions are of two types, topicals and generics. A topical would be advance notice of information, say about a particular volcano like Vesuvius. A generic would give advance warning that volcanoes—one unnamed, or many, would be in the news. Having brought the viewer to the tube, the news managers are not going to let him get away like the fish at the edge of the boat. Viewers are given, during the newscasts, shots of something called "bumpers." These are advance notices of what is to follow the advertising breaks. Sustaining and complementing all of the news are graphics, flashing lights, painted and lighted globes, maps and charts, and sonic supports.

Finally television has accomplished another Orwellian triumph, one over time itself. Time is not easy to master. It is tough and evasive. Philosophers, theologians, poets, the people, scientists have all tried to comprehend it. Failing that, they have tried to control it through arbitrary measurement. Try anything was the theory: drops of water, sand in a glass, notched wheels moved by weights or springs, electrical impulses, ions.

Over the centuries, time was wasted and saved. It was lost and found, released and regained. It was taken out and put in. It was measured. There was free time and borrowed time.

Then came radio and television. Time which had never before been sold—it had been bartered with Faust and a few others—now was offered for sale. If offered for sale time had to be graded. Old categories of time were cast out. Time was reclassified, as "prime," "choice," and "good." These grade differentiations, incidentally, are the same used in grading beef.

Not limiting their treatment of time to commerce, the radio/television media also attacked the philosophical conceptions of time. Although most philosophers hold that no measurable segment of time is like any other, radio/television says "not so." There is such a thing as "equal time," and also "unique time." Thus they have identified Maude's time, and Mary Tyler Moore's time, and other kinds of time.

Finally, radio/television asserted a control over time which theologians have denied to God. There was no time before God created the world, says St. Augustine, but once started, time was to run its course. Television interviewers, regularly and without apology say, "We are out of time," to which we can only add, "forever and forever, Amen."

Along with these language changes and cultural changes, there has been, especially in the post–World War II years, a change in the structural and institutional control and direction of life in the United States, which change has contributed to depersonalization and the reduction of individual responsibility and control over both private and public life. The change has been to give more and more power over more and more aspects of life to corporations, or to be more precise to "the Corporation." Before World War II corporations reflected something of the personalities of their founders, or of their officers. People knew that Sewell Avery was president of Montgomery Ward. Today Montgomery Ward is owned by Mobil Oil, or was when this article was being written. Curtis, Sloan, Kettering, and others were identified with General Motors, now headed by persons with names such as Smith and Murphy. Carnegie and Mellon were remembered. Corporate structure was essentially feudal. Persons had rights within the corporation, in many cases better and more secure than the rights of persons working in other corporations, or without the protection of the corporate feudal system. Such security remains attractive to many today, with General Motors (GM) offering, for those who work for it, the most complete security. In its last contract GM has agreed to provide legal services or to finance legal services for its employees. We can anticipate a time when GM will have its own court system, with possible appeal to outside, constitutional courts. GM may next be following the old precept that the religion of the prince is the religion of the people. Our most serious concern should not be over the identifiable feudal corporations, but rather over the general exercise of corporate power in our society, reflecting as it must the limitations of the corporate conscience. Corporations are essentially like members of a choir of angels (if we know what angels are like), each one having the same soul as all the others. Thus the soul of a large corporation is identical with the soul of a small one. Eight automobile-producing corporations would differ only accidentally, and all would act under the direction of the principle that the basic purpose of the corporation is to make money within the law for stockholders, and also to pay officers adequately.

As early as 1831, James Kent, a legal scholar of his time, said that we had made it too easy to organize corporations, pointing out that we had gone far beyond what was permitted either under the Roman law, or the English common law. He saw danger in giving too much economic power to an institution of limited moral, social, and political responsibility.

At the beginning of this century Woodrow Wilson warned against even calling corporations "legal persons," for they were not persons and should not be credited with personality or treated as though they were anything but what the law had made them, he wrote.

Yet we today stand by, seemingly helpless, wringing our hands over the behavior of our creatures, not unlike a Frankenstein complaining because of the misbehavior of his monster. About 80 percent of the nation's economic activity is controlled by or is the responsibility of corporations. With the help of liberal reformers, such as Common Cause, the Federal Elections Law of 1975–76 encouraged through legalization the establishment of corporate political action committees which are becoming the major source of congressional campaign funds.

A third significant area in which power has been transferred to corporate units is in their control over military technology and weapons research in the military-industrial complex, which President Eisenhower warned the nation of in his farewell address. It might have been better if he had sounded the warning in his first inaugural.

The fourth area in which corporate power is operative is in control of foreign policy, where multinational corporations have taken on the attributes of sovereign nations, not seeking justice, or liberty, or happiness, but the best "bottom line."

The fifth field of growing corporate influence, now being encouraged through moral persuasion and tax concessions, is that of education, religion, and culture, through increased corporate contributions to such institutions and activities, while personal and governmental support is discouraged. The Amway Company recently financed a European trip for the National Symphony of Washington, at the same time as it was introducing its products and its methodology to that continent.

And then there is bureaucracy. "Legally," Hannah Arendt wrote in her book *The Origins of Totalitarianism,* "government by bureaucracy is government by decree and this means that power, which in a constitutional government only enforces the law, becomes the direct source of all legislation. Decrees, moreover, remain anonymous (while laws can always be traced to specific men or assemblies) and therefore seem to flow from some over-all ruling power that needs no justification." "There is no general principle," she continues, "which simple reason can understand behind the decree, but ever changing circumstances which only an expert can know in detail."[6]

Bureaucracy has the potential to carry a democratic society beyond de Tocqueville's warning of the danger of the "tyranny of the majority" over minorities. The ultimate, integral, corruption of democracy is that through the bureaucratization of control over more and more areas of individual and social life; the majority tyrannizes itself.

One thinks of the recent action of the Federal Bureau of Investigation (FBI) in setting up "Abscam," as a result of which one senator and a number of congressmen and other public officials, encouraged to perform illegal acts, have been convicted and sentenced to prison. When the head of the FBI was interrogated concerning the operation of the "scam," he said that no one person was responsible, that it had come up through the agency. Despite this action, the FBI remains an agency, with lines of authority and responsibility reasonably intact. More dangerous are bureaucracies such as the Federal Elections Commission, which has great and arbitrary power over the electoral process by which the government is chosen; the Federal Communications Commission (FCC), with far-reaching power (much of it, fortunately, not yet used, although its field is that of radio and television, which Nicolas Johnson, once head of the FCC, declared was an instrument suitable for use only in a totalitarian society); and the Internal Revenue Service, with authority to intervene in almost every private and social area of American life—business, financial, private, and noncommercial—and to exercise its power largely exempted from the constitutional protection of privacy, equal protection of the law, due process, and the ultimate principle that one is "innocent until proved guilty."

We approach what John Ahearn of Stanford University described, in an essay written in 1979, as a state of "entropy." In thermodynamics, entropy is defined as a measure of the randomness, chaos, and disorder of a system, leading to the final state of inert uniformity, an undifferentiated mass with the common denominator, the average, and the mean all being the same—the condition Henry Adams marked as the continuing, ever-present threat to civilization.

1984 approaches.

Notes

1. Norman Podhoretz, "If Orwell Were Alive Today," *Harper's*, January, 1983, pp. 30–37.
2. Irving Howe, "Enigmas of Power," *The New Republic*, Special Year-End Issue, 187, no. 26 (December, 1982): 32.
3. Howe, "Enigmas of Power," 32.
4. See *The Collected Essays, Journalism and Letters of George Orwell*, ed. Sonia Orwell and Ian Angus, 4 vols. (New York: Harcourt Brace Jovanovich, 1968), 4:136.
5. *CEJL* 4:136–37.
6. Hannah Arendt, *The Origins of Totalitarianism*, new ed. with added prefaces (New York: Harcourt Brace Jovanovich, 1973), 243, 244.

Nineteen Eighty-Four
and the Eclipse of Private Worlds

Francis A. Allen

To answer fully why for over a generation a novel has remained embedded in the consciousness of persons in widely differing situations and of varied backgrounds and convictions would be, perhaps, to say more about the society than the work of art. Orwell's *Nineteen Eighty-Four*, whatever its limitations, has amply demonstrated its power to strip bare many of the half-realized fears of persons inhabiting the Western world in our time, and of giving the terrors a tangible shape. The book has transcended a merely literary influence. Just as many persons who have never read *Don Quixote* speak of tilting at windmills, so too Big Brother is regularly denounced from public platforms and in newspaper columns by persons unable to account for the origin of the term. When one inquires more precisely about which fears of modern men and women are identified and confirmed in Orwell's somber vision, more than one answer may be forthcoming. Some may point to Oceania's systematic debasement of language, for example, or to the extinction of memory by the deliberate falsification of the past. Yet it seems likely that for most readers the particular horror evoked by the society imagined in *Nineteen Eighty-Four* stems from its brutal and premeditated destruction of the private worlds of its members.

One familiar with the general outlines of Orwell's life can hardly be surprised to discover him championing the value of individual privacy.[1] What may be unexpected is the comprehensiveness of his view. Orwell, for all his political concerns, was not a systematic analyst; and *Nineteen Eighty-Four* is not a philosophic treatise. Yet the novel manages to encompass, either by description or nuance, the most significant dimensions of the privacy concept treated in the enormous philosophical, legal, and sociological literature that surrounds the subject.[2] Some of the dimensions of particular importance to the novel need to be identified at the outset.

The point that should first be made is that it is artificial and distorting to attempt a too rigid separation of Oceania's assault on the private worlds of the party members from its aggressions on other human and humanistic values. Thus the destruction of history and memory, the creation of Newspeak, along with the abandonment of the rule of law and the more direct intrusions on personal intimacy and seclusion may all be seen, from one vantage point, as part of the state's comprehensive assault on the private worlds of its subjects. The point requires emphasis, for one of the factors that lessens the coherence of modern polemics surrounding the idea of privacy is the fact that privacy values are so often inextricably intertwined with other values—freedom and volition, speech and literary creation, intimacy and family values, meditation, the practice of religion and politics—to such a degree that a consensus on what are the distinctive features of the privacy value has proved elusive and, so far, unattainable.[3]

Yet is is clear that all aspects of state policy in Oceania do and are calculated to unseat the private worlds of the party members. Early in the novel Winston Smith muses that "nothing was your own except the few cubic centimeters inside your skull."[4] Inexorably, the state acts to occupy that constricted cavity as well. The destruction of memory and history and certainly the debasement of language represent efforts at thought control. Such concerns become the inevitable preoccupation of totalitarian regimes, for as the theorists of the People's Republic of China have perceived, the political society cannot occupy the totality of human life so long as "dangerous thoughts" in individuals persist.[5] Even though the internal mental phenomena of the party members escape direct surveillance by the state's ever-present telescreens, the regime may nevertheless achieve a more stunning victory over the private lives of persons: it may determine what thoughts the party members entertain.

The destruction of memory and history as forms of thought control deserves a closer look. In demolishing the external deposit of the past Oceania goes far toward destroying the private pasts of individuals, for without these external signs and objects, memory unreinforced fades and vanishes. Thus the individual is evicted from his most important private realm; he becomes dependent on the state for memory itself. This victory of the state encompasses another: the state achieves not only the extinction of the past but also of the individual's capacity to value the past as an essential condition of full humanity. Even the rebel Julia has been induced to believe that the past is unimportant and that it is the natural condition of humankind to live in the "endless present" created by the Party (p. 129).

Scorn of the past has a familiar ring. One of the many ironies of the mind set of the rebellious young persons on American campuses in the late 1960s was that arising from the effort to escape the past by suppressing and disregarding it. Bernard Shaw causes his character, Julius Caesar, to respond with contemptuous unconcern when informed that the magnificent repository of the past, the library of Alexandria, is in flames. It is the memory of mankind that is burning, he is told. "It is a shameful memory," he replies. "Let it burn."[6] Before the response is applauded, it is well to note that it is a *Caesar* who makes the reply. Many in the 1960s college generation failed to perceive that it is the past, especially the ideals and aspirations given birth in the past, that provides the primary defense against the aggressions of the present and the best hope for avoiding a future determined by the inhumanities of the present. Stifling the past cripples criticism of the present.[7]

Another, and to Orwell an obviously vital, dimension of Oceania's assault on the private worlds is its suppression of artistic creativity. One of the novel's arresting insights is contained in the episode in which Winston Smith, having determined to keep a diary, discovers that the encroachments of the state upon his life have seemingly deprived him of the power of expressing himself or, indeed, of remembering what he had intended to say (p. 10). Like Virginia Woolf, Orwell recognized the writer's need for a room—and a world—of one's own.[8] Orwell's commitment goes further, however. As a recent biographer asserts, it is the flourishing of individual creative values of the many, not merely of the few, that was Orwell's aspiration.[9] There is surely nothing of aesthetic ivory-towerism in his position. The "invasion of literature by politics" was inevitable in these times, he wrote. "[A]n awareness of the enormous injustice and misery of the world, and a guilt-stricken feeling that one ought to be doing something about it, . . . makes a purely aesthetic attitude toward life impossible."[10] Recognition of the inescapable intrusion of "politics" into the artistic consciousness, however, in no way mitigated Orwell's scorn for writers who surrender their private worlds and prostitute themselves to a party line and for those who in his time were "rebelling against the idea of individual integrity" (*CEJL* 4:60).

The private world is not only a world of solitude; it is also the world of intimate relations. With equal purpose Oceania moves to extinguish or attenuate those relations. The diminution of the family in Western society possessed ominous political implications for Orwell. "A deep instinct warns," he wrote in 1946, ". . . not to destroy the family which in the modern world is the sole refuge from the state" (*CEJL* 4:91). That the truly totalitarian state must conceive of the family and personal relations of love and friendship as its rivals was not an insight original with Orwell,[11] but his particular vision of the political attack on intimacy finds striking corroboration in some of the ideological writing and policies of the People's Republic of China in the recent past. In the Chinese literature relations between the sexes have been identified as "the love problem," a problem presumably to be solved or at least severely contained by the state. The cult of personality in the Mao regime may find its analogue in Oceania's prescribed sessions of group adulation for Big Brother and hate for his enemies. Both may be seen as efforts to force transference of emotion from the intimate world of personal relations to the public realm.[12]

The implications of the state's assault on intimacy transcend the merely political, however. If the cultivation of personal relations requires a degree of privacy, and if the experiencing of intimacy is indispensable to full humanity,[13] Oceania's policy is radically inhumane. For the Party member society is drab, gray, and tedious. Existence is shallow; there are no resonances. "Tragedy," muses Winston Smith, "belonged to the ancient time when there was still privacy, love, and friendship, and when the members of a family stood by one another without needing to know the reason" (p. 28).

Orwell in passing identifies another characteristic of societies bent on destruction of the private worlds of individuals. Winston Smith knows that in Oceania there is no law against keeping a diary. "[N]othing was illegal, since there were no longer any laws" (p. 9). He is also aware, however, that if caught doing so, he will be punished by death or a twenty-five-year term in a forced labor camp. Orwell correctly perceives that the penal law does not simply unleash the punitive power of the state, but that it also constricts state powers; for acts that fall outside the legal definitions of crime fall outside the state's authority to punish.[14] Any developed society seeking to maintain lines separating the private worlds from the public cannot risk reliance on the good will of officials or on a general understanding to accomplish the end. The understanding must be elaborated in the society's enforceable norms.[15] The rule of law may not be a sufficient condition for the flourishing of private worlds, but it is an indispensable one.

It is unnecessary to canvass all the strategies employed by Oceania in its war on the private worlds of its subjects, but one final, undergirding assumption of its policy must be examined. "Who will deny," asked Isaiah Berlin, "that political problems . . . depend logically and directly on what man's nature is taken to be?"[16] In portraying a political society that founds its policy on the assumption of the total malleability of human nature, Orwell gave expression to one of his most searing concerns. Before the outbreak of World War II, he wrote,

> In the past every tyranny was sooner or later overthrown, or at least resisted, because of "human nature," which as a matter of course desired liberty. But we cannot be at all certain that "human nature" is constant. It may be just as possible to produce a breed of men who do not wish for liberty as to produce a breed of hornless cows. The Inquisition failed, but then the Inquisition had not the resources of the modern state. (*CEJL* 4:380–81)

The final alteration or destruction of Winston Smith's nature through the horror of the rats serves to warn what the resources and purposes of the modern Western state may come to be.[17]

The outrages inflicted on humankind by the Nazi regime remain sufficiently vivid to provide effective warnings of the dangers implicit in a theory of human nature founded on a crude biologism. But the perils residing in the theory of complete malleability of human character and personality seem less apparent, especially to those committed to rapid and fundamental changes in social arrangements.[18] Yet liberal societies have traditionally eschewed doctrines of extreme environmentalism in fashioning their policies.[19] The liberal assumption has been that there are certain basic attributes of human nature that may be modified but not eradicated, that there are certain things that a society and its agencies cannot achieve and ought not to undertake. Indeed, no intellectual stance is more subversive of liberal values than Oceania's postulate of the total malleability of human nature. Paradoxically, the dangers of the concept may be enhanced when those possessed of political power are motivated by goals of social well-being. For if an idyllic human condition is within the capacities of organized society, if thoughts and deeds of individuals can be conditioned to achieve some all-encompassing harmony that realizes the full possibilities of human existence, then those exercising political power may feel morally mandated to subject the most intimate aspects of human life to extreme state interventions. Concepts like human freedom, dignity, and privacy may prove insufficient to contain policy founded on such assumptions.[20]

An attack on the private worlds as deliberate and all-encompassing as that of Oceania must be regarded as nothing short of an effort to extirpate the fact of uniqueness in human life. It must be seen, at the same time, as a crusade to destroy the remnants of the pluralistic society that arose in the Western world and that expresses, however imperfectly, the value of the human individual. Orwell's imagined society thus poses disturbing issues. What forms of individualism are tenable in our time? How, in a technological age which makes totalitarian societies possible, are the values of individuality to be preserved?

Orwell's delineation of a society committed to the destruction of private worlds may be seen as containing, among other things, an urgent message for the public policy of modern pluralistic states. An initial response to the novel's forebodings might take a form such as this: if the preservation of the values of human individuality depends on the drawing and maintaining of clear lines separating the public realm from the private, let us by all means build walls about the private worlds; let us build them boldly and high, and defend them against any who would weaken or penetrate them. Yet reflection on the nature of human aspirations and human affairs quickly leads to the conviction that exhortation is not enough, that the defense of the private realm in our time requires more than good will and moral fervor. One way to give point and poignancy to Orwell's vision is to inquire why threats to private worlds have arisen in Western culture and why the defense of the privacy value is beset by such formidable difficulties. In identifying the nature of the difficulties reference will be made at several points to the ambivalent treatment given the privacy value in American law. The legal experience is worth pursuing not because the aspects it presents are necessarily the most important of our concerns, but rather because in the law one often finds the most precise and abundant evidence bearing on the character and magnitude of the problems to be confronted. One looks to the law, then, for insights about the nature of the particular problems encountered in the defense of private worlds and why they are so hard.

The concept of the private world is obviously central to the liberal society, but support for the value has not been confined to the recent centuries of the modern era since that society came into being. The Christian tradition, for example, not only maintains the distinction between what is God's and Caesar's, but also separates the public from the private and emphasizes the importance of the latter to the living of a sanctified life.[21] Nineteen hundred years after the birth of Christ, that which is trivial, seductive, and evil continues to be described in many churches and households by the word *worldly*. Much else in the Western cultural tradition reinforces the privacy value, as, for example, Montaigne's temperate disquisition on the legitimacy and pleasures of solitude.[22]

Yet deep countercurrents emerged early in the history of Western culture and continue strong in modern America. The society envisioned in Plato's *Republic* is one in which the good life is conducted in the public world almost to the exclusion of the private.[23] The persisting populist and egalitarian tendencies in American society have often weakened defense of the privacy value, the concept of a protected private world being seen at times as elitist and at others as sinister.[24]

In the post-Vietnam, post-Watergate world, new and exotic manifestations of populist attitudes have burgeoned, many of which express hostility to the private world. One prominent attribute of the Vietnam college generation was its tendency to confuse the personal and the political.[25] Similar confusions plague the larger society, and identifying the boundaries that separate the public from the private creates continuing uncertainty and unease. Characteristic phenomena of the present and recent past include the rise of investigative journalism under the banner of "the people's right to know," the flourishing of the gossip industry, "sunshine" laws, the encounter movement. Resistance to the ideal of "openness" either in professional or private life has become for many the deadly secular sin. Suspicion of or hostility to the privacy value in contemporary America, however, represents more than a fad or an aberration of the popular culture. Similar suspicions have been expressed in sober social analysis. Some of the analysts have found little more in the defense of the private world than a pathological effort to escape legitimate social obligations and involvements. This strand of thought, although encompassing great diversity of expression and assumptions, tends on the whole to see in the search for privacy evidence of alienation.[26]

The epidemic of alienation, the weakening of social purposes in American society, the "Balkanization" of American politics into narrow limited-issue interest groups, have all attracted the serious concern of thoughtful observers, and rightly so.[27] If in fact such afflictions are the product of the liberal society's allegiance to the privacy value, its costs are substantial indeed. There is reason to doubt, however, that the critics' indictment can be sustained.

Underlying the argument of some of the critics is the assumption that the private and public worlds coexist in a state of antagonistic rivalry, that enhancement of the former is most often achieved at the expense of the latter. There are probably few in these times who do not share the critics' concern for the state of our public life or who would contest the proposition that loyalites in American society are often too narrowly drawn and that social purposes wither and languish. Nor is it possible to give assurances that privacy will not often be used for ignoble and selfish ends, just as other great privileges such as freedom of speech or of economic enterprise may be employed in destructive and inhumane activity. These concessions, however, do not detract from the assertion that enhancement of the quality of the public life, if it occurs, will result, not from the weakening, but the strengthening of the private worlds. The flourishing of liberal societies entails a movement of energy, thought, and humane objectives from the private to the public realms. It is in the private worlds that friendship, compassion, and the other life-enhancing values are first and most strongly experienced. Such virtues are not likely to be reflected in public life if their movement from the private world is obstructed or weakened.

The rewards of the private world are gained principally by persons who have attained some measure of autonomy and personhood. Indeed, for those who have failed to achieve these qualities, privacy may constitute not a blessing but a terror. For such, privacy becomes equated with loneliness, alienation, anomie. One recalls the observation of Søren Kierkegaard: "[P]eople shudder at solitude to such a degree that they know no other use to put it to but (oh, admirable epigram!) as a punishment for criminals."[28] Perhaps persons of complete autonomy do not require solitude to discover who they are, what they believe, and how to stand against the compulsions of the state or the forces of conformity in their society. But whether such perfectly autonomous beings exist may be doubted. Even the great religious leaders of the past reveal careers of withdrawal and reentry into the world of their fellows. Moreover, high levels of autonomy are not attained all at once. They are secured in a process of becoming, and the process includes periods of withdrawal into the private world. This is not a prescription for alienation, but rather of constructive socialization.[29] That, at least in our culture, a modicum of privacy enhances rather than obstructs socialization is suggested by the American utopian experiments in the nineteenth century and the more recent history of the kibbutz in Israel. In both instances the fact of extreme group surveillance appears to have eroded community cohesiveness rather than strengthened it.[30]

A much more persuasive diagnosis of alienation in modern society locates its causes not in the pursuit of privacy, but rather in losses in the reality and the sense of personal autonomy. The commitment to social purposes is weakened, in part because of a widespread perception of the futility of individual effort in defining and achieving social goals. A sense of helplessness is produced by the vulnerability of the individual in every aspect of his life to the aggressions of state power and those of the giant aggregations of private wealth. The feeling is enhanced by the manifold invasions of areas formerly deemed part of the private realm, and, perhaps equally importantly, by apprehensions of greater incursions in the future. The damage done by the telescreens in Winston Smith's world stems not alone from the fact that he is under actual surveillance and hence stripped of power to control what information about himself is communicated to the state. It arises also from the fact that he is uncertain when Big Brother is watching or whether his surveillance ever ceases. Again, it should not be overlooked that political alienation of many persons in American society, in particular many members of the intelligentsia, has resulted from a political style, populist in origin, that reveals small regard for personal privacy and at times results in gross assaults upon the private worlds of individuals. The McCarthy era, to cite only one series of events, confirmed the antipolitical biases of many intellectuals, attitudes founded on over a century of American experience.[31] There is ample reason to suppose that the losses in personal autonomy that underlie alienation are exacerbated by the invasions of the private world characteristic of modern technological society. If this is true in any significant part, the indicated response is not the further constriction of the private world but rather its more effective defense.

Nineteen Eighty-Four's affirmation of the importance of the private world to human interests and humane values eases the burden of its modern defenders. It is, however, one thing to affirm, quite another to define and protect. These latter difficulties reveal themselves most clearly in the legal experience, and consulting that history may contribute to their understanding. The private world encompasses some of the most basic of human aspirations; inevitably such aspirations are reflected in jurisprudential reflections and in the definitions of legal rights. Yet the "legalization" of the private world gives rise to perplexing problems, and its results are often tentative and unsatisfactory.

The difficulties are in the first instance conceptual in nature. Privacy has proved to be a mercurial idea, one difficult to capture within the confines of a legal formula. Not all privacy claims are of the same kind or of similar importance. They arise in extraordinary profusion, and they tend to adopt the coloration of the particular context from which they arise. The rights of privacy visualized in the law of torts to protect individuals from unwelcome public exposure by other private persons are significantly different from the constitutional right against compelled inquiry by the state or against the unsanctioned invasion of homes or papers by police functionaries. The right of a woman to determine when or if she is to bear a child is different from either.

Although the privacy value is the subject of considerable legal attention, no completely satisfactory analytical structure defining and supporting the various privacy interests has to date emerged. In such a situation the disorderly conduct of concepts can be anticipated, and that expectation is amply realized in much of the judicial literature. Some judges have promoted a bold and imperialistic expansion of the privacy concept. Thus in the well-known case of *Griswold v. Connecticut* Justice Douglas for the Court invalidated a state statute that provided criminal penalties for "any person who uses any drug . . . or instrument for the purpose of preventing conception."[32] The interest that the state statute was said to have offended was a constitutional right of privacy. And where does the right come from? It is not to be found in the express language of the Constitution, said Justice Douglas; the right has its origins in "emanations" from the "periphery" of several Bill of Rights provisions.[33] But why the privacy rationale? The Fourteenth Amendment forbids a state to deny "liberty" without due process of law, and the injury done by the statute might be thought to fit comfortably into that historical category. But the category had been engulfed in all too much history. "Substantive due process" doctrines were employed by the old Court at the turn of the century to invalidate such legislation as that limiting the hours of labor of workmen, and the present majority was unwilling to revive doctrines tainted by such uses in the past.[34]

Since the case of *Meyer v. Nebraska* in 1923, the Supreme Court has announced a small number of decisions, including those in the abortion cases,[35] that are said to delineate a sphere of interests, denominated privacy concerns, in such areas as marriage, procreation, and child rearing.[36] The cases are, as one commentator observed, "a rag-tag lot."[37] Many of them appear to speak principally to values other than those now attributed to them. How broadly or narrowly the constitutional right of privacy is to be drawn in the future, and by what processes of reasoning such questions are to be resolved or even thought about, remains obscure. These efforts of the Court to give constitutional definition to the privacy interest are not the products of principled decision making, and whatever social benefits they confer do not include that of strengthening the rule of law.

A very different and perhaps equally dubious reaction to the privacy value can be found in the reductionist positions taken by other courts and by some legal commentators. These writers and judges, far from urging an amorphous inflation of the privacy concept, believe it in most situations to be extraneous and unnecessary. Typically, it is said, questions of privacy are associated with other interests and values— interests in reputation, in the protection of property from trespass or appropriation, and the like. Proper resolution of such disputes is facilitated by proceeding directly to the consideration of such interests unencumbered by reference to the privacy concept.[38]

It may be doubted, however, that such a rigorous purging of privacy from the vocabulary of the law best serves our long-term interests.[39] It is clear that in much modern discourse, both within and outside the legal arena, there is reluctance to confront fundamental issues of the private world and that the shyness is often displayed even when the privacy concern is real and in need of identification and consideration. The tendency to evade basic issues may well be encouraged by the absence of an established conceptual system persuasively and usefully articulating the privacy values. Thus in the debates that have arisen from time to time in the last two decades concerning the use of lie detectors in the hiring practices of public and private employers, discussion tends to wind down in questions about the technical reliability of the polygraph, leaving fundamental concerns of human dignity unidentified and unanalyzed.[40] The use of so-called rehabilitative techniques on persons convicted of crime or suffering from mental disorder, especially such procedures as psychosurgery, aversive conditioning, and extreme drug therapies, tends to be opposed, if opposed at all, on grounds that they do not work, are unreliable, or produce unfortunate side effects. Remaining unstated and unconsidered are questions of the propriety in a liberal society of the government's manipulation of human beings by penetrating or engulfing their conscious defenses.[41]

The difficulties encountered in the legal defense of the private world, however, are not confined to problems of definition and articulation, important as these matters are to the life of the law. Even more significant is the circumstance that the claims of the private realm are by their nature contingent rather than absolute. In a famous dissenting opinion, Justice Brandeis referred to a "right to be let alone— the most comprehensive of the rights and the right most valued by civilized men."[42] Yet clearly no individual can be both in society and also wholly immune to its demands. The right to be let alone, however broadly drawn, will not prevent government from limiting individual volition and penetrating solitude by insisting, for example, that persons maintain their premises in ways that do not offend the health, fire, or building code, or hand over substantial fractions of their wealth and income to the tax collector. The values of the private world are not our only values, and the defense of that world consists largely in struggles over where boundaries dividing the private from the public and the social are to be drawn. Unhappily there is no calculus that unfailingly locates the borders of these realms in positions guaranteeing optimum social and personal advantages. In a liberal state, unlike Oceania, attacks on the private realm are ordinarily launched by those who, often sincerely, profess attachment to the privacy value, but who in the particular instance urge that a larger value is gained by a constriction of the private world.

There is, of course, nothing surprising in this. The fashioning of all basic legal and constitutional immunities involves problems of balancing interests and values (although some have dreamed that First Amendment rights can be defined as absolute).[43] Seeking equilibrium between centrifugal and centripetal tendencies is the constant preoccupation of liberal societies. Yet if the problems of maintaining the values of the private world are not unique in this respect, their defenders are, nevertheless, often in positions of comparative disadvantage. In a world of conflicting values and interests the most important question may often be, who has the burden of persuasion? It might be thought that, given the importance of the private world to the most fundamental liberal values, the onus of proof should be placed on those who seek to justify invasions of the private realm on the ground that larger social interests are being served. In many areas of American law and policy precisely the opposite presumption is being applied. Paul Freund observed over thirty years ago that "on the whole, the active proselyting interests have been given greater sanctuary [in our law] than the quiet virtues or the right of privacy."[44] Although the intervening decisions of the Supreme Court, of course, do not demonstrate the tendency with complete consistency, the proposition remains essentially valid.[45]

An especially stern test of our commitment to privacy values is to be found in the area of criminal law enforcement. Before the decision of the abortion cases and their antecedents, the lawyer speaking of "the rights to privacy" was most likely referring to the protections afforded by the Fourth Amendment to the United States Constitution. The contingent nature of those rights is made apparent in the language of the amendment itself. It is only "unreasonable" searches and seizures that are forbidden. Privacy may be invaded and papers and other evidence seized, provided formalities of justification have been satisfied and the official conduct does not transgress the scope of the authorization. Nevertheless, the bulwark of the Fourth Amendment is constantly besieged by claims of social interest and expediency and for constriction of the rights it protects.[46] It may be instructive to consider why this is true.

The first and perhaps most important reason is that Fourth Amendment privacy rights are most often asserted by persons who have something criminal to hide. In a period of extreme public sensitivity to crime, like the present, many in the community tend to regard the Fourth Amendment simply as a refuge for felons. Attitudes of this sort are strongly represented in contemporary conservative political movements. At first glance this may appear paradoxical, for all experience testifies that in the administration of criminal justice, governmental power frequently oversteps its proper bounds; and the containment of the public force in these areas for the protection of individual and group values may be regarded as an essentially conservative objective. What might be seen as a natural and inevitable concern of the American conservative, however, is often neutralized by a perception that relegates most criminal defendants asserting rights of privacy to the category of "the others," persons whose interests are wholly separate from and antagonistic to his own. The "criminal classes," a phrase much used by affluent persons in nineteenth-century Britain and the United States, captures this sense of distance with great precision. The dichotomy of the criminal and noncriminal classes is strengthened when, as in modern America, criminal tendencies are widely seen as the particular attributes of racial and ethnic minorities.[47]

Even when privacy values in criminal justice administration are identified and it is recognized that a police establishment ignorant of and hostile to such values constitutes, in the long run, a peril to the entire community, the claims of privacy may be perceived as weak, speculative, and remote when compared to the insistent demands of law enforcement. Vigorous judicial enforcement is also inhibited by the fact that courts are agencies of government and under constraint to permit legislatures and administrative personnel to perform, and within limits to define, their own functions. Once the legislature initiates a penal policy that, for example, criminalizes the use of drugs and alcohol, gambling, and certain forms of sexual expression, the courts will often respond by conceding authority to the enforcement agencies to perform their difficult duties; and the concessions tend toward the limitation of constitutional inhibitions on governmental action. However persuasive the case for contemporary penal policy in these areas, the fact plainly stated is that it has substantially constricted the boundaries of the private world in American society.[48]

The implications of these developments are more somber than is sometimes understood. A contagion effect sets in. Attitudes formed in the context of counterespionage or organized crime are readily transmittable to surveillance of the activities of politically suspect groups or even of political rivals. Watergate taught us that.[49] Sometimes in responding to the exigent claims of law enforcement the courts with insufficient awareness appear willing to open wide the gates of the private world to state power. In the famous "pen register" case, a prevailing majority of the present Supreme Court held that the government, without a warrant, may acquire evidence of the phone numbers dialed by a suspected person, apparently on the ground that because the caller necessarily discloses this information to the telephone company it cannot be deemed private.[50] Yet in an interdependent technological society one cannot function or even survive without a plethora of limited disclosures. If the tendency of this decision continues and if, as against government, the citizen is not permitted to maintain the limitations on his limited disclosures, then we shall have ceded an enormous tract of the private world to uninhibited state scrutiny.

The canvass of dilemmas and difficulties encountered in the legal experience does not and is not intended to suggest that the record of the law in defining and protecting the limits of the private world is simply one of waste and futility. In Oceania there is no law, and maintenance of the values of human individuality is hardly conceivable without it. Yet if the private world is to have meaning in the postmodern age, we must be disabused of the notion that all that is required of us is to permit the law to undertake its initiatives and pursue its objectives. The law ultimately reflects the struggle of interests and values going forward in society, and the future of law is one of the interests at stake in the struggle. That there are dimensions to the social and ethical issues in dispute that transcend the merely legal is best demonstrated by a scrutiny of the legal experience itself.[51]

Given a political society as intent as Oceania's to blot out the past, it is perhaps not surprising that the reader of the novel is left in doubt about how the regime, firmly ensconced in Winston Smith's day, had established itself. Orwell tells us only a little about the events that led to the reality of 1984. Although the history of the previous half-century is shadowy, one deduces that Oceania did not emerge from an established Hitler-like or Stalin-like dictatorship. Rather it appears in some way to have evolved principally from the Western capitalist societies of Britain and the United States. One suspects that a warning is being issued here, and the suspicion is strengthened when Orwell is found writing in one of his best-known late essays, "In our age, the idea of intellectual liberty is under attack from two directions. On the one side are its threatened enemies, the apologists of totalitarianism, and on the other its immediate, practical enemies, monopoly and bureaucracy" (*CEJL* 4:367–68).

The notion that the modern threat to individual autonomy and the other values fostered by the private world comes not alone or even principally from the state, but rather from society itself, has been frequently advanced in the recent past. The great dichotomy is not that of public and private; it is that of the social and the private.[52] In short, it is modern culture that subverts the private world, and, according to some who have addressed the question, the true issue is how the grip of society can be eased or the culture overthrown. One striking aspect of the analysis is the fact that it is embraced by persons occupying positions along the entire ideological spectrum. The attack on modern Western culture is joined by proponents of the liberal society, but more especially by representatives of the political left and of the political right.[53]

Before proceeding with a consideration of the argument and the evidence invoked to support it, one preliminary matter requires attention. Either as a political tactic or as a rhetorical embellishment, some who attack Western society as depersonalizing and hence as dehumanizing have argued that the true enemy of the private world is not the state and that the defenders of that world need not maintain their traditional wariness of state intrusion.[54] Such assurances convey no conviction and deserve no credit. Any governmental organism commanding the sorts of electronic and computer technology that are available today in all developed nations must be regarded not simply as a potential but as an active antagonist of the private world. Any government, like our own, that supports a National Security Agency with technical capacity to sweep the atmosphere and collect radio messages in the process of transmission, to identify and record them, has earned our serious concern. This is all the more true when the agency has over the years often acted with dubious legality, and has displayed a consistent impatience with statutory, administrative, and constitutional restraints on its operations.[55] We shall ill serve our vital interests if in our haste to indict Western culture we underestimate the current massive and burgeoning threat of state power.

Yet one need not assume the diminishment of the political threat to recognize the force of the argument of those who indict modern culture for its devastating effects in the private realm. According to the picture drawn, the inhabitants of the Western world, with its mass media, mindless popular entertainment, and advertising, are being manipulated and conditioned, not in the fashion of Oceania's tyrannical rule over Party members like Winston Smith and Julia, but rather in a manner closer to its handling of the lower orders of society, the proles. An even more direct literary expression of the thesis is found in a work of the late Per Wahlöö, the well-known Swedish writer of detective fiction. The book, known in this country under the title *Murder on the Thirty-First Floor*, pictures a society in which all means of public communication have fallen under the control of a single private corporation. The resulting censorship and thought control exceeds anything that could possibly be achieved by the state through force. Community acceptance of the monopoly is gained, first, through corrupting the public taste by providing an unrelieved diet of pap and drivel. "The cover word for this," it is remarked, "is 'harmless entertainment.' "[56] For the small minority of critical intellectuals not amenable to control by such means, the corporation devises a different tactic. A journal of social and literary criticism is established. Contributors are well paid and allowed complete freedom to attack any aspect of social life. The magazine is carefully edited and printed month after month, year after year—but the issues are never circulated.

The picture painted in this critique is one of a culture that incapacitates persons from valuing or making fruitful use of the private world. In *Nineteen Eighty-Four* the telescreen that may be dimmed but never turned off constitutes a primary symbol of the state's intrusions into the private lives of its subjects. Yet how great are the differences between such a society and one in which persons who because of cultural constraints, loneliness, apathy, and diminished sense of personhood can never bring themselves to turn off the television set? And what is seen on television may often consist of education in the devaluation of privacy. Much of the "harmless entertainment" consists of revelations into the intimate lives of media personages. Recently a columnist in a women's magazine gushed, "I now wake up . . . to find myself in the midst of a coast-to-coast explosion. Suddenly everybody is gossiping—freely, presumably unguiltily and loving it."[57] A journal of large circulation and as bereft of redeeming social purpose as can well be imagined, in a triumph of distortion and euphemism, advertises itself as attractive to persons "with inquiring minds." If, even with their complicity, we scrutinize the lives of public personalities as if they were animals in a zoo, have we not suffered losses in human dignity of all persons and reduced the value of privacy in our own lives?[58]

Other expressions of the policy of Oceania have been identified in contemporary Western society. We are developing, some have said, our own versions of Newspeak. Thus Herbert Marcuse argued that the technological culture promotes a language of overwhelming concreteness, highly functional in character, ill adapted to conceptual thinking, and discouraging to criticism and evaluation.[59] Perhaps of more immediate concern is our apparent inability to inculcate language facility of any sort in many of our young. Because it has become familiar it no longer startles us that it is possible for young persons to complete their studies in what are ostensibly the great universities without gaining a command of language above the level of technical literacy and without acquiring sufficient understanding of language to respect it. Such persons are deprived of a capacity essential to autonomy, and lack adequate defenses against the aggressive inroads of political propaganda and cultural imperatives into their private worlds.

It is argued by critics on the right that the very assumptions of a liberal society unleash the assaults of popular culture on certain vital aspects of privacy. The unrestrained license of speech and publication mandated by that society denies refuges and living space free from recurrent manifestations of overt sexuality to individuals and families desiring such freedom.[60] Even the huckstering of hammers and saws takes place in a synthetic atmosphere of blatant sensuality, even the sale of candy bars to children. These phenomena are importantly implicated in the rise of political activism within fundamentalist religious groups. Such activism may at first appear inconsistent with one important strand of the fundamentalist tradition, the premillennialist stance. According to this view, culture and politics are irredeemable, and efforts at social reform are both futile and pernicious: the latter because such activity diverts the faithful from the truly essential tasks of personal salvation and the conversion of others.[61] The proper stance thus requires disregard of and separation from the larger society. But members of these groups have discovered that separation is increasingly difficult to achieve. Modern culture, particularly through the media and the public schools, penetrates the bastions that they have thrown around themselves and their families.[62] The aggressive political program of the fundamentalists may rest less on optimism about the redemption of American society than on a determination to make effective their separation from the moral contaminations of society. It reflects a purpose to construct areas of privacy for themselves, however destructive the agenda may be to the autonomy and privacy of persons committed to different values and perceptions. The liberal society thus creates its own enemies, and provides them with their most effective weapons.

The critique of modern culture is many-faceted, but the overarching allegation is that it produces human beings crippled in character and personality, incapable of autonomy, lacking in identity, leading lives of despair, and prone to violence. One recalls a recent rash of instances of persons falsely claiming to have found dangerous foreign objects in packaged food and drugs. Most often motivation for the claims appears to include a thirst for attention, a craving for an identity created by a minute's exposure before a television camera. If it is argued that the behavior is merely that of a lunatic fringe, the answer is that the form a society's lunacy takes may have much to say about the attributes of the prevailing culture. The tendency in American society to identify fame with notoriety is surely not one confined to an eccentric few. There is reason to suspect that the tendency points to a weakening of the sense of self, a shrinking of what Erikson calls "ego identity": in short, a condition in many persons that renders the concept of the private world unfathomable and ultimately frightening.[63]

In an almost perfect phrase, Montaigne asserted that "a man must flee from the popular conditions that have taken possession of his soul."[64] It is hard advice. Given the force of the intrusions in the modern world, both those launched by the state and those created by the prevailing culture, where is the man to flee? And, even more difficult, how may the "popular conditions" be altered and made less threatening to his private realm? In much of the current literature, especially that coming from the left, a strong note of fatalism is sounded about the capacity of Western society to cure itself. That society, it is asserted, is impotent to confront the drift toward destruction of the private worlds by measures short of an overturning of social institutions and a complete recasting of social, political, and economic relations. If the prescription is rejected, then inevitably the Western world will keep its rendezvous with the cold day in April when the clocks are striking thirteen.

It is a somber forecast and one sufficiently buttressed by evidences and omens to be taken seriously. Yet the diagnosis and prescription are hardly disinterested. The cure proposed, moreover, may prove more virulent than the disease. Still, troubling questions persist: Is Western society any longer capable of producing and nourishing an individualism appropriate to the times? Will it prove able to hold back the threatened eclipse of the private worlds?

There may, indeed, be reason to hope that, despite evidences of decay, Western individualism is a hardier plant and its roots more firmly anchored than the critics of the modern state and contemporary culture allow. The values of human autonomy and uniqueness are susceptible of many forms of expression. Manifestations of the ideals that emerged in the early decades of the Industrial Revolution do not represent their only possible expressions. The rejection or modification of some earlier manifestations does not necessarily entail surrender of the values themselves. [65]

The critical issues in the defense of the private world may prove to be questions of will and strategy. There is evidence that the desire to promote and defend some privacy interests has waned. But not all the evidence points in the same direction. In the course of the past two decades a stronger outcry than ever before has been raised against certain intrusions into the private realm. The widespread protest against subliminal advertising supplies one illustration. A proliferation of statutory enactments dealing with a broad spectrum of privacy intrusions and a plethora of judicial decisions concerning related issues provide other examples. [66] It is true, of course, that the growing public sensitivity to at least some privacy issues and the reaction of legislatures and courts may itself constitute evidence of increasing and intensified assaults against the private world in the United States. Harold Laski once remarked that fundamental questions are only asked in a society whose body politic is diseased. [67] The burgeoning of law relating to the rights of individuals is indicative of a crisis of liberty that has persistently afflicted the Western world since World War I. But if modern concerns reflect an ominous challenge to the private world, they are also part of a defensive response. And response is vital to any hope that Oceania is not to be the ultimate destination of Western society.

There is irony and danger in the fact that a strategy for defense of the private world necessitates struggle in the public arena. Such a strategy necessarily entails more than the framing and enforcement of legal measures, but the existence of enforceable rights constitutes a vital part of it. The rise of electronic and computer technology and their ready availability to government and private business groups enormously complicates the devising of strategy. We cannot rid ourselves, even if we would, of these techniques. The genie of technology, having been let out of the bottle, cannot be forced back in. As a result the private world lies continuously under the shadow of power capable of being used for invading and obliterating the private realm. These exigencies, however, provide opportunities for the creation of policy. We are unable to eliminate such threats, but there are ample occasions for mandating uses of technology that minimize instead of magnify interferences with private lives. [68] Nor should the importance of the defense of privacy values by courts and legislatures to the development of personal attitudes be overlooked. Learned Hand once suggested that the freedoms of the First Amendment thrive only among a people capable of valuing them.[69] Yet it is also true that debates on freedom-of-speech issues in the Supreme Court since 1917 have done much to educate public attitudes, and that modern support of the values springs in important part from the advocacy of great judges, sometimes expressed in dissent.[70] So also adjudication of interests vital to the private world may contribute to the formation of a vigorous public opinion and hence produce effects going far beyond the particular issues adjudicated.

Yet there are limits on what may be demanded or expected from law and public policy. If the private world is successfully defended, the outcome will result in principal part from the importance that a great many individuals attach to the private realm and the uses to which they put it. It is surely not paradoxical that the survival or loss of the privacy value depends most importantly on what is done by individuals in their private lives. What is done may, in turn, depend importantly on how well institutions dedicated to cultivation of the life of the mind and aesthetic sensibility perform their tasks, and whether those efforts can escape submersion in the mindlessness this society spawns. There are no guarantees. The case for hope is an uneasy one, but this is a time when all liberal hopes rest on uneasy premises. As this becomes increasingly clear, many persons will return to *Nineteen Eighty-Four* to be reminded of what is at stake.

Notes

1. One recalls the provision in Orwell's will: "[I]n case any suggestion should arise I request that no memorial service be held for me after my death and that no biography shall be written." See Bernard Crick, *George Orwell: A Life* (Boston: Little, Brown, 1980), 404.
2. Perhaps the most useful general discussion of privacy and the issues of policy that surround it is still Alan F. Westin, *Privacy and Freedom* (New York: Atheneum, 1967). An interesting interdisciplinary canvass of views is provided in *Privacy*, ed. J. Roland Pennock and John W. Chapman (New York: Atherton, 1971). Cited in subsequent references as Pennock, *Privacy*.
3. In Ruth Gavison, "Privacy and the Limits of Law," (*Yale Law Journal* 89 [1980]:421) an important, if not entirely successful, effort is made to

define the essence of the privacy concept and to distinguish it from other values with which it is frequently associated.

4. George Orwell, *Nineteen Eighty-Four* (New York: Signet, 1981), 26. Subsequent page references to Orwell's novel will be included parenthetically in the text.

5. ". . . the state bears a burden of ensuring that a preponderance of good thoughts exists in the brains of the citizens." See Donald J. Munro, *The Concept of Man in Contemporary China* (Ann Arbor: University of Michigan Press, 1977), 53. The classic discussion of the "brainwashing" phenomenon is Robert Jay Lifton, *Thought Reform and the Psychology of Totalism* (New York: Norton, 1961).

6. *Caesar and Cleopatra* in *George Bernard Shaw: Seven Plays* (New York: Dodd, Mead, 1951), 407.

7. It is interesting that one of the most forcible statements of this point was made by Herbert Marcuse, whom many in the 1960s generation adopted as their mentor.

> Remembrance of the past may give rise to dangerous insights, and the established society seems to be apprehensive of the subversive contents of memory. Remembrance is a mode of dissociation from the given facts, a mode of "mediation" which breaks, for short moments, the omnipresent power of the given facts. Memory recalls the terror and the hope that passed. Both come to life again, but whereas in reality the former recurs in ever new forms, the latter remains hope. And in the personal events which reappear in the individual memory, the fears and aspirations of mankind assert themselves—the universal in the particular. (Herbert Marcuse, *One-Dimensional Man* [Boston: Beacon Press, 1964], 98–99.)

8. "Serious prose, in any case, has to be composed in solitude." "The Prevention of Literature" in *The Collected Essays, Journalism and Letters of George Orwell*, ed. Sonia Orwell and Ian Angus, 4 vols. (New York: Harcourt Brace Jovanovich, 1968), 4:68. Hereafter cited as *CEJL*.

9. Crick, *Orwell*, 406.

10. Orwell, "Writers and Leviathan," *CEJL* 4:408–9. Compare the comment of Albert Camus in *Resistance, Rebellion, and Death* (New York: Modern Library, 1963), 109.

> In the midst of such a din the writer cannot hope to remain aloof in order to pursue the reflections and images that are dear to him. Until the present moment, remaining aloof has always been possible in history. When someone did not approve he could always keep silent or talk of something else. Today everything is changed and even silence has dangerous implications. The moment that abstaining from choice is looked upon as choice and punished and praised as such, the artist is willy-nilly impressed into service.

See also Francis Allen, *The Crimes of Politics* (Cambridge, Mass.: Harvard University Press, 1974), 2–3.

11. See Orwell's review of Zamyatin's *We*, where the theme of constraints on intimacy in a totalitarian state is also developed (*CEJL* 4:73).

12. "[O]f all totalitarian regimes to date [the People's Republic] appears to be the most ambitious and determined to impose officially prescribed patterns of morality and of marital, family, and sex relationships. Its apparent aim is to 'politicize' all personal relationships and to obliterate any distinction between private and public concerns." See Paul Hollander, "Privacy: A Bastion Stormed," in *Twelve Problems of Communism* 6 (November-December 1963):1.

13. A fuller development of this theme may be found in Charles Fried, "Privacy," *Yale Law Journal* 77 (1968):475.

14. See Francis Allen, *The Decline of the Rehabilitative Ideal* (New Haven: Yale University Press, 1981), 66–68.

15. See John R. Silber, "Masks and Fig Leaves," in Pennock, *Privacy*, 235.

16. Isaiah Berlin, "Does Political Theory Still Exist?," in *Philosophy, Politics and Society*, 2nd ser., ed. Peter Laslett and Walter G. Runciman (Oxford: Blackwell, 1962), 22.

17. Not only in *Nineteen Eighty-Four* but also in Zamyatin's *We* and Aldous Huxley's *Brave New World* societies are described dedicated to changing the nature of persons through overwhelming the individual's conscious defenses. In Zamyatin's work a form of psychosurgery is described. "The latest discovery of our State science is that there is a center for fancy—a miserable little nervous knot in the lower region of the frontal lobe of the brain. A triple treatment of this knot with X-rays will cure you of fancy" (*We*, trans. Gregory Zilboorg [New York: E. P. Dutton, 1959], 167).

18. Cf. "We know of no relevant constraints placed on social processes by human biology. There is no evidence from ethnography, archeology, or history that would enable us to circumscribe the limits of possible human social organization. What history and ethnography do provide us with are the materials for building a theory that will itself be an instrument of social change." Sociobiology Study Group of Science for the People, "Sociobiology—Another Biological Determinism," in *The Sociobiology Debate*, ed. Arthur L. Caplan (New York: Harper and Row, 1978), 24–25.

19. For a discussion of Sigmund Freud's rejection of concepts of total malleability, see Paul Roazen, *Freud: Political and Social Thought* (New York: Knopf, 1968), 159, and Lionel Trilling, *Freud and the Crisis of Our Culture* (Boston: Beacon Press, 1955), 48, 53–55.

20. Allen, *The Rehabilitative Ideal*, 42–45.

21. ". . . study to be quiet, and to do your own business, and to work with your own hands as we commanded you." 1 Thess. 4:11. See Hannah Arendt, *The Human Condition* (Chicago: University of Chicago Press, 1958), 74.

22. *The Essays of Eyquem de Montaigne*, trans. Charles Cotton, in *Great Books of the Western World*, ed. R. M. Hutchins, 54 vols., vol. 25 (Chicago: Encyclopedia Britannica, 1952), bk. 1, essay 38.

23. ". . . Plato whose political plans foresaw the abolition of private property and an extension of the public sphere to the point of annihilating private life altogether." Arendt, *The Human Condition*, 30. The second chapter

of her work describes the nature of the distinction between the public and private realms in the classic age, and contrasts the modern situation (pp. 22–78).

24. Pennock, *Privacy*, xv; Westin, *Privacy and Freedom*, 27–28, 40.

25. It has recently been asserted that the leading figures in the 1960s cultural revolt "tended to obliterate the distinction between the personal and the public, to politicize their own private experiences and feelings, to see their own emotional condition as a social issue" (Meg Greenfield, "About John Lennon," *Newsweek*, 29 December 1980, 68). John Chapman wrote: "Strictly speaking, the relations of men who lack the capacity to enjoy and sustain privacy can be neither personal nor political; they must rather be said to be politicized. In their personalities, power will occupy the gap left by privacy, and their political manners will degenerate toward violence." See "Personality and Privacy" in Pennock, *Privacy*, 240.

26. Michael A. Weinstein has contributed a roll call of the modern critics, or in some cases opponents, of the privacy value and an analysis of their arguments: "The case for reducing privacy to some other condition has been argued along two lines. First, privacy may be interpreted as a fall from the primal condition of social communion or personal wholeness. If the argument proceeds in this way, privacy is itself evil and the demand for privacy is an expression of false consciousness. . . . Second, privacy may be interpreted as an anonymity which allows a person to escape from his social responsibilities" ("The Use of Privacy in the Good Life," in Pennock, *Privacy*, 88, 92).

27. On "Balkanization," see the comments of Kevin Phillips quoted in Norman J. Ornstein and Shirley Elder, *Interest Groups, Lobbying and Policymaking* (Washington, D.C.: Congressional Quarterly Press, 1978), 222. On the decline of social purposes see Allen, *The Rehabilitative Ideal*, 18–29, 86–89, and the materials there cited.

28. Søren Kierkegaard, *The Sickness Unto Death*, trans. Walter Lowrie (New York: Doubleday Anchor, 1954), 198.

29. Paul Freund, "One Concept or Many," in Pennock, *Privacy*, 195–96.

30. Westin, *Privacy and Freedom*, 59. See also Bruno Bettelheim, *The Children of the Dream* (New York: Macmillan, 1969), 251.

31. The most exhaustive treatment of this and related matters is to be found in Edward Shils, *The Torment of Secrecy: The Background and Consequences of American Security Policies* (Glencoe, Ill.: The Free Press, 1956). On the McCarthy era, see pp. 192–200.

32. 381 *United States Reports* (hereafter cited as U.S.) 479 (1965). The criminal defendants in the case were not marital partners who used birth control substances but rather employees of a birth control clinic who provided materials and instructions to clients and were charged as accessories to the statute's violations.

33. "The present case, then, concerns a relationship lying within the zone of privacy created by several fundamental constitutional guarantees." Idem, 485. See Robert Bork, "Neutral Principles and Some First Amendment Problems," *Indiana Law Journal* 47 (1971):1–35.

34. Two members of the Court, Justices Harlan and White, however, would have rested the decision on versions of due process theory.

35. These include such cases as *Meyer v. Nebraska*, 262 U.S. 390 (1923); *Pierce v. Society of Sisters*, 268 U.S. 510 (1925); *Skinner v. Oklahoma*, 316 U.S. 535 (1942); *Eisenstadt v. Baird*, 405 U.S. 438 (1972); *Roe v. Wade*, 410 U.S. 113 (1973).

36. Philip B. Heyman and Douglas E. Barzelay, "The Forest and the Trees: Roe v. Wade and Its Critics," *Boston University Law Review* 53 (1973): 765, 772–76.

37. Donald Regan, "Rewriting Doe v. Wade," *Michigan Law Review* 77 (1979): 1569, 1639.

38. A leading instance of this style of scholarship is to be found in William Lloyd Prosser, *Handbook of the Law of Torts*, 4th ed. (St. Paul: West Publishing Company, 1971), 804–14.

39. A considered attack on the "reductionists" is made in Gavison, "Limits of Law," 460–67. Compare Freund, "One Concept," 98: "It would be misleading to incorporate a right of privacy into a legal rule, it would be impoverishing to exclude it as the term of a legal principle."

40. Westin, *Privacy and Freedom*, 237–39.

41. Accounts of such procedures may be found in Stephen J. Chorover, *From Genesis to Genocide: The Meaning of Human Nature and The Power of Behavior Control* (Cambridge, Mass.: MIT Press, 1979), and Stephen J. Sansweet, *The Punishment Cure: How Aversion Therapy Is Being Used* (New York: Mason/Charter, 1965). See also Ralph Neville, "Ethical and Philosophical Issues of Behavior Control," delivered at American Association for the Advancement of Science, December 27, 1972, p. 4.

42. *Olmstead v. United States*, 277 U.S. 438, 478 (1928).

43. See, e.g., "Free Speech and Its Relation to Self-Government," in Alexander Meiklejohn, *Political Freedom: The Constitutional Powers of the People* (New York: Harper, 1960), 20–21; Laurent B. Frantz, "The First Amendment in the Balance," *Yale Law Journal* 71 (1962):1424.

44. Paul Freund, *On Understanding the Supreme Court* (Boston: Little, Brown, 1949), rev. and incorporated into *The Supreme Court of the United States: Its Business, Purposes and Performance* (Cleveland: World Publishing Co., 1961). It has been suggested that the preference for the active rather than the passive values has been manifest in other branches of the law. In Morton J. Horwitz, *The Transformation of American Law* (Cambridge, Mass.: Harvard University Press, 1977), it is argued that the emerging American property law in the early nineteenth century favored active, entrepreneurial values over those of "quiet enjoyment."

45. *Erznoznik v. Jacksonville*, 422 U.S. 205 (1975). In Richard A. Posner, "The Uncertain Protection of Privacy by the Supreme Court," *Supreme Court Review* 1979, p. 173, this decision is described as one in which the privacy value was improperly submerged in the interest of other values.

46. Outstanding discussions of the Fourth Amendment cases include Wayne Lafave, *Search and Seizure* (Boston: Little, Brown, 1978); Anthony Amsterdam, "Perspectives on the Fourth Amendment," *Minnesota Law Re-*

view 58 (1974):349; James B. White, "The Fourth Amendment as a Way of Talking About People," *Supreme Court Review*, 1974, p. 165.

47. See Allen, *The Rehabilitative Ideal*, 30–31.

48. Allen, "Majorities, Minorities, and Morals: Penal Policy and Consensual Behavior," *Northern Kentucky Law Review* 9 (1982):1.

49. Allen, *The Crimes of Politics*, 71.

50. *Smith v. Maryland*, 442 U.S. 735 (1979). See also *United States v. Miller*, 425 U.S. 435 (1976).

51. Some of the factors that limit the effectiveness of the law's defense of the private world stem from the fact that law and its institutions are part of the public realm. Thus a person suffering from an invasion of privacy by another may be deterred from seeking legal redress because the judicial proceeding may have the effect of publicizing even further whatever it may be that the complainant has wished to keep private.

52. The threefold division of human life into the public, the social, and the private appears with varying emphasis in the work of Arendt, *The Human Condition*, and Marcuse, *One-Dimensional Man*.

53. Thus on the left, see Marcuse, *One-Dimensional Man*, and, on the right, Walter Berns, "Privacy, Liberalism, and the Role of Government" in *Liberty and the Rule of Law*, ed. Robert L. Cunningham (College Station, Texas: Texas A & M University Press, 1979); Earnest Van den Haag, "On Privacy" in Pennock, *Privacy*, 149.

54. "The real enemy of privacy . . . today . . . is not government" (Berns, "Privacy, Liberalism, and the Role of Government," 214); Van den Haag, "On Privacy," 168. Cf. Marcuse, *One-Dimensional Man*, x.

55. See James Bamford, *The Puzzle Palace: A Report of America's Most Secret Agency* (Boston: Houghton Mifflin, 1982), *passim*, an indispensable book despite its literary deficiencies.

56. Per Wahlöö, *Murder on the Thirty-First Floor* (Stockholm: Norstedt, 1964; English ed., London: Joseph, 1966; Pantheon, 1982), 112.

57. LeBarre, "Gossip! Why We All Love It," *Family Circle* 66 (August, 1976).

58. Stanley Benn, "Privacy, Freedom, and Respect for Persons" in Pennock, *Privacy*, 14–15.

59. Marcuse, *One-Dimensional Man*, 94–95.

60. Berns, "Privacy, Liberalism, and the Role of Government."

61. The leading discussion is George M. Marsden, *Fundamentalism in American Culture: The Shaping of Twentieth-Century Evangelicalism, 1890–1925* (New York: Oxford University Press, 1980). It is, of course, true that other strands of fundamentalist belief mandated active involvement in public controversy, as in the temperance movement. See Marsden, *Fundamentalism*, 228. See also Joseph R. Gusfield, *Symbolic Crusade: Status Politics and the American Temperance Movement* (Urbana: University of Illinois Press, 1963).

62. The bizarre physical assault on Supreme Court Justice Byron White in the summer of 1982, it will be recalled, was justified by the attacker on the ground that television was bringing four-letter words into his home.

63. Cf. Chapman, "Personality and Privacy," in Pennock, *Privacy*, 248: "These reflections suggest that . . . the prospects for privacy depend on the num-

ber of persons who grow up psychically insecure. For these people would tend to become indifferent to privacy, both their own and that of others, and to seek relief in group identification and in symbolic aggression, or worse, in real aggression against the society and those they sense to be different."

64. Montaigne, *Essays*, 1:38.
65. Cf. Chapman, "Personality and Privacy," in Pennock, *Privacy*, 237.
66. A major piece of such legislation is the Privacy Act of 1974, 5 U.S.C.A. § 522a. The act contains the following congressional findings:

> (1) the privacy of an individual is affected by the collection . . . of personal information by Federal agencies. (2) the increasing use of computers and sophisticated technology . . . has greatly magnified the harm to individual privacy. . . . (4) the right to privacy is a personal and fundamental right protected by the Constitution of the United States. . . . (§2 Pub. L. 93-379 (1974))

Other federal statutes include the Privacy Protection Act of 1980, 42 U.S.C.A. §2000aa, aa5, 7, 11–12, and the Privacy Protection for Rape Victims Act of 1978, 28 U.S.C.A. App. §§412, 1103. Much comparable legislation has been enacted by the states. Thus an Associated Press dispatch, dated August 30, 1982, reported that all fifty states, Puerto Rico, and the District of Columbia now have laws regulating the privacy of criminal history records. As late as 1974 only nine states had such laws or regulations.

67. Harold Laski, *Political Thought in England from Locke to Bentham* (New York: H. Holt, 1920), 212.
68. Westin, *Privacy and Freedom*, 365–99.
69. Learned Hand, *The Spirit of Liberty: Papers and Addresses*, ed. Irving Dilliard, 3d ed. (New York: Knopf, 1960).
70. See especially the opinions of Justices Holmes and Brandeis in *Abrams v. United States*, 250 U.S. 616 (1919); *Gitlow v. New York*, 268 U.S. 652 (1925); *Whitney v. California*, 274 U.S. 357 (1927).

George Orwell
as Political Secretary of the Zeitgeist

W. Warren Wagar

Huxley versus Orwell

One of the less heated quarrels in modern literature and politics, but not one of the less grisly, pits Aldous Huxley against George Orwell. Both writers are remembered for novels depicting a hell half here already and soon to engulf us all. The question is, which vision hews more closely to the coming reality, *Brave New World* or *Nineteen Eighty-Four?*

Huxley, reviewing his own work near the end of his life, argued that although *Nineteen Eighty-Four* had looked more plausible in the darkest days of the Cold War, it was now (1958) pretty much out of date. *Brave New World* was plainly winning the race. In the age of Khrushchev, even the Soviet Union had learned that sugar works better than whips.[1]

Orwell was no longer available to fight back, but he did comment on *Brave New World* more than once in his abundant critical writings. In 1946, for example, he compared it unfavorably to Yevgeny Zamyatin's *We*, complaining that Huxley had missed a decisive point. His dictators had no motive to rule, neither economic exploitation nor "the desire to bully and dominate. There is no power hunger, no sadism, no hardness of any kind."[2] Orwell failed to see how such a society could arise or sustain itself. He put his money on *We*, and shortly thereafter, he invested the last precious remnant of his time and energy and health in the writing of his own version of *We*, which became *Nineteen Eighty-Four*.

Another quarter-century has passed since Huxley chided Orwell. Khrushchev has departed from the stage, along with his successor Brezhnev. The new incarnation of Big Brother is a former head of the Thought Police. The latest edition of Centrifugal Bumblepuppy is called Pac-Man, and someone by the name of Shultz has inherited the role of Mustapha Mond, although it will be a long time before we see a performance to rival that of Henry Kissinger.

In short, *Brave New World* and *Nineteen Eighty-Four* continue to sell briskly, and the debate drags on, between the partisans of Huxley

177

and Orwell, to determine which nightmare better describes the world system inexorably advancing to devour us.

The easiest way to settle the issue, as Erich Fromm once hinted, is to see *Brave New World* as a picture of the probable evolution of the Western industrial democracies and *Nineteen Eighty-Four* as a model of what mankind would be like under Soviet rule. But Fromm goes on to stress the underlying similarity of the two visions, and of Zamyatin's as well. Despite differences in detail, all three negative utopias agree that the worst thing imaginable is the demolition of personal freedom and identity by a bureaucracy of experts in human engineering.[3]

I concur with Fromm. In some measure because of Orwell, and Huxley and Zamyatin, and their many fellow dystopists—including C. S. Lewis, Kurt Vonnegut, Jr., Ray Bradbury, and Anthony Burgess—the abolition of the autonomous self is, indeed, the deepest fear of recent Western high culture. It is our collective Room 101.

But the qualifying phrase "in some measure" needs repeating. I am not the kind of intellectual historian who harbors fantasies about the omnipotence of the pen. All that the Orwells and Huxleys have done is to reinforce anxieties already well ensconced in Western consciousness. If the anxieties had not been long fermenting in our psychic underworld, the books that best articulate them would not have proved popular, and most likely would not even have been written.

Such a thought is, of course, horrifying to every true Orwell enthusiast, and might have spoiled his fun, too. Few intellectuals of Orwell's generation prized so highly their self-image as prowling lone wolves, despised and misunderstood by every faction, *au-dessus* (or *au-dessous*) *de la mêlée*. He even dressed as a lone wolf. His good friend Malcolm Muggeridge recalls their first meeting at a Fleet Street restaurant. Orwell turned up "in a sort of proletarian fancy dress; an ancient battered sports jacket and corduroy trousers, not actually tied up with string as in old comic drawings, but of the kind that could still be bought in those days in working-class districts and in seaside towns where fishermen live." Orwell looked quite odd, especially for an old Etonian. But in this, "as in other matters, Orwell was ahead of his time; his costume is now *de rigueur* in public schools and universities, and is more or less the uniform of the middle- and upper-class young."[4]

The point is not without significance. Orwell's hatreds, his values, his ideas, his tastes, even his affectations have prospered remarkably well in the decades since his death. His earlier books have been dusted off and revived. *Nineteen Eighty-Four* is the most influential single volume in the whole history of speculative or futurist fiction, surpassing even *Brave New World*.

But clearly George Orwell cannot take all the credit for himself.

He was just fortunate enough to be able to say precisely what everyone wanted to hear at precisely the time they wanted to hear it, with precisely the right penumbra of auxiliary illusions and preconceptions. What I mean by all this is not intended to be mysterious. George Orwell, his *Nineteen Eighty-Four*, his other writings, and the flesh-and-blood man who invented them all, Eric Blair, expressed the dominant world view in the high culture of late capitalism.

Before anyone rushes to the conclusion that I am a Marxist parrot angry with Orwell for tilting my perch or pissing on my crackers, let me ask a question. What *should* be the deepest fear of Western high culture in the period since 1949, when *Nineteen Eighty-Four* was first published? What is the surest, the most unambiguous, and the most overwhelming threat to mankind in the year 1984? Suppression of freedom by bureaucrats? Capitalist exploitation of workers? Pollution of the ecosystem by industrial wastes? Unemployment? Starvation and poverty in the Third World? Negative growth in the gross world product?

None of the above. Quite unforeseen by Karl Marx, the greatest horror confronting mankind in 1984, as in every other year since 1949, is the countdown to nuclear oblivion. It began in 1949, when the acquisition of fission bombs by the Soviet Union ensured a nuclear arms race.

Even before 1949, in the age of tanks, machine guns, U-boats, warplanes, and heavy artillery, close to one hundred million people lost their lives in wars, and civilization almost collapsed twice. Without question the good chance of a third and final world war should scare us more than anything. Without question it does not. In the Western bourgeois democracies what we fear most is the accelerating erosion of personal autonomy by the machinations of big government, or big business, or both. The Zeitgeist sets a higher value on the mystique of the self than on mere physical survival.

To appreciate this, just compare the quality in speculative fiction of fantasies of terminal wars with fantasies of all-engulfing superstates. The superstates win any comparison, hands down. Even when the terminal war tale is quite choice, on the order of Walter M. Miller's *A Canticle for Leibowitz* or Russell Hoban's *Riddley Walker*, it generally turns out that the author's chief obsession is the diabolical cleverness of modern man, rather than war or destruction as such. The same authors could have written the same novels and made the same points—well, more or less—without staging a nuclear world war at all.[5]

It may also be worth bearing in mind that Huxley and Orwell both erected their imaginary superstates in the ruins of imaginary Armageddons. The world of Our Ford came into being as a result of the horrors of the Nine Years' War. "There was a choice between World Control and destruction."[6] The baleful regimes of Big Brother and his counterparts in Eurasia and Eastasia see to it that no atomic wars of the sort that had ravaged the planet in the mid-1950s will ever occur again. War making continues, but on a limited basis, and entirely for domestic reasons. Just as freedom is really slavery, so war is really peace. And Orwell's protagonists, like Huxley's before them, do not thank Big Brother for the privilege of staying alive. What is staying alive, compared with being free? Better dead than Red.

Of course one may object that George Orwell was a fervent socialist, and therefore it is unfair to imply that he prized liberty above equality and above human life. Much ink has been spilled to defend or to assail Orwell's socialist credentials, but the argument seems pointless. He called himself a "democratic Socialist," and I am satisfied that during his last fifteen or twenty years on earth, he was just such a thing. The words are sufficiently elastic to permit many political thinkers of many shades of persuasion to shelter under them. Orwell made as plausible a socialist as most Englishmen of his generation who wore the badge.

For that matter, the mature Orwell belonged to a venerable line of socialists who can be traced well back into the nineteenth century. To adapt a phrase of Julian Symons, they were socialists of the heart rather than the slide rule,[7] writers like Charles Kingsley and William Morris, drawn to the cause by compassion or guilt or nostalgia for simpler ages, rather than by hard-boiled socioeconomic analysis and theory. Orwell was such a socialist.

He was also such a man, a man of the heart rather than science and reason. In the war of the world views, which has raged in the history of Western thought since at least the Renaissance, he pitched his tent in the camp of the romantics. Since a variant of romanticism has prevailed throughout the twentieth century among the avant-garde intellectuals and artists of the Western countries, Orwell's allegiance was well timed, and helps to explain his continuing popularity. As we shall see, the unique blend of views that Orwell espoused has given him a high standing not only with the avant-garde but also with a broader, middlebrow reading public.

The War of the World Views

Let me define my terms. As I use the phrase, a world view is closely akin to Wilhelm Dilthey's *Weltanschauung*, a set of orchestrated replies to the big questions about truth, beauty, goodness, and reality.[8] In the crudest terms, Western intellectual history since the Renaissance may be reduced to a struggle between essentially subjective and essentially objective world views.

At first, and continuing from medieval times, the dominant world view was a mixture of subjectivist Christian and Greek ideas, drawn chiefly from Platonism, with bits of Aristotle tossed in for good measure. By the late seventeenth century, at the time of Paul Hazard's *crise de la conscience européenne*, the paradigm had shifted to an objectivist value system grounded in the physics, mathematics, and logic of Descartes, Newton, and Locke. Near the close of the eighteenth century, beginning in the Germanic world, thought reverted to a more subjective configuration of basic assumptions, the romanticism of Goethe, the German idealists, Wordsworth, and Chateaubriand. The paradigm shifted once more in the middle decades of the nineteenth century, to the positivism of Comte and Mill and Zola. The latest shift dates from the end of the nineteenth and the early decades of the twentieth century, leading to the establishment of a new orthodoxy among the avant-garde, a neoromantic world view that has been variously dubbed anti-intellectualism, antipositivism, and irrationalism. Its harbingers were thinkers and artists such as Nietzsche, Freud, and Gauguin, and its partisans in the twentieth century proper have included at least three-quarters of our guiding spirits.

Caveats are in order. A world view may be "dominant," but in the history of modern Western civilization, it never enjoys exclusive possession of the available intellectual terrain. The previously dominant world view continues to wield influence and attract followers, as do still earlier *Weltanschauungen;* and near the end of its reign, the dominant world view has already called forth its dialectical opposite, which captures some of the best and the brightest of the oncoming generation.

Nor should one expect a given world view to flourish in a chemically pure state in any of its adherents. No mind of any depth or subtlety subscribes to the values of one world view, and one only. Traces of others are always detectable. The same is true of national cultures. Each arrives somewhat earlier or later at the dominant world view than other national cultures, and in each country the proportion of adherents to dissenters at the zenith point is somewhat different. The German-speaking world, for example, produced relatively fewer champions of the Enlightenment and of positivism than did the English- and French-speaking worlds.

Notice, too, that I define dominance as possession of the loyalties of the avant-garde, the intellectual and artistic cutting edge, where the "latest" and "newest" and most "original" ideas and values are circulating. In the 1770s, let us say, it was the poets and playwrights of the *Sturm und Drang* school who occupied the cutting edge in Germany. They helped shape the course of all Western literature for seventy years. In the 1840s, in the same country, the cutting edge of thought was occupied by such great debunkers of romanticism as

Feuerbach and Marx. But in good time what is advanced may become the property of everyone. The formulas of romantic music, to choose an extreme example, so advanced when they were invented by Beethoven and Schubert and Berlioz, are now embedded in the most commonplace film scores and jukebox ballads.

It follows that a world view is not a particular ideology or the philosophy of a class, but something like the costume in which Orwell appeared at the restaurant on Fleet Street, a set of intellectual and artistic clothes worn during a given epoch in the history of culture. At one time, one set of clothes is fashionable, and then the fashions change. As it happens, the more subjective world views tend to go down best with conservative or reactionary thinkers, and the more objective with radical thinkers, but there is no necessary correspondence between the two. It is quite possible (and quite common) for a socialist to be a romantic and for a reactionary to be a positivist. To some not inconsiderable extent the oscillation between world views of the two principal families is a function of the internal history of ideas. A given configuration of values, applied rigorously enough over a sufficient period of years, loses its freshness, becomes associated with sclerotic *doyens* of the various fields of endeavor, and must finally be overthrown by fierce young Turks.

To return now to the subject at hand, why should one categorize Orwell as a romantic or a neoromantic? In *Nineteen Eighty-Four*, for example, Winston is the quintessential romantic hero—apart from the flaw in his character that makes him too easy a prey for O'Brien—and a spokesperson for the romanticism in Orwell himself. At the same time, *Nineteen Eighty-Four* is a small masterpiece of irrationalist political thought. Twentieth-century intellectuals like it because it addresses some of the central themes of the currently ascendant world view. But the novel appeals to a broader public because it trades so skillfully on the now firmly established popular taste for the values of romanticism. It goes without saying that *Nineteen Eighty-Four* has also sold millions of copies because it makes effective propaganda for "our" side in the Cold War. Yet it would not be so effective if it were not so marvelously attuned to a wide array of reigning assumptions. The adverb is a tribute to Orwell, the literary craftsman. He did not invent the reigning assumptions.

All the same, how can one be certain of Orwell's affiliations in the war of the world views? Was he not, in many ways, an old-fashioned rationalist? Did he not devote some of his most scornful pages to assaults on the neoromantic quacks and faddists of his day?[9]

A superficial acquaintance with Orwell might yield all kinds of misleading impressions. He took no part, it is true, in the various formal revivals of irrationalist religiosity, including mysticism, that afflicted his contemporaries. He was not a philosophical idealist. Unlike so many irrationalists, he did not deny the existence of an objectively knowable external universe. Breaking down faith in such a universe was perhaps the foremost objective of O'Brien's brainwashing of Winston in *Nineteen Eighty-Four*. Even Orwell's way of expressing himself seems to identify him with an older generation. He wrote in a particularly clear, straightforward prose style, prose "like a window pane,"[10] and his novels generally follow the techniques and conventions of Edwardian realism.

But it is literally impossible for any one writer to embrace all the modes of expression of a given world view, even if he belongs to it heart and soul. Orwell's quarrels with his fellow neoromantics were intramural affairs, and even when he appeared to lean toward positivism, he was often not leaning in that direction at all.

A good place to make a start in unraveling Orwell's thought is Bernard Crick's superb and sympathetic biography, and especially its introductory essay, which offers Crick's assessment of the man and his work. In discussing Orwell's journalism and essays, the most explicit sources of his ideas, Crick notes that certain themes recur.

> . . . love of nature, love of books and literature, dislike of mass production, distrust of intellectuals, suspicion of government, contempt for and warnings against totalitarianism, advice on making, mending or growing things for yourself, anti-imperialism and anti-racialism, detestation of censorship, and praise of plain language, plain speaking, the good in the past, decency, fraternity, individuality, liberty, egalitarianism and patriotism.[11]

As I count the items on this revealing list (none is omitted), a little more than half could be advocated by exponents of any world view, depending on the definitions of terms and the reasons chosen for advocacy. The others, such as "love of nature," "dislike of mass production," "advice on making, mending or growing things for yourself," and "praise of . . . the good in the past," are characteristically romantic and neoromantic themes. Not one is unambiguously positivist or neopositivist. There is nothing about science and reason, nothing about objectivity and empiricism, nothing in a favorable sense about law or logic or technology or mathematics or the material base of social relations and the natural order.

But a list of themes is only suggestive. We must dig deeper. Above all, we must apply pick and shovel to Orwell's political thought, its negations and its affirmations alike.

Orwell's Politics: Negations

The ruling passions of George Orwell's political conscience were never obscure. What he most feared was the subjection of the individual to the domination of experts in behavioral engineering, although he would not have described his villains in quite those terms. He saw them as tyrants, drunk on a limitless thirst for power, who used brainwashing, thought control, terror, torture, and the unrelenting bureaucratic regulation of every facet of life as means to their satanic ends. What Orwell most treasured was the autonomous self, the self-determined, self-disciplined, hard, active man who stands alone and bows his head to no one.

First, his fear. It was a matter both of fear and of loathing. Orwell spent much of his brief literary career jousting with his fellow intellectuals, not in a spirit of amiable rivalry, but in anger. He ridiculed the flower children of his day for their supposed softness and rootlessness, but he saved his hottest anger for what might be called the professional intellectuals: men and women with well-developed creeds, the brainy, the cliquish, the superior folk who had no real faith in the working man, and who, he knew in his bones, were always obscenely eager to prostitute themselves in the service of absolute power. As he commented in 1942, such people liked to run in packs, each of which lasted about five years.

> I have been writing long enough to see three of them come and two go—the Catholic gang, the Stalinist gang, and the present pacifist, or, as they are sometimes nicknamed, Fascifist gang. My case against all of them is that they write mentally dishonest propaganda and degrade literary criticism to mutual arse-licking.[12]

Orwell did not limit his scorn to small fashionable literary cliques. Whenever he had an opportunity to view the intelligentsia in the round, as in his wartime volume on the outlook for socialism in England, *The Lion and the Unicorn*, he reviled them without mercy. The working man was splendid, even the upper classes were morally sound, although misguided and oppressive, but the intellectuals . . . ! All through the 1930s this unruly lot, Orwell wrote, had badly weakened national morale, never offered a single "constructive suggestion," and indulged in "irresponsible carping." Intellectuals exhibited the "emotional shallowness" of people "who live in a world of ideas and have little contact with physical reality." Severed from "the common culture of the country," they could do little but whore after foreign ideologies like Marxism. "The Bloomsbury highbrow," he concluded, "with his mechanical snigger, is as out of date as the cavalry colonel."[13]

The same strictures appeared again in 1947 in *The English People*, one of Orwell's most insufferably charming efforts, where he dismissed the British intelligentsia "from Carlyle onwards" as a herd of power-worshiping Machiavellians.

> The ruthless ideologies of the Continent—not merely communism and fascism, but anarchism, Trotskyism, and even ultramontane Catholicism—are accepted in their pure form only by the intelligentsia, who constitute a sort of island of bigotry amid the general vagueness.[14]

The English common man, Orwell noted in still another essay, "is still living in the mental world of Dickens, but nearly every modern intellectual has gone over to some form of totalitarianism."[15]

Examples could be multiplied, but there is really no need. D. A. N. Jones, in his "Arguments against Orwell," does a good job of reviewing the wholesale denunciation of the English intellectuals in which Orwell indulged, and there are ample scholarly analyses of the matter by William Steinhoff and Alex Zwerdling, among others.[16] Although Steinhoff and Zwerdling let Orwell off too easily, they quote him at length, and his fury speaks for itself.

In due course Orwell was moved by his personal involvement in the Spanish Civil War, by spotty reading in modern history and politics transcending the English experience, and by all the cataclysmic events of the late 1930s and 1940s in Stalin's Russia and Hitler's Europe to take a wider view of the role of intellectuals in the contemporary world. In Britain the intellectuals may have cut a pitiful figure, but elsewhere? Elsewhere, their ideas and their cleverness and their contribution to public life amounted to more than impotent scheming and bawling. Elsewhere, increasingly, intellectuals were engaged in the building of leviathan states, as the satraps and counselors of tyrants, or as tyrants in their own right.

Orwell distilled his thoughts on the intelligentsia in *Animal Farm* and *Nineteen Eighty-Four*, two complementary visions of what will happen to all mankind if power falls into the hands of the typical sort of modern intellectual. The pigs lead the revolution in *Animal Farm* because they are the brainiest of the beasts, the intellectuals of the four-footed community, and the inventors of "a complete system of thought, to which they gave the name of Animalism."[17] This last is the most delicious of Orwell's many delicious phrases. The words trip lightly on the tongue, but the irony is heavy. Anyone who knows Orwell's prejudices will find it irresistibly funny, although the humor is of the purest black.

In *Nineteen Eighty-Four*, the intellectuals are once again in power. We meet only one supremely intelligent person in the whole novel, the Grand Inquisitor O'Brien, Orwell's Mustapha Mond. There is also an Outer Party, pigs of lesser intellect and weaker will, represented by Winston, Julia, Syme, Parsons, and various others, who serve the regime with differing degrees of enthusiasm and are not spared from Orwell's contempt. Even Winston and Julia are contemptible, not because they attempt to overthrow Big Brother and not because they are romantics, but because they fall so easily for the totalitarian claptrap of a counterrevolutionary credo that demands the renunciation of personal autonomy and human decency no less thoroughly than Ingsoc. The key passage, often remarked by critics, is O'Brien's questioning of the lovers when he initiates them into the "Brotherhood." Winston and Julia are willing to commit acts of murder, sabotage, treachery, suicide, even to throw sulphuric acid into a child's face, if the Brotherhood requires it.[18] They agree to all this without any intimidation whatever. In short, they are representative modern intellectuals.

At one level, *Animal Farm* and *Nineteen Eighty-Four* may be read as essays in irrationalist political theory. Like such modern masters of the subject as Georges Sorel, Vilfredo Pareto, and Graham Wallas, Orwell is telling us that man is not the calculating machine of utilitarian rationalism, but a creature driven by emotions, which can be manipulated to advantage by politicians, who are themselves anything but the sage and rational beings they appear to be in their robes of state. The ferocious will to power of politicians exploits the gullibility and greed of everybody else.

But there is another level. Orwell sees a roughly inverse relationship in life as it is lived between intellect and morality. The best people (or animals) in his fiction are most often the stupidest; the worst are the smartest. Although he launches no frontal attack on intelligence or reason or science, as such, the fact remains that in Orwell's universe, the people most to be feared are those whose keen minds give them the power and the arrogance—the diabolical will—to lord it over their inferiors.

Orwell's one major attempt to construct a theoretical framework for his view of the future comes in his analysis and adaptation of the writings of James Burnham, and especially of Burnham's *The Managerial Revolution*. He reviewed *The Managerial Revolution* at some length in 1946, and as Steinhoff and others have shown, he incorporated much of its substance into the excerpts from the "Book" of Emmanuel Goldstein in *Nineteen Eighty-Four*.[19] As summed up by Orwell himself, Burnham's position is simply that power in the future will pass, is already passing, into the hands of

the people who effectively control the means of production: that is, business executives, technicians, bureaucrats and soldiers.

. . . Each society will be hierarchical, with an aristocracy of talent at the top and a mass of semi-slaves at the bottom.[20]

In Goldstein's explication, Oceania is no more or less than a Burnhamite society. The new aristocracy, writes Goldstein, is composed mostly of "bureaucrats, scientists, technicians, trade-union organizers, publicity experts, sociologists, teachers, journalists, and professional politicians."[21] The Inner Party, with less than 2 percent of the population, is "the brain of the State" and the Outer Party, with 13 percent, is "the hands." Membership in each is determined not by heredity, but by competitive examination. The rest of the body social, the proles, are the common laborers. Thus, as in Burnham, Oceania keeps "the ablest people at the top."[22]

In other words, what Orwell offers us in *Nineteen Eighty-Four* is just one more variation on a theme as old as Plato's *Republic* or Bacon's *New Atlantis*, brought up to date in the nineteenth century by Auguste Comte and carried into the twentieth by H. G. Wells in *A Modern Utopia:* the project of a society managed by the cognoscenti. The nature of the expert knowledge that matters most may change from era to era, from philosophy to science to human engineering, but it is the same hoary ideal: enlightened despotism. In Orwell, the despots are enlightened only in the sense that they know how to manipulate people. Their ultimate aim is power. Nevertheless, in the age of big government, big business, and big communications, they are the knowers of what needs knowing.

In the war of the world views, belief in the efficacy and rationality of government by the cognoscenti was a utopia of many *philosophes* of the French Enlightenment and many positivists of the nineteenth and early twentieth centuries. It harmonized well with the notion that mankind should submit to the rule of reason and to the laws of nature disclosed by science. I like to call it "technocracy," in the most literal sense of "government by know-how." Elsewhere I have described it as the "most successful of all utopian visions."[23] What sometimes bars us from viewing it as utopian, perhaps, is the grim determination of most of its protagonists to define their project as a matter of science rather than utopian "fantasy," and the equally grim resolve of romantics and neoromantics to find it absoutely dystopian.

So in the final showing Orwell and Aldous Huxley were fellow travelers. *Nineteen Eighty-Four* belongs to the tradition of satirical criticism of the positivist utopia that has its roots in the *Gulliver's Travels* of Orwell's beloved Jonathan Swift and continues in our own century with *Brave New World* and such other major texts as E. M. Forster's "The Machine Stops," Zamyatin's *We*, and C. S. Lewis's *That Hideous Strength.*[24]

Where Orwell parts company with the Huxleys and the Lewises is only in the relatively smaller attention he assigns to the grip of science and technology on the imaginations of the dystopian ruling class. Some of the differences may be explained, to follow George Woodcock, simply by Orwell's lack of any real training or experience in such matters.[25] Zamyatin was reacting against a veritable cult of science and technology mounted in the early days of Lenin's Russia, and against his own education as an engineer. Huxley had grown up in the shadow of his grandfather, Thomas Henry Huxley, the greatest apostle of the scientific world view in late Victorian England, and of his scientist brother Julian. Orwell's only passionate interests were politics and literature.

But when Orwell did trouble himself to say something about science and technology, he spoke in the authentic accents of the contemporary neoromantic. At the start of a telling piece in *Tribune*, "What Is Science?" he used the word favorably to mean a "method of thought which obtains verifiable results by reasoning logically from observed fact," but he went on to water down his own definition to something not much more elaborate than rationality or even common sense.[26] As Bernard Crick observes, Orwell had a habit of reducing all knowledge to common sense.[27] Moreover, the main point of "What Is Science?" was not to praise scientific method, but to warn against the amorality, arrogance, and political stupidity of scientists. The scientific specialist, bereft as he usually is of any insight into history or politics, willingly throws himself at the feet of dictators. He makes bombs on command and gladly swallows any nonsense he is told to believe. Stuffing the average human being with more science in school would

> narrow the range of his thoughts and make him more than ever contemptuous of such knowledge as he did not possess: and his political reactions would probably be somewhat less intelligent than those of an illiterate peasant who retained a few historical memories and a fairly sound aesthetic sense.[28]

Orwell had been even more explicit on the topic of science and scientists in 1941 in his essay "Wells, Hitler and the World State." What made Wells no longer worth reading, he feared, were his obsolete notions of the goodness of science. Wells always assumed that the "scientific man" was on the side of progress and virtue, and the "romantic man" on the side of reaction and villainy. But history since 1914 proved him wrong. Science and scientists had enlisted in "the service of ideas appropriate to the Stone Age." The airplanes that Wells prophesied with such gusto had been used mostly to drop bombs. (It conveniently slipped Orwell's mind that before 1914 no one foresaw the military uses of aviation in more gruesome detail than Wells.) At any rate, events had shown that "the equation of science with common sense does not really hold good."[29]

But in the main, Orwell was more prone to ignore science than to inveigh against it. What touched him viscerally was the transformation of human life and the landscape by technology. On this point he was quite plain and quite consistent from the first. In *The Road to Wigan Pier*, in *Coming Up for Air*, in various essays, in *Nineteen Eighty-Four*, and elsewhere, he conjured up one nightmare vision after another of modern urban industrial civilization. "I wasn't born for an age like this," he complained in one of his better *Adelphi* poems. In youth he had known simple joys, fish in a shaded stream, horses, ducks in flight at dawn, but in the streamlined world of the 1930s "Horses are made of chromium steel / And little fat men shall ride them."[30] One thinks, too, of the marvelous passage in *Coming Up for Air* when the hapless George Bowling bites into his first synthetic sausage and looks for somewhere to spit it out. "It gave me the feeling that I'd bitten into the modern world and discovered what it was really made of. . . . Everything slick and streamlined, everything made out of something else."[31] Later, he returns to his boyhood village and finds his beloved fishing hole converted into a rubbish dump for tin cans by the managers of a new sham-Tudor housing development.

The heart of the problem, Orwell argued in his review of a book by Herbert Read, was that although technology may give us good things, the more dependent we become on it, the more freedom we must expect to lose. An authentically decentralized society would be unable to sustain "the kind of air-conditioned, chromium-plated, gadget-ridden existence which is now considered desirable and enlightened." Such an existence required a "repressive apparatus" of central control. Just as sadly, "the machine has frustrated the creative instincts and degraded aesthetic feeling."[32] Orwell's preference, stated many times, was for a society not unlike Morris's in *News from Nowhere*, a society without costly luxuries or runaway technology, a society where as many goods as possible were made by hand by craftsmen. Technology, he warned, was like a dangerous drug, to be used "grudgingly and suspiciously."[33]

In *Nineteen Eighty-Four*, of course, Orwell took his analysis of the future of technology a step further. Here technology and science as well had been placed at the service of the state, instead of the other way round. Bit by bit, the Party was phasing out progress in both, authorizing research to continue only in weaponry and in techniques of thought control. Eventually, after the mechanisms of absolute mastery had been perfected, including the eradication of orgasms by neurosurgery, science itself would disappear, and technology would become as stagnant and limited as in *News from Nowhere*, to a hideously different effect. But it would have been the scientists and the engineers who had made it all possible, right through to their own well-deserved self-destruction.

Orwell's Politics: Affirmations

The positive half of Orwell's politics is just as important as the negative, but less convoluted. He attached the highest priority in his political thought to saving the autonomy of the individual. He was a socialist and a democrat primarily because he saw in democratic socialism the best way to protect the individual against the remorseless advance of technocratic totalitarianism.

In this regard, too, Orwell was the legatee of both the romantic and the irrationalist world views. The alienated tragic hero of romanticism and the absurd yet curiously unbowed antihero of irrationalism provide the obvious models. If Orwell shifted uneasily back and forth between the two, still the autonomous self that he sought to defend was never the blank tablet, the atomic integer, or the pleasure-seeking and pain-avoiding *homme-machine* of positivism and the eighteenth-century Enlightenment.

Alan Sandison has devoted a whole volume to the thesis that the provenance of Orwell's political morality was the Protestant Reformation, and its protoromantic image of the self as free, responsible, guilty, predestined, God-fearing, and defiant all at the same time. With the help of Erik Erikson, he shows some of the striking parallels between the course of Orwell's life and Luther's. He analyzes Protestant asceticism, activism, and self-loathing, all Orwellian qualities, along with stern censoriousness, a penchant for oversimplification, and missionary fervor. In Sandison's reading, *Nineteen Eighty-Four* turns out to have its spiritual foundations in the contest between the solitary Protestant conscience (Winston) and the Church of Rome (O'Brien, the Party).[34]

Sandison overworks a few apt passages from Orwell's oeuvre, but his arguments are seductive, especially in light of the affinities between the Protestant mystique and romanticism. He has put his finger on what matters most in understanding Orwell's individualism. It was an essentially religious faith, with all the theology secularized and internalized. God (for Orwell) was not dead: he merely became mortal, the quintessence of each mortal self.

What happens to nature in such a world view? Is it silent and opaque, as in the philosophy of Camus? No. Here Sandison associates Orwell with the sturdy empiricism of the late Renaissance. Orwell, he points out, rejoiced unsentimentally in the solid facticity of the sensed world. He needed a "belly-to-earth" contact with nature, to guarantee the objective existence of the self now that an external deity was no longer available to do the job.[35] Again, Sandison exaggerates. Most of the time, at least, Orwell rejoiced in nature with the sensibility of an early romantic. His nostalgia, his yearning for old simplicities, his delight in animals and conventional rustic beauty are all too obvious.

But Orwell's "empiricism" is worth a closer look, to see what it may conceal. Consider the interrogation of Winston at the end of *Nineteen Eighty-Four*. Winston is asked to deny the most fundamental facts of nature and history and experience. He resists. Somehow it is vitally important not to yield. He is not asked at this point to deny himself or his love for Julia, only externals—the stars, gravity, the sum of two and two. Yet they matter, as something to hold on to, and by which to be held. They satisfy his hunger for an absolute certainty higher than any merely human words or human claims, a need that Orwell felt all through his life, but a need that could be filled only by something akin to the Christian faith in God, not by the tentative and ever-mutable knowledge of empiricism. If Orwell's God was the autonomous self, his unscientific passion for an unquestionable universe was his surrogate for God's Holy Word.

As Isaac Deutscher put the matter bluntly, in another context, Orwell "was anything but a sceptic. His mental make-up was rather that of the fanatic, determined to get an answer, a quick and a plain answer, to his question."[36] When the Party at last breaks Winston's rigid belief in external reality, he is a dead man. The crude goings-on that follow in Room 101 are almost superfluous. O'Brien reminds one of Wither, the archvillain of *That Hideous Strength*, who had progressed from Hegel to Hume to pragmatism to logical positivism to the void of absolute nothingness, believing in no reality at all. In Lewis's Augustinian theology, the absence of being denotes the Great Nullity himself, Satan; and Wither is Satan's wholly sworn bondman.[37]

Assorted Predilections

These, then, are the axial tenets of Orwell's political doctrine, the doctrine given its ultimate expression in *Nineteen Eighty-Four*: the attack on totalitarianism as an infernal engine of the intelligentsia and the substitution of faith in the autonomous self and a trustworthy cosmos for faith in God. His ties to romanticism and neoromanticism extend, of course, in many other directions, each of which deserves its own essay. I have space only for a synopsis.

Already mentioned is the romantic character of Orwell's socialism, a socialism of the heart, a political religion of "common decency," analyzed in a penetrating recent study by James Connors.[38] Casting aside Marx and every other serious effort to understand the dynamics of capitalism as a system of social relations, Orwell embraced only the sentimental or affective dimension of socialism. Raymond Williams says it best in his critique of *The Lion and the Unicorn*, where Orwell likened England to a family with the "wrong members" in control. Orwell's failure to grasp the structural realities of class conflict was a function both of his economic illiteracy and of his deep emotional need for the "family" that was England.[39]

Other commentators, including Connors, have noted the powerful links between Orwell's socialism and a simple Sunday-school version of Christian morality, as taught by the itinerant workman from Nazareth. Orwell occasionally had a kind word for Christian morality himself.[40] Woodcock compares his political faith to Tolstoy's vision of Christianity, Steinhoff connects it with evangelical Protestantism, and Crick makes good polemical use of a neglected review essay by Orwell from 1946, in which he followed socialism back through Morris, Whitman, and Rousseau (romantics all) to Winstanley and "the early Christians and the slave revolts of antiquity."[41]

In the same category is Orwell's tortuous love of the common people, as hard-won as a monk's love of hair shirts or begging bowls; and his generally more robust patriotism, which he always regarded as a necessary underpinning of a genuinely democratic socialism. Both were intensely romantic affections, in Orwell's case, and further evidence of his all but insatiable need for roots.[42] One could go on: his love of nature as encountered in the English countryside, his nostalgia for golden early days, his conservative views of womanhood and the family, the symbolism of the paperweight and the dream of "the old, rabbit-bitten pasture" in *Nineteen Eighty-Four*, Bowling's memory of Lower Binfield in *Coming Up for Air*. "He fed from the earth, like Anteus," writes Woodcock, "and his happiest recollections of youth, like his happiest letters, were concerned in some way or another with rural experiences."[43]

There was also a nastier side to Orwell's romanticism, identified by Terry Eagleton as "a tough, swaggering sense of self-righteous masculinity," which erupted on rare occasions into actual physical brutality.[44] As Steinhoff remarks, "he was a man of action not averse to violence."[45] Orwell despised men who were fat or gay or soft, such as the Deputy Commissioner Macgregor in *Burmese Days* or Winston's fellow tenant Parsons in *Nineteen Eighty-Four*. Although one must say this with due caution, Orwell even had a weakness for the heroic and macho aspects of fascism. He empathized with the parades, the patriotism, the stern attacks on bourgeois hedonism, the hairy virility of it all. Despite his many firm denunciations of fascism, he seldom experienced any sort of abdominal revulsion in contemplating its doings. The death camps of the Holocaust barely caught his notice. Nothing said in his novels about the behavior of Fascists, for example, can stand up to the physical ferocity of his depiction of an anti-Fascist meeting in *Coming Up for Air*, a prototype of the Two Minutes Hate in *Nineteen Eighty-Four*.[46] His model for totalitarianism was invariably Stalin's Russia, not Hitler's Germany; Bolshevist antifascism, not fascism.

In one memorable wartime book review, which Woodcock twists into an argument for Orwell's sense of fair play and "moral courage," our two-fisted author admitted that he had "never been able to dislike Hitler." He would have gladly murdered the man, but he "could feel no personal animosity. The fact is that there is something deeply appealing about him. One feels it again when one sees his photographs." Orwell found in them the face of a suffering and self-sacrificing hero. "In a rather more manly way it reproduces the expression of innumerable pictures of Christ crucified."[47] Patently, what Orwell was up to had nothing to do with fair play. He saw something of himself in Hitler, because something of himself was there. As Woodcock concedes, Orwell's pen portrait of Hitler calls vividly to mind any number of Orwellian antiheroes.[48]

But the last word on the subject should be Orwell's own, from his 1941 essay proclaiming the obsolescence of H. G. Wells. "The people who have shown the best understanding of Fascism," he wrote (pointedly excluding Wells, who understood nothing about it in Orwell's judgment), "are either those who have suffered under it or those who have a Fascist streak in themselves."[49] In the second group he lists Jack London and Rudyard Kipling, but he was probably also thinking of a third chap: if not George Orwell, then at least Eric Blair.[50]

The Consequences of George Orwell

This study comes to its close with a few summary judgments on the consequences of George Orwell, especially in his role as the political secretary of the Zeitgeist. After his death in 1950, he became steadily more important. The popular taste for romanticism continued undiminished, and perhaps expanded. The avant-garde continued to ring changes on the now almost venerable world view that I have termed irrationalism. Western intellectuals were caught up in the ideological, political, military, and economic contest between the superpowers, and most Western socialists joined Orwell in not only preferring but also aligning with Natopolis.[51] In all this, Orwell was just the man for the times. Romantic, neoromantic, and obsessive anticommunist, he could not fail to please. With aid from a few of his younger living contemporaries—Koestler, Ionesco, Camus, Grass—Orwell was virtually the conscience of Western man in the 1950s and early 1960s. Nor has his reputation suffered unduly in the years since then.

But I am bound to report that the consequences of George Orwell, from 1950 to 1984, have been mostly disastrous. It is absurd to blame Orwell, in any ultimate sense. He was as good a man as most, and a first-class writer. Nevertheless, it might have been better for mankind if he had never lived.

The worst results of Orwell's work can be tallied under three headings: what he did for Western socialism, what he did for the Cold War, and what he did to increase the chances of an irrevocable final hot war.

To English socialism, and to socialism throughout the Atlantic community, Orwell left behind the message that politics is a dirty, irrational business; that a socialist is well advised to rely on common sense and instinct rather than elaborate dehumanizing alien ideologies such as Marxism; that a man, including a socialist, isn't worth much unless he is an ardent patriot well rooted in his native culture; that most of the intelligentsia is rotten; that the common people are our only hope, although they happen to be almost invincibly passive and naive and incapable of lifting a finger on their own behalf; and that revolution is a bad dream. As Raymond Williams argues in reviewing *Animal Farm*, Orwell "is opposing here more than the Soviet or Stalinist experience. Both the consciousness of the workers and the possibility of authentic revolution are denied."[52]

Citations can be found in Orwell's work to refute Williams, but a writer must be judged not only by what he says, but by what he says most effectively, and with the greatest conviction. The picture of the working class and of revolution in *Animal Farm, Nineteen Eighty-Four*, and several other key texts gives no grounds for reasoned confidence in the future building of socialism anywhere in the world. In the case of Great Britain, where Orwell's anti-intellectual and defeatist perversion of democratic socialism exerted the deepest influence, his writings encouraged the illusion swallowed by one Labour politician after another that the best policy was to let the trickle-down from postwar affluence erode class distinctions bit by bit, with a shove now and then from Parliament. It might not be the millennium, but the only alternative, as anyone who read Orwell could tell you in a flash, was the unspeakable horror of Napoleon, Big Brother, and the Thought Police.

The result has been not the emergence of democratic socialism throughout the Atlantic community but the extension of the power of capital and the state apparatus that protects and collaborates with capital. Bureaucracy and technocracy have grown, much as Burnham had foreseen in 1941. Some genuine revolutions, as in China, have gone awry in Orwellian ways, learning nothing from his warnings, but in the Atlantic bourgeois democracies the moderate leftists and neoconservatives who have heard and heeded Orwell have not brought democratic socialism one day closer.

In the realm of international politics, *Nineteen Eighty-Four* deserves Deutscher's epithet of "ideological superweapon in the cold war."[53] Although Orwell's principal concern in writing the book was to convince Englishmen and others in the Atlantic community not to succumb to the direful songs of a fusty old German siren with a big black beard, what his novel has done is to help convince innumerable Atlantic citizens that almost anything is worse than falling one missile, one spacecraft, or one sphere of influence behind the Soviet Union. As Orwell said himself, the best alternative to the polarization of power in the postwar world was a unified socialist Western Europe, but, failing that, it behooved all men of good will to rally behind the Stars and Stripes.[54] Yet if Orwell had written nothing else, the moral of *Nineteen Eighty-Four* would have been clear to the simplest reader, like the news vendor in New York who told Deutscher that he should read the book to find out why "we must drop the atom bomb on the Bolshies."[55] Ironically, the writer who made a career out of opposing absolutism was an absolutist himself, in the rigidity and ferocity of his political credo. *Nineteen Eighty-Four* has terrified whole generations.

> But it has not helped them to see more clearly the issues with which the world is grappling; it has not advanced their understanding. It has only increased and intensified the waves of panic and hate that run through the world and obfuscate innocent minds. *1984* has taught millions to look at the conflict between East and West in terms of black and white, and it has shown them a monster bogy and a monster scapegoat for all the ills that plague mankind.[56]

Another tragic consequence of Orwell's politics, and of *Nineteen Eighty-Four* in particular, is its insistence on making personal freedom a higher value, in effect an infinitely higher value, than world peace and world order. He was not alone in this, of course. But he did a great deal to popularize the priority. In the result, any number of well-meaning people think they would rather be "free," which can mean a variety of things, than submit to even a benevolent world technocracy or dictatorship.

But what if the best we can do for the next hundred years is to preserve our skins as a species? What if this does mean a division of the planet into three zones of hegemony, as in *Nineteen Eighty-Four*, and a tacit agreement to avoid and prevent total war? What if it means a global directorate of businessmen and commissars? What if it means either or both of these, and some of us working underground as well to transform the emergent world order when the time is right into an authentically socialist world republic? Orwell once or twice paid lip service to the idea of a people's world state, but more often he thought of it as a Wellsian dream, in most ways hopelessly out of date.[57] His real allegiance was to the self, the romantic genius picturesquely estranged from everything and everybody, who must always be free to feel exactly what he feels and to say exactly what he pleases. Perhaps in some distant century a socialist world state would arrive. In the meantime socialists had to defend freedom by playing their part in the arena of armed world politics—even to the point of wearing the livery of the lords of Natopolis.

The consequences, once again, are clear. Although he knew that a total war with nuclear weapons would be suicidal, Orwell was much more afraid of a nuclear stalemate, which the Superpowers would exploit to consolidate their power on the home front. World annihilation was just not an Orwellian nightmare. By convincing so many of his readers that other things were worse or more likely (no matter how fantastically exaggerated), he joined Zamyatin, Huxley, and all their *confrères* in making it easier for Western electorates to invest billions of tax dollars in the doomsday arms race.

At least we have been spared one mercy. George Orwell died in early middle age in 1950. He did not live to join the ranks of the neoconservatives, as Norman Podhoretz smugly contends he would have done.[58] We have been spared his appearances on "Firing Line" with Bill Buckley, his discovery and patronage of Aleksandr Solzhenitsyn, his first Holy Communion at the side of Malcolm Muggeridge, his sentimental acceptance speech in Stockholm after winning the Nobel Prize.

Or perhaps Podhoretz is wrong, after all. Perhaps the romantic in Orwell would have compelled him to play the good gray Steppenwolf right to the end, sedulously shunning all cozy cliques from his fastness in the Hebrides. Replying to Podhoretz, Christopher Hitchens reminds us that in the late 1940s Orwell was invited to make common cause with the forerunners of today's neoconservatives many times— "and just as many times he pushed the poisoned chalice from his lips."[59]

We shall never know. All we can say with reasonable sureness is that George Orwell adhered throughout his mature years to a world view that fused nineteenth-century romanticism and twentieth-century irrationalism in his own particular way. It was a potent mix of prevailing values. It does much to explain why his writing has clicked so well till now. When the Zeitgeist moves on again, to a new positivism, it may do what it did to poor old Wells, and leave him far behind.

Notes

1. Aldous Huxley, *Brave New World Revisited*, in *Brave New World and Brave New World Revisited* (New York: Harper and Row, 1960), 2–3, 21.
2. *The Collected Essays, Journalism and Letters of George Orwell*, ed. Sonia Orwell and Ian Angus, 4 vols. (New York: Harcourt Brace Jovanovich, 1968), 4:73. Hereafter cited as *CEJL*.
3. Erich Fromm, "Afterword," in George Orwell, *Nineteen Eighty-Four* (New York: Signet Classics, 1961), 260–61.
4. Malcolm Muggeridge, "A Knight of the Woeful Countenance," in *The World of George Orwell*, ed. Miriam Gross (London: Weidenfeld and Nicolson, 1971), 168.
5. See W. Warren Wagar, *Terminal Visions: The Literature of Last Things* (Bloomington: Indiana University Press, 1982).
6. Huxley, *Brave New World*, in *Brave New World and Brave New World Revisited*, 36.
7. Quoted in George Woodcock, *The Crystal Spirit: A Study of George Orwell* (Boston: Little, Brown, 1966), 27.
8. See W. Warren Wagar, *World Views: A Study in Comparative History* (Hinsdale, Ill.: Dryden Press, 1977), 4–8.
9. See, for example, George Orwell, *The Road to Wigan Pier* (London: Secker and Warburg, 1959), 173–74. Muggeridge adds, "He was always going on about nancy poets and pacifists and sandal-wearing vegetarians with what seemed to me unnecessary and unfair virulence" ("A Knight of the Woeful Countenance," 172).
10. *CEJL* 1:7. Cf. Woodcock, *The Crystal Spirit*, pt. 4.
11. Bernard Crick, *George Orwell: A Life* (London: Secker and Warburg, 1980), xvii.
12. *CEJL* 2:229.
13. George Orwell, *The Lion and the Unicorn: Socialism and the English Genius* (London: Secker and Warburg, 1962), 38–40. Also in *CEJL* 2:74–75.
14. George Orwell, *The English People* (London: Collins, 1947), 14, 22. See also p. 46, where he applauds the English for preferring "instinct to logic, and character to intelligence." *The English People*, like *The Lion and the Unicorn*, was reprinted in *CEJL*, where the three passages quoted here and above may be found in 3:7, 16, and 36.
15. *CEJL* 1:459.
16. D. A. N. Jones, "Arguments against Orwell," in *The World of George Orwell*, ed. Miriam Gross, 154–61; William Steinhoff, *George Orwell and the Origins of 1984* (Ann Arbor: University of Michigan Press, 1975), chaps. 4–8; and Alex Zwerdling, *Orwell and the Left* (New Haven: Yale University Press, 1974), especially chap. 2.
17. George Orwell, *Animal Farm* (New York: Signet Classics, n.d.), 26.
18. George Orwell, *Nineteen Eighty-Four* (New York: Signet Classics, 1961), 142.
19. See Steinhoff, *George Orwell and the Origins of 1984*, chap. 3, "The Influence of James Burnham," and especially p. 43.
20. *CEJL* 4:160–61.

21. Orwell, *Nineteen Eighty-Four*, 169.
22. Orwell, *Nineteen Eighty-Four*, 172–73.
23. See W. Warren Wagar, "The Steel-Gray Saviour: Technocracy as Utopia and Ideology," *Alternative Futures: The Journal of Utopian Studies* 2, no. 2 (Spring 1979):38–54.
24. Orwell reviewed *That Hideous Strength*, although the review was unfortunately not reprinted in *CEJL*. See Steinhoff, *George Orwell and the Origins of* 1984, 225n.58.
25. See Woodcock, *The Crystal Spirit*, 215.
26. *CEJL* 4:10 and ff.
27. Crick, *Orwell*, xxi.
28. *CEJL* 4:12.
29. *CEJL* 2:143.
30. *CEJL* 1:5.
31. George Orwell, *Coming Up for Air* (New York: Harcourt, Brace, 1950), 27.
32. *CEJL* 4:49.
33. See Woodcock, *The Crystal Spirit*, 242–49, for a lucid discussion of Orwell's negative view of technological progress.
34. See Alan Sandison, *The Last Man in Europe: An Essay on George Orwell* (New York: Barnes and Noble, 1974).
35. See Sandison, *The Last Man in Europe*, chap. 2, "Operating inside Nature."
36. Isaac Deutscher, "*1984*—The Mysticism of Cruelty," in *George Orwell: A Collection of Critical Essays*, ed. Raymond Williams (Englewood Cliffs, N.J.: Prentice-Hall, 1974), 129.
37. C. S. Lewis, *That Hideous Strength* (New York: Macmillan, 1946), especially p. 420.
38. James Connors, " 'Who Dies If England Live?': Christianity and the Moral Vision of George Orwell," in *The Secular Mind: Transformations of Faith in Modern Europe*, ed. W. Warren Wagar (New York: Holmes and Meier, 1982), 169–96.
39. See Raymond Williams, *George Orwell* (New York: Viking, 1971), chap. 2, "England, Whose England?"
40. See the discussion in Connors, " 'Who Dies If England Live?'," 187–90.
41. See Woodcock, *The Crystal Spirit*, 283; Steinhoff, *George Orwell and the Origins of* 1984, 213; and Crick, *Orwell*, 351–52.
42. See Muggeridge, "A Knight of the Woeful Countenance," 174–75.
43. Woodcock, *The Crystal Spirit*, 61.
44. Terry Eagleton, "Orwell and the Lower-Middle-Class Novel," in *George Orwell: A Collection of Critical Essays*, ed. Williams, 11. See also Crick, *Orwell*, 87–88 and 178–79.
45. Steinhoff, *George Orwell and the Origins of* 1984, 86.
46. See Orwell, *Coming Up for Air*, 169–80.
47. *CEJL* 2:13–14; and see Woodcock, *The Crystal Spirit*, 57.
48. Woodcock, *The Crystal Spirit*, 58. Sandison makes the same point in *The Last Man in Europe*, 41.
49. *CEJL* 2:144.
50. Yet another way of gauging a writer's allegiance in the war of the world views is to ascertain which authors he himself reads and admires, and

why. Here, too, Orwell turns out to have had pronounced romantic and neoromantic predilections. His favorite authors included Shakespeare, Swift, Dickens, Charles Reade, Poe, Housman, Kipling, and the early— the fin-de-siècle irrationalist—Wells. In mature years he learned to take pleasure in some of the principal neoromantic moderns, such as Eliot, Lawrence, and Joyce. Also relevant is Orwell's choice of the authors who were being translated into Newspeak in *Nineteen Eighty-Four:* "Shakespeare, Milton, Swift, Byron, Dickens, and some others. . . . When the task had been completed, their original writings, with all else that survived of the literature of the past, would be destroyed" (p. 256). The Party was selecting for mutilation only baroque and romantic masters whom Orwell particularly loved or respected, which doubles the horror of it all. Instead of being allowed to disappear with dignity, they too, like Winston, had to be "cleansed"!

51. On Orwell and "Natopolis," see E. P. Thompson, "Inside *Which* Whale?" in *George Orwell: A Collection of Critical Essays,* ed. Williams, 80–88.
52. Williams, *Orwell,* 73.
53. Deutscher, "The Mysticism of Cruelty," 119.
54. See, e.g., *CEJL* 4:323, 370–75, and 398.
55. Deutscher, "The Mysticism of Cruelty," 132.
56. Deutscher, "The Mysticism of Cruelty," 132.
57. See *CEJL* 2:140–41; and Orwell, *The Lion and the Unicorn,* 50, also in *CEJL* 2:80.
58. Norman Podhoretz, "If Orwell Were Alive Today," *Harper's* January, 1983, pp. 30–37.
59. Christopher Hitchens, in Hitchens and Podhoretz, "An Exchange on Orwell," *Harper's,* February, 1982, p. 56.

Afterword: The Inner Heart

William R. Steinhoff

The logic of *Nineteen Eighty-Four* requires that Winston Smith learn to love Big Brother. Given the conditions Orwell describes nothing less than this is acceptable, and yet one wonders why Winston could not have continued to resist until he was killed. Is it evident that force and fraud will always succeed? Is pain applied by superior intelligence irresistible? Outside the novel the answers to these questions are clear: some human beings, at least, never give in. History is full of examples of heroic resistance to tyrannical power; there are martyrs of all sorts—religious, scientific, political—who did not succumb to seemingly intolerable pain however crudely or ingeniously applied.

Recall for a moment some details from the story of Bishop Ridley and Bishop Latimer stripped to their shrouds, chained to the stake, with gunpowder hung about their necks.

> Then they brought a fagot, kindled with fire, and laid it down at Ridley's feet. To whom Latimer spake in this manner—"Be of good comfort, brother Ridley, and play the man; We shall this day light such a candle by God's grace in England, as I trust shall never be put out."[1]

Of Latimer we learn that he received the flame as if embracing it, and that Ridley in his agony said repeatedly, "Let the fire come to me; I cannot burn." What reason is there that Winston Smith could not act as these martyrs did?

The bodily pain that Winston endures is the least of the tortures he undergoes. Nevertheless it is very great. And it is the first step in the process by which Winston's body is weakened, his intellectual beliefs refuted, and his love for Julia destroyed. When first attacked in the Ministry of Love he knows that

> never, for any reason on earth, could you wish for an increase of pain. Of pain you could wish only one thing: that it should stop. Nothing in the world was so bad as physical pain. In the face of pain there are no heroes, no heroes, he thought over and over as he writhed on the floor, clutching uselessly at his disabled left arm.[2]

201

Passages like this would not be nearly so emotionally persuasive if they were not grounded in Orwell's lifelong experience with his own weak body whether in Spain or in the hospitals where he spent so much time. "How the Poor Die" gives a vivid report of his treatment at a French charity hospital and of how he "lay down again, humiliated, disgusted and frightened by the thing that had been done to me."[3] The following passage in *Nineteen Eighty-Four* is only one of those preparing the reader to accept Winston's response to danger.

> It struck him that in moments of crisis one is never fighting against an external enemy but always against one's own body. Even now, in spite of the gin, the dull ache in his belly made consecutive thought impossible. And it is the same, he perceived, in all seemingly heroic or tragic situations. On the battlefield, in the torture chamber, on a sinking ship, the issues that you are fighting for are always forgotten, because the body swells up until it fills the universe, and even when you are not paralyzed by fright or screaming with pain, life is a moment-to-moment struggle against hunger or cold or sleeplessness, against a sour stomach or an aching tooth. (P. 86)

But Winston's vulnerability is even greater than this suggests.

As his story shows, Bishop Latimer was confident that history, human memory, and objective reality could not be tampered with. He had a faith, and he believed that it would be triumphantly vindicated in the future. Winston Smith has no such faith, and much of Orwell's novel is devoted to showing why the vital supports of faith—like a belief in objective reality and the possibility of truthful history—might, given the state of contemporary life, be credibly withdrawn in his representation of Oceania. Winston is like the arbitrary victims of Nazi Germany who supposedly would never be remembered because no one could prove that they had ever existed. Nevertheless, he knows he exists. Why can't he enact his martyrdom on the platform of his own mind? Why can't he, if only silently, say "I am free inside my own head, and I declare that I am right and the Party wrong?" The answer to these questions does not, I suggest, lie wholly in O'Brien's power to inflict pain and in his superior intelligence.

Orwell's sense of the importance of ideas is demonstrated by the emphasis he gives them in the conflict between the rebel and the Party. A question that perplexed him for a long time is this: can a human being be "free" inside his head? If he knows the truth will it set him free? In *A Clergyman's Daughter* the brutalizing effects of field labor reduce Dorothy to the condition of a mindless animal,[4] but Bozo the Screever in *Down and Out in Paris and London* thought that anyone, rich or poor, could live the same life. "You just got to say to yourself, 'I'm a free man in *here*'—he tapped his forehead,—'and you're all right.' "[5] The contrary response appears early in Orwell's fiction in such characters as Gordon Comstock of *Keep the Aspidistra Flying* and Flory in *Burmese Days*. He says of Flory, the rebel against British imperialism,

> Time passed, and each year Flory found himself less at home in the world of the sahibs, more liable to get into trouble when he talked seriously on any subject whatever. So he had learned to live inwardly, secretly, in books and secret thoughts that could not be uttered. Even his talks with the doctor were a kind of talking to himself. . . . But it is a corrupting thing to live one's life in secret. One should live with the stream of life, not against it.[6]

One of the principal themes of Orwell's fiction is in fact the destructive effect of the isolation and consequent loneliness of a human being living in a hostile society. To live with the stream of life means that one has found a Brotherhood to belong to. Gordon Comstock mistakenly supposes that he can successfully separate himself and his poems from the money-dominated world around him. Winston needs O'Brien just as much as he needs Julia.

> The greatest mistake is to imagine that the human being is an autonomous individual. The secret freedom which you can supposedly enjoy under a despotic government is nonsense, because your thoughts are never entirely your own. Philosophers, writers, artists, even scientists, not only need encouragement and an audience, they need constant stimulation from other people. It is almost impossible to think without talking. If Defoe had really lived on a desert island he could not have written *Robinson Crusoe*, nor would he have wanted to. (*CEJL* 3:133)

Is Winston Smith free within the "few cubic centimetres inside his skull" and reduced to loving submission only by O'Brien's torture? I believe that Orwell shows us that Winston contributes to his own defeat. He is in some measure on O'Brien's side because he shares O'Brien's ideas.

One reason that Orwell wrote *Nineteen Eighty-Four*, he says, was to draw out "to their logical consequences" the "totalitarian ideas [that] have taken root in the minds of intellectuals everywhere" (*CEJL* 4:502). These ideas, given classic statement by Machiavelli, are epitomized by Lenin's "Who, Whom?" Mao Tse-tung's "All power comes out of the barrel of a gun," and Stalin's "How many divisions does the Pope have?" Orwell, on the contrary, rejected the view that politics is only an incessant struggle for power among men whose weapons are force and fraud, and he did not think that the end justified the means. He feared, however, that the new and growing class of intellectual-bureaucrats, imbued with Machiavelli's ideas, secretly wished "to destroy the old equalitarian version of Socialism and usher in a hierarchical society where the intellectual can at last get his hands on the whip" (*CEJL* 4:179).

For a considerable time in the novel it seems that Winston quite heroically clings to his faith in the commonsense view of objective reality expressed in the equation "two plus two equals four," but a review of O'Brien's "catechism" throws a different light on the state of his soul. When O'Brien, posing as a fellow conspirator against the Party, asks Winston and Julia "in general terms" what they are prepared to do on behalf of the Brotherhood, Winston replies, "Anything that we are capable of." The questions then grow more specific: die for the cause? commit murder? spread venereal disease?

> "If, for example, it would somehow serve our interests to throw sulphuric acid in a child's face—are you prepared to do that?" (P. 142)

The answer is always yes until O'Brien asks,

> "You are prepared, the two of you, to separate and never see one another again?"
> "No!" broke in Julia.
> It appeared to Winston that a long time passed before he answered. For a moment he seemed even to have been deprived of the power of speech. His tongue worked soundlessly, forming the opening syllables of one word, then of the other, over and over again. Until he had said it, he did not know which word he was going to say. "No," he said finally. (Pp. 142–43)

The difference between Julia's quick response and Winston's long hesitation is significant, though not crucial. Julia's is in keeping with her characteristic decisiveness and may even be linked to her "I'm not literary, dear," in the sense that she is not an intellectual, not temperamentally reflective as an intellectual is supposed to be, and "the difference between truth and falsehood [does] not seem important to her" (p. 127). Winston is more timid and more inclined to think about possibilities before he replies. What is more important is the nature of the questions and what the answers imply. As the questions grow more specific the actions they call for become more revolting. It is the willingness to "throw sulphuric acid in a child's face" that most reveals the inner corruption of all three characters. They believe that the end justifies the means—any means. The note touched here has already been sounded in the book. Julia has told Winston at their first rendezvous that members of the Inner Party are "not so holy as they make out." They had enjoyed her favors too.

His heart leapt. Scores of times she had done it; he wished it had been hundreds—thousands. Anything that hinted at corruption always filled him with a wild hope. Who knew? Perhaps the Party was rotten under the surface, its cult of strenuousness and self-denial simply a sham concealing iniquity. If he could have infected the whole lot of them with leprosy or syphilis, how gladly he would have done so! Anything to rot, to weaken, to undermine! He pulled her down so that they were kneeling face to face.

"Listen. The more men you've had, the more I love you. Do you understand that?"

"Yes, perfectly."

"I hate purity. I hate goodness. I don't want any virtue to exist anywhere. I want everyone to be corrupt to the bones."

"Well, then, I ought to suit you, dear. I'm corrupt to the bones." (Pp. 104–5)

This note is sounded again at another critical point. In one of their dialogues Winston tells O'Brien that the proles will finally triumph. "In the end they will beat you. Sooner or later they will see you for what you are, and then they will tear you to pieces" (p. 222). And when O'Brien points out the unlikelihood of revolt from that quarter Winston, lacking any belief in God, falls back on "something in the universe . . . some spirit, some principle" and finally, the spirit of Man.

"You are the last man," said O'Brien. "You are the guardian of the human spirit. You shall see yourself as you are. Take off your clothes." (P. 223)

What he sees in the mirror is what O'Brien calls "a bag of filth." "Do you see that thing facing you? That is the last man. If you are human, that is humanity" (p. 224).

Even now Winston considers himself morally superior to O'Brien and the Party with their lies and cruelty, resting his claim on the fact that he has not betrayed Julia. But can he assert his claim to moral superiority after accepting the principle that the end justifies the means? He had supposed that loving Julia was compatible with performing unspeakably evil acts in the cause of the Brotherhood. The result is the corruption of intellect and spirit.

Much earlier Orwell has tried to clarify what Winston means by the spirit, the secret self that the Party cannot control. Julia and Winston once believed that, as he said, "Confession is not betrayal. What you say or do doesn't matter; only feelings matter. If they could make me stop loving you—that would be the real betrayal" (p. 137).

> She thought it over. "They can't do that," she said finally. "It's the one thing they can't do. They can make you say anything—*anything*—but they can't make you believe it. They can't get inside you."
>
> "No," he said a little more hopefully, "no; that's quite true. They can't get inside you. If you can *feel* that staying human is worth while, even when it can't have any result whatever, you've beaten them." (Pp. 137–38)

"Staying human" means here fidelity to private loyalties and echoes the same idea in *Burmese Days*. "We sell our souls in public and buy them back in private, among our friends."[7] Winston's mother "possessed a kind of nobility, a kind of purity, because the standards she obeyed were private ones" (p. 136). So with the proles. "They were not loyal to a party or a country or an idea, they were loyal to one another. . . . The proles had stayed human. They had not become hardened inside. They had held on to the primitive emotions which he himself had to relearn by conscious effort" (p. 136). Elsewhere, "staying human" is likely to be connected to some truth of individual perception, as when Orwell praises E. M. Forster for preferring T. S. Eliot's poetry in 1917 because it was " 'innocent of public spirit.' "[8] Sometimes it is associated with the truthful account of the details of existence, however disgusting, as these appear, for example, in Orwell's accounts of his experiences in Spain. If one is faithful to the truth even pain is conquerable.

> But if the object was not to stay alive but to stay human, what difference did it ultimately make? They could not alter your feelings; for that matter you could not alter them yourself, even if you wanted to. They could lay bare in the utmost intimate detail everything that you had done or said or thought; but the inner heart, whose workings were mysterious to yourself, remained impregnable. (P. 138)

From one point of view *Nineteen Eighty-Four* is a dramatic contest between two intellectuals. Their conflict emphasizes intellectual issues—the nature of objective reality, the possibility of truthful history, the significance of memory. As it turns out, however, it is on the battleground of the inner heart that the conflict is decided. For Winston the final test once seemed to be a commonsense assertion. "Freedom is the freedom to say that two plus two make four. If that is granted, all else follows" (p. 69). His touchstone changes, however. Late in the process of his conversion, in a moment of reverie, he believes that he still "loves" Julia, that he is not yet defeated. "He obeyed the Party, but he still hated the Party. In the old days he had hidden a heretical mind beneath an appearance of conformity. Now he had retreated a step further: in his mind he had surrendered, but he had hoped to keep the inner heart inviolate" (p. 231). In order to do this Winston realizes that, paradoxically, he has to practice a variation of doublethink, even facecrime, to try to deceive, not the Party but himself.

> For the first time he perceived that if you want to keep a secret you must also hide it from yourself. You must know all the while that it is there, but until it is needed you must never let it emerge into your consciousness in any shape that could be given a name. From now onwards he must not only think right; he must feel right, dream right. And all the while he must keep his hatred locked up inside him like a ball of matter which was part of himself and yet unconnected with the rest of him, a kind of cyst. (P. 231)

In his fantasy he dramatizes the moment when he will be shot in the back of the head, but in the ten seconds before that happens "the world inside him would turn over." They would have killed him before they realized that the "flaw in the pattern" had not been removed. "They would have blown a hole in their own perfection. To die hating them, that was freedom" (p. 231). So the definition of freedom has changed; it is located in the inner heart, not in the mind. But unlike the martyrs of the Reformation Winston has undermined the spiritual basis that can sustain either hatred or love. This is finally driven home to him as he listens to the "sound track of the conversation he had had with O'Brien on the night when he had enrolled himself in the Brotherhood" (p. 222). He is like Rubashov in *Darkness at Noon*, of whom Orwell said that he had forfeited "any right to protest against torture, secret prisons, [and] organized lying" because he had been corrupted by his acceptance of the Communist party's philosophy.[9] Orwell condemned the assumption that evil is acceptable if it furthers a good cause and he incidentally observed that in practice "the Machiavellian system fails, even by its own test of material success."[10] The destruction of Nazi Germany showed that dishonesty is not the best policy. "The fact that this shallow piece of naughtiness can—just because it sounds 'realistic' and grown-up—be accepted without any examination does not speak well for the Anglo-American intelligentsia."[11]

Winston Smith cannot finally resist O'Brien because the emotional and intellectual grounds on which he stands began to be fatally eroded when he accepted O'Brien's leadership in the rebellion he thought they were planning. The pain he endures later on is terrible, but as

Orwell shows us he might have held out if first his mind and then his spirit had not been corrupted. He is a victim but not a martyr because he has been betrayed by what is false within.

Notes

1. This famous account from John Foxe's *Acts and Monuments* is quoted here from *The Book of Martyrs: a History of the Persecution of the Protestants by John Foxe* (London: James Nisbet, n.d.), 345.
2. George Orwell, *Nineteen Eighty-Four* (New York: New American Library, 1981), 197. Subsequent references to the novel appear parenthetically in the text.
3. George Orwell, "How the Poor Die," in *The Collected Essays, Journalism and Letters of George Orwell*, ed. Sonia Orwell and Ian Angus, 4 vols. (New York: Harcourt, Brace, Jovanovich, 1968), 4:225. Subsequent references appear in the text as *CEJL*.
4. George Orwell, *A Clergyman's Daughter* (London: Secker and Warburg, 1960), 121–38.
5. George Orwell, *Down and Out in Paris and London* (New York: Berkley Pub. Corp., 1959), 120.
6. George Orwell, *Burmese Days* (London: Secker and Warburg, 1955), 69–70.
7. Orwell, *Burmese Days*, 69.
8. *CEJL* 2:239.
9. George Orwell, review of Arthur Koestler's *Darkness at Noon* in *The New Statesman and Nation*, January 4, 1941, p. 16.
10. George Orwell, "Why Machiavellians of Today Fall Down," *Manchester Evening News*, January 20, 1944.
11. Orwell, "Why Machiavellians Fall Down."

Contributors

Joseph Adelson — *Professor of Psychology*
The University of Michigan

Francis A. Allen — *Edson R. Sunderland Professor of Law*
The University of Michigan

Richard W. Bailey — *Professor of English Language and Literature*
The University of Michigan

Gorman Beauchamp — *Associate Professor of Humanities*
The University of Michigan

Bernard Crick — *Professor of Political Science*
Birkbeck College, University of London

Ejner J. Jensen — *Professor of English Language and Literature*
The University of Michigan

Eugene J. McCarthy — *Former United States Senator from Minnesota*
Woodville, Virginia

Alfred G. Meyer — *Professor of Political Science*
The University of Michigan

William R. Steinhoff — *Professor of English Language and Literature*
The University of Michigan

Leslie Tentler — *Associate Professor of History*
The University of Michigan-Dearborn

W. Warren Wagar — *Professor of History*
State University of New York, Binghamton

Alex Zwerdling — *Professor of English*
University of California, Berkeley